FREEDOM AND PLANNING

IN AUSTRALIA

A. CAMPBELL GARNETT

Freedom & Planning
—in—
AUSTRALIA

The University of Wisconsin Press

Agent for the Continent of Europe
W. S. Hall & Co.
457 Madison Avenue
New York 22, New York

PRINTED IN THE UNITED STATES OF AMERICA BY THE
BUSINESS PRESS, INC.—LANCASTER, PENNSYLVANIA

TO MY AUSTRALIAN SISTERS

GRACE AND ALICE

Preface

I HAVE lived half my adult life in my native land of Australia and half in my adopted country, the United States. This book is an attempt to interpret the spirit and social order of my former homeland to those among whom I now live. It would not be fair to either if I did not frankly criticize as well as praise. Such evaluations, of course, are inevitably colored by my personal point of view. But I believe I have not been doctrinaire, and I have striven to be objective.

I have not attempted to write a political and economic history of Australia, but have sought to tell enough of the national story, with emphasis on its most interesting and relevant features, to enable the American reader to catch the spirit of the country and to understand the discussion of its present problems. I have also occasionally injected a word to the Australians themselves that I hope may be constructive and enable them to see themselves through the eyes of one who has come to know and appreciate the American point of view.

America has, rather unwillingly, become the hub upon which turns the future of the world. Australia is a small country, but one of strategic importance and kindred spirit in the world that now revolves around the American axis. Americans are therefore rightly interested in Australia, and it is important for both peoples that they understand each other. It is important to Australia because she needs the support and understanding of America. It is important to America because Australia is a social laboratory in which are being tried out many experiments that have a bearing on America's own internal problems. Similar experiments are being made, and are somewhat farther advanced, in New Zealand; but the Australian experiments are more relevant to America's own problems, the country being much more fully industrialized and having, in her federal system, a political structure more like that of the United States.

Most, though not all, of the social experiments in Australia are either the work of the Labor Party or have been carried through with its aid. For the fourth time in Commonwealth history Labor obtained power in the federal government in October, 1941, through the defection of two "Independent" supporters of the former government. In 1943 the party confirmed this success by winning a large majority in both houses and proceeded to put through a program of social legislation embodying important advances in what are often called the "Social Service State" and the "Cooperative Commonwealth." This program was again confirmed by the decisive victory won in the general elections of September, 1946—the first time that Labor has ever won two successive federal elections. Another three years was therefore given for establishing the policies and tendencies of the last few years, which are described in the later chapters. This means that they can be regarded as accepted features of the political structure of the Commonwealth, for experience shows that social advances, once firmly established, come to be adopted unreservedly by all parties in Australia.

The parties opposed to Labor at the present time are the Liberal and the Country parties. They usually work together in fairly close cooperation. The Country Party first entered the political scene in 1918. The Liberal Party was formed by the fusion of the former Conservative and Liberal parties early in the century. It has several times changed its name, although it has remained essentially the same organization. To avoid possible confusion I have adopted the practice of referring to the party opposed to Labor not by its official name but simply as the "non-Labor" or "anti-Labor" party.

In the preparation of this book I have received aid from the Special Research Committee of the University of Wisconsin. My thanks are also due those many Australians, some of them old friends, who aided my research during the six months I spent in the country gathering material (February to August, 1946). They are far too numerous to mention by name; I may only say that I have received the utmost courtesy and enthusiastic aid from cabinet ministers and members of parliament of both parties, from captains of industry and trade-union leaders, from university professors and civil servants. Without such assistance, which not only guided me to the relevant published material but often made available personal manuscripts and private reports, it would have been impossible to gather in so short a time the information here presented.

My special thanks, however, are due the gentlemen who have contributed the essays on the present policies of their respective parties which comprise Chapters XI, XII, and XIII. These papers (written during my visit to Australia in 1946) present the personal interpretations of the writers, all of whom, however, are well qualified to speak for their parties. W. C. Taylor was then vice-president of the New South Wales branch of the Australian Labor Party. Dr. Lloyd Ross is a former secretary of the New South Wales Railwaymen's Union and a present official in the Department of Postwar Reconstruction. Dr. Grenfell Price is a former Liberal member of the federal parliament and author of several notable books on Australian problems. C. G. Kerr is Public Relations Officer of the Liberal and Country League of South Australia. The Honorable J. P. Abbott is a Country Party member of the federal parliament and a former Minister of the Crown. Their papers will greatly assist the reader to arrive at an accurate concept of the political life of Australia in this postwar era.

My thanks are due also to the following for permission to use quotations: to Angus and Robertson of Sydney for verses by Henry Lawson and A. B. Paterson; to Tyrrel's of Sydney for the quotation from Robert D. Barton's *Reminiscences of a Pioneer;* and to Miss Sheila Sibley and the editors of *Salt* for the "Ballade of the Convict's Daughter." I should like to express my gratitude also to Professor Arthur H. Robinson and Miss Edith J. Bond of the geography department of the University of Wisconsin for preparing the map which appears on the end papers.

A. Campbell Garnett

The University of Wisconsin
May, 1949.

Contents

FREEDOM AND PLANNING

IN AUSTRALIA

-1-

The Land and the People

AUSTRALIA is John Bull's substitute for the American colonies lost in 1776. It was in 1770 that British interest in science and exploration led to the discovery of the pleasant and fertile lands of its eastern seaboard. The existence of this "Terra Australis" had long been vaguely surmised from the reports of many navigators, but little was known of it beyond what had been revealed by the pirate-adventurer William Dampier, who in 1688 visited the dismal desert of the northwestern coast and left a vivid description of it.

A century later Captain Cook was dispatched with a party of scientists from the Royal Society of London to observe the transit of Venus at Tahiti, and subsequently to do a little exploring of the Southern Ocean. After leaving Tahiti he circumnavigated New Zealand, which Tasman had discovered in 1642. Having proved that this was merely a large group of islands, he struck westward across the twelve hundred miles of the Tasman Sea. When the east coast of Australia came in sight, near its southernmost point, he proceeded northward along the coast, proving the continental dimensions of the territory, and sailed home around the northern point to report his discovery of a land where "most sorts of grain, fruit, roots, etc. of every kind would flourish," and containing provender for "more cattle, at every season of the year, than can possibly be brought into the country."

At that time, however, Britain had colonies and troubles enough. Not until eighteen years later, in 1788, did the government think seriously of making practical use of Cook's discovery. The revolt of the American colonies had deprived His Majesty of three million of his most vigorous subjects and a realm of far greater possibilities than their homeland, and neither the king nor his government was in a mood to experiment with another that might prove equally troublesome and unprofitable. What eventually drove them to action was not the vision of a new and happier Britain overseas, but the problem of caring for the teeming population of their prisons, which the harsh criminal laws of the time were constantly crowding to overcapacity.

Prior to the American Revolution it had been the custom to pay contractors so much per head to transport English convicts to Virginia and Maryland, where they were sold as slaves. Some sixty-six thousand persons convicted of the less serious crimes were disposed of in this way. Those found guilty of major crimes were hanged. But now the jails and prison hulks were again filled to overflowing. Furthermore, a demand for change was in the air: it was being said that the function of punishment was to reform, not destroy. People had been listening to John Howard, the prison reformer. They had been reading Beccaria's *Treatise On Crimes and Punishment*. They had been influenced by Rousseau's faith that no man is so bad that he cannot be made good for something. When sent to America, even as a slave, the prisoner had been given a chance of a new life and reformation of character. In the British jails of the day his body decayed and his soul became depraved. Public opinion demanded that something be done about it, and the government responded by sending a fleet of convict ships to New South Wales.

At first Australia was merely a place where the outcasts of British society were given a chance to enjoy independence and decency once more. But soon it became a haven where any poor man might find a better opportunity, where servants could rise to equality with their masters, where new forms of freedom could be developed for the benefit of mankind. This did not, of course, happen all at once; nor is the process even yet complete. Ancient shackles are not readily removed from men's minds, nor are better social orders easily devised. And this land where new social experiments were to be made proved to be no paradise of plenty, but a region which yields her gifts only to the strong of heart and keen of mind.

Some geographical facts.— Economically John Bull's substitution of Australia for the American colonies was a poor bargain. At the present stage of scientific knowledge and at modern American standards of living the United States could probably accommodate 200 million people. Under similar conditions Australia could probably support a population of 20 to 30 millions, the most recent estimates being nearer the lower figure. Today the population is just over 7,500,000, and twenty-five years ago it was only 5,500,000. This is extremely small for a country which has almost exactly the same area as the United States exclusive of Alaska, and which was opened up for settlement at about the same time as the trans-Mississippi states. In those states a population of over 40 million is now living in an area about three-fifths the size of Australia.

The slow growth of population is in part attributable to Australia's distance from Europe. Even today it takes thirty days to travel from London to Perth by the short route through the Suez Canal, and another ten days to Sydney. Before the days of steam the journey usually took from four to six months. But the more fundamental reason for both the slow growth and the low estimates of the country's ultimate carrying capacity is the arid character of the greater part of its area.

Australia lies south of the equator in the same latitudes as North Africa and the Sahara, and the southern states of the United States and Mexico. But its tropical and subtropical areas lack the mountains and plateaus which bring rain to much of Mexico, and its much greater land mass adds to the heat and aridity. At the same time, having a broad sea between its tropical coast and the equator, these areas are less dry than the Sahara.

The northern (tropical) area is watered in the summer by the southern monsoon. This creates a strip of woodland across the extreme north, much of which, however, is too rugged to be useful. Below this, where the monsoon is less severe, is a strip of grassland which contains much good cattle country. Because of the high evaporation the grass disappears at the point where the monsoonal rain falls as low as twenty inches. And because of the long dry season very little of this tropical area is suitable for agricultural development.

In the southern (temperate) region a considerable area in the southwestern corner and a larger area in the southeast are watered by winter rains. Here wheat can be grown and, in favored districts, fruits and vegetables.

East of a line running due north from Melbourne and lying on both sides of the Great Dividing Range, which runs down the entire east coast, is a region where rains are uniform winter and summer. This is the most favored part of Australia. Between the sea and the mountains, which are comparable in height with those of the eastern part of the United States, and which in most parts are within sight of the sea, there are beautiful, well watered slopes, ranging from a tropical jungle in the far north, through magnificent dairy and farming country in the long central region, to giant eucalyptus forests in the south. Over the mountains stretch the great park-like plains where sheep thrive under ideal conditions and wheat grows in abundance.

West of this region the rainfall peters out, and here, between the northern grasslands and the southern wheat fields, lie the vast region of arid lands and great stretches of sandy desert. In these areas, with the help of an artesian water supply, a great pastoral industry has a precarious but usually profitable existence. In this region, however, a handful of resourceful men suffice to tend the sheep and cattle that rove over thousands of square miles.

In the north the climate is hot and often humid, yet in this region a quarter of a million white Australians live and work, largely in the open air, and rear healthy families free from diseases carried by native populations elsewhere in the tropics. In the temperate zone, which includes three-fifths of the continent, the other seven and a quarter million inhabitants enjoy a climate resembling that of California or Texas. But even in this favored part the really well watered area is relatively small, and much of that is too mountainous to be of use for agriculture.

From twenty to thirty millions, therefore, appears to be the maximum population that Australia can sustain well; and for that number she also has adequate resources of coal and iron and a fair supply of other minerals. By American standards such a population is not large, nor does it offer much relief for the overcrowded conditions of other lands.

But a nation of seven and a half millions of vigorous and democratic people, with prospects of growing to twenty or thirty millions, is a human unit of considerable importance in the affairs of the world. So even from the economic standpoint John Bull's substitute for his American colonies is not to be despised.

It is not for its economic contribution, however, that Australia is of the most importance to the world, but rather for what its people are and have done. For here is one of the new nations of the globe that has gone far in casting off the shackles of the past. Here is a democracy that has dared to venture and experiment in new forms of freedom and new methods of social organization and control. In an age when man's mastery over physical things has made him a danger to himself it seems worth while to study the methods and the thoughts of a people who are making their own distinctive experiments in democracy.

Self-government.— Australia today is a British "dominion." This means that she is one of a group of independent nations which all recognize the same king, the others being Great Britain, Canada, South Africa, New Zealand, India, Pakistan, and Ceylon. With some reservations on the part of the last three, they together constitute the British Commonwealth of Nations. Several of them also control certain territories that are not self-governing. Thus Australia controls part of New Guinea; New Zealand controls part of Samoa (the other part being an American possession); and both control several other small Pacific islands. South Africa controls the mandated territory which was formerly German Southwest Africa. Great Britain controls a large number of territories in Africa, Asia, and other parts of the world which are in various stages of approach to self-government. It is only these that are correctly spoken of as the British Empire. The Dominions constitute the British Commonwealth of

Nations, or, in accord with a recent gesture to the Asiatic Dominions, simply the Commonwealth of Nations.

It is sometimes hard for Americans to comprehend the degree of independence the different Dominions have. Great Britain is merely one Dominion of seven. Her parliament and government have no legal authority over the others, nor have theirs over Great Britain. The king is a constitutional monarch who acts on the advice of his ministers. He lives in Great Britain and appoints representatives (usually called "governors," though they do not govern) in the other Dominions. These governors are appointed, however, on the advice of the government of the Dominion concerned, not on that of the British government. Usually the governor chosen is an English or Scottish gentleman heartily approved by the king, but not always. George V protested strongly when in 1931 J. H. Scullin's Labor Government nominated Chief Justice Isaac Isaacs, a brilliant Australian-born Jew and chief justice of the High Court of Australia. But Prime Minister Scullin insisted upon his nominee, and His Majesty made the appointment. All the Dominions have the right to secede from the Commonwealth at any time, or to remain neutral in time of war. Both these rights have been exercised by Eire. And in 1939 the parliament of South Africa voted by only a narrow margin in favor of a declaration of war.

The ties that bind the nations of the Commonwealth together are not to be found in any authority of one over the other, but simply in such bonds as common blood, sentiment, and culture, and in common strategic and economic interests. In internal affairs they are quite independent. In external affairs they try to work together in the common interest. In matters of foreign policy the government of Great Britain, being the strongest and most experienced, tends to take the lead. But the others do not always follow.

This has been very clearly demonstrated at recent international conferences, beginning with the conference of the United Nations at San Francisco, where Australia and New Zealand led the revolt of the smaller nations against the Big Four policy endorsed by Great Britain and the United States.

This national independence and political democracy Australia has attained only by slow degrees. If we would understand the spirit that now animates her, if we would assess her institutions and understand the trends that point to the future, we must look at the road by which she has come. In this first part of this book, therefore, we shall review some of the salient events of Australia's lively political history. In the remaining chapters we shall examine her most distinctive institutions and policies and the ideas that lie behind them.

Convict days.— Captain Arthur Phillip, who in 1787 was put in charge of the first convict fleet and subsequent settlement in New South Wales, was a man of remarkable ability and wisdom. The convicts were exceedingly poor material with which to begin the building of a nation, and the soldiers and officers in charge of them were little better. Even worse, few of them had had any practical experience as farmers. The result was that for several years the colony had to be fed largely by supplies from England. In its very first year, when one of the supply ships was wrecked, the colony escaped starvation only because of the courage, firm discipline, and wise example of Governor Phillip. He shared privations with the prisoners, throwing his own food supply into the common store. He took upon himself the risk and fatigue of exploration and attended carefully to every detail in the management of the settlement. The disciplinary measures he took in dealing with offenders were often severe, but not unjust according to the standards of the time.

Phillip's health permitted his remaining in charge of the settlement for only five years. After his retirement control fell into less able hands. Soldiers and officers of the New South Wales Corps, especially organized to police and guard the settlement, were underpaid and ill chosen. They and the few free settlers who had come out proceeded to enrich themselves by many forms of graft at the expense of the convicts. Only the worst of the latter were actually kept in prison and chain gangs; many were given "ticket of leave," which gave them freedom to work or farm for themselves within a given district. Some were pardoned on condition that they remain in the colony, and others whose terms had expired also chose to remain. Still other convicts were indentured to work for a very small wage for some officer-farmer, free settler, or emancipated convict; and these were often badly exploited.

A caste system soon developed. The former convicts or "emancipists" were despised by the free settlers, officers, and soldiers, who excluded them from their society, even though some were men of culture who had acquired some property. Members of this upper caste were dubbed "exclusionists" and "pure merinos." But for several years they controlled the colony and enriched themselves while the unfortunate products of the convict system suffered and often became further degraded.

In 1809, however, the colony came under the control of Governor Lachlan Macquarie. The New South Wales Corps was abolished, and the country was policed by the regiment Macquarie brought with him. His control was therefore absolute and he used it to reform the administration. He believed in encouraging the emancipated convicts and tried to break the caste system by appointing many of them to positions of importance and inviting some of them to dine at Government House. This shocked and angered the "pure merinos," but Macquarie held to his course. He secured large sums from the British government to expend on public works, including a road over the Blue Mountains behind

Sydney which opened up to the sheep raiser the park-like plains of the nearer interior. He strove, however, to develop the land by putting small farmers on agricultural blocks rather than letting it fall into the hands of pastoralists building up large estates.

There is no doubt that Macquarie genuinely had at heart the interests of the unfortunates committed to his charge. He made the convict colony really perform the function for which it had been created—to give another chance to men and women who had (partly through their own fault) become the victims of the harsh social system of their homeland. But he also made enemies; and he made mistakes. His power was absolute and he sometimes abused it. He was recalled in 1821 after a commission of inquiry had censured his administration as too arbitrary, much too favorable to the emancipists, and unwise in the restrictions it placed on the development of large pastoral estates.

Macquarie's administration marks the beginning of the end of the convict era. He had made New South Wales attractive to free settlers. He had not wanted them, but they had come. Toward the close of his administration they began to come in large numbers, for the land had been proved exceptionally suitable for sheep. Anyone who could afford to buy a small flock of merinos and grubstake himself for a year could squat on a broad selection, hire a few convicts for shepherds at almost nominal wages, and with the help of emancipists and other migratory workers at shearing time proceed to grow rich without much effort. It was not long before the free settlers began to outnumber the convicts and emancipists. The children of convicts and emancipists also grew up as free citizens and for the most part proved themselves worthy pioneers. Their numbers, however, were not great, for of a total of 137,161 persons transported to Australia only 20,209 were women. The flow of convicts to New South Wales was stopped in 1840. That to Tasmania, where the worst convicts had been sent and treated with great brutality, ceased in 1853. Between 1850 and 1867 ten thousand were sent to Western Australia at the request of settlers needing labor. But that marked the end of the system. Meantime, by 1850, the population had grown to 405,000, and by 1860 to well over a million.

In another way, too, Macquarie's administration represented the end of an era. The criticism of his arbitrary ways led to the beginning of self-government. This took the form of a nominated council of free citizens which at first was merely advisory to the governor but rapidly gained greater power, especially after elected representatives were added. In 1850 an act of the British parliament provided for representative government on the British parliamentary model in New South Wales, Tasmania, and the newly established colonies of Victoria and South Australia.

The squatters.— In New South Wales land was at first distributed freehold in small lots—thirty acres to an unmarried emancipated convict, fifty to a married one, fifty to a private or free civilian, and one hundred to commissioned or noncommissioned officers with convicts assigned to work for them. By 1802 they were growing enough grain for the colony, and thereafter, since distances from overseas markets made export difficult, they turned their attention to sheep and cattle farming. This required larger areas of land. Therefore, in 1804, the British government adopted the policy of granting large tracts of land and assigning large numbers of convicts to work that land to people of means who would invest money in the colony, the size of the grant being proportionate to the capital invested. One family, the Blaxland brothers, for example, invested six thousand pounds, and re-

ceived eight thousand acres and eighty convicts. Later, settlers were allowed to add to their estates by purchase of
Crown lands at auction sales.

In a land so vast, defended only by a thin sprinkling of
ill-armed and poorly organized aborigines, it was impossible to
make energetic men conform to legal processes of occupation.
Squatters with a few sheep moved into unoccupied areas.
Some of these men were ex-convicts, but more were free
settlers. Most of them were too poor to take up land in the
legal way, but others were young adventurers of good family.
They opened up the country in defiance of the law, and most
of them prospered. Soon they began to press for recognition of their claims, and in 1836 the Legislative Council
passed an act allowing any man to occupy land in the outer
areas of the colony upon payment of a license fee of ten
pounds a year. Three years later, when a tax of a penny
per head was levied on sheep and threepence on cattle, the
revenue thus obtained was used to provide police protection
for the squatters' rights. For an annual fee of ten pounds
a man might buy a license to "squat" upon a leasehold estate
large enough to support four thousand sheep, and there was
no limit to the number of licenses he might hold. Very
rapidly, therefore, the squatters divided up into great sheep
ranches all the land fit for pasture and soon began to agitate
for security of tenure. The British government did not
wish to allow pastoralists to fix their grip upon land that it
might later wish to subdivide into smaller agricultural holdings, but the squatters were becoming rich and influential.
In 1847 Orders in Council were passed classifying the land
as "settled," "intermediate," and "unsettled." The settled
land (near towns and near the coast) could be leased for only
a year at a time; intermediate land for eight years; unsettled
land for fourteen. Most of the land in question fell into
the third class and could, it was stipulated, be purchased by

the lessee, and by him alone, for a pound an acre. This figure was so high that few wished to buy, but the squatter felt safe in the possession of his very cheap lease.

This stipulation ended the era of squatters' agitation. From this time on they became supporters of the established order. Being now secure in the possession of their great estates, they opposed the political efforts of subsequent decades to "unlock the land" once more, in order to make room for the small farmer. With wealth and security the squatters grew in power and became a ruling class, a landed gentry, an aristocracy founded on wool and convict labor, just as that of the American South was founded on cotton and slavery.

The Wakefield theory.— Without the supply of assigned convict labor the squatters in New South Wales could not have built up their large estates. For who will willingly work for another when he can find land of his own and become his own master? But despite their value to employers the convicts and ex-convicts created a very undesirable element in the population. Men of vision, therefore, interested in the future of the Australian colonies, cast about for some better means of supplying labor to settlers and colonial capitalists who needed it. Some suggested the introduction of Asiatics under a system of indenture, but the evil results of American slavery were sufficiently well recognized to prevent the adoption of this course. Instead, attention was directed to an ingenious scheme devised by the English colonial theorist, Edward Gibbon Wakefield.

Wakefield saw that free laborers could not be expected to work for wages in the colonies if they could get free land, nor could they be made to work for very long if land was cheap. His solution of the problem, therefore, was to raise the price of land. This would ensure that laborers brought out as free immigrants would have to work for wages for several years in order to save enough to buy land of their own. When one group of immigrants had saved enough money to buy land, or when people with capital came out prepared to buy, more land should be sold and the proceeds used to bring out new laborers for the expanding needs of the colony. If the price was fixed right and wages were fair, this process could go on until the colony was fully occupied.

Wakefield urged that a new colony, free from convict labor, be established on these lines somewhere in Australia. He insisted that it be promised self-government, with features in its constitution drawn from the radical People's Charter of 1839, as soon as it had attained a population of fifty thousand. He interested a number of notable Englishmen in his scheme, including John Stuart Mill, the economist and philosopher, George Grote, the historian, and the statesman, Earl Grey. South Australia was selected as the most suitable site for a beginning, and in 1834 the "South Australian Association" secured the passage of an act authorizing the creation of a colony on Wakefield's plan.

The colony was established at Adelaide in 1836, but it was nearly wrecked during the first few years by its own theoretical success. The immigrants brought out with the proceeds of the first land sales proceeded to offer higher prices for the land close to the city bought by the first-comers. This started a boom, which received fresh impetus from every land sale and every new batch of immigrants. Landowners, instead of going out to clear their farms and start producing, remained in the city to speculate in land. Laborers had no work to do, and the governor was forced to employ them in building public works for which the British taxpayer eventually had to pay. When the British government finally called a halt, the colony was bankrupt. The colonists, however, then got to work on the land and by 1842 the crisis was over. By 1850 South Australia had a thriving population of 63,700.

The price of land in South Australia had been fixed first at twelve shillings an acre and a little later at a pound. And since it was impracticable to charge more in one colony than in another, these prices were also adopted elsewhere. But in New South Wales, and especially in the newly opened part which later became Victoria, it was impossible to keep squatters off the free land. Thus that part of Wakefield's plan which was designed to maintain a constant flow of labor for the owners of land did not work very successfully; though a large part of the proceeds of land purchases was applied to the assistance of immigration, the supply of free labor rarely equaled the demand in any of the colonies. The plan did not, as was hoped, enable the younger sons of English gentlemen to obtain cheap estates and plenty of laborers and tenants in the colonies. Except for the diminishing number of assigned convicts Australia became a country where free settlers worked their land, tended their sheep themselves, and paid good wages to those who helped them as station hands or in harvesting and shearing.

Gold, wool, and immigrants.— In 1851 Australia had a population of 437,000 engaged almost entirely in the pastoral industry and a little agriculture. This population was spread thinly over all the land in the temperate zone having a sufficient rainfall to provide pasture. But in that year gold fields were discovered which proved to be extremely rich. A rush set in from all parts of the world, including experienced prospectors from California, although the great majority were British. The census of 1861 showed a total population of 1,250,000, of whom more than 92 per cent had been born either in Great Britain or in Australia itself.

Not only had the population nearly trebled during the decade but it had changed greatly in character. Whereas the assisted immigrants of the past had been drawn chiefly from the poorer classes and had come out expecting to work for years as laborers and servants, the newcomers were independent adventurers who paid their own passage and looked for quick returns on the gold fields. They were an orderly set, though they carried arms; and they introduced into the Australian gold fields very little of the lawlessness that was so common in the mining regions of California and Alaska. They represented all classes of the community; many were drawn from the ranks of the Chartists and Irish revolutionaries. Most of them were men and women of exceptional courage and vigor, traits which are usually accompanied by a mentality above the average. Some realized their hope of making a quick fortune, but the great majority were disappointed. For most of these latter a return to the old lands was difficult if not impossible; they had to make their homes in the new country. But they were not the type of people to be content to become mere servants or laborers for the squatters who had preceded them, taken up all the good land, and dominated colonial society.

The spirit of the diggers is shown by an incident that occurred in 1854, known as the Eureka Stockade. The Legislative Council of New South Wales and that of Victoria, controlled by the squatters, imposed a license fee of thirty shillings a month for the privilege of digging for gold. Granted the propriety of taxing the new industry in some manner, this tax was unjust in that it fell with equal force on the man who was digging without any luck and the one who was making a fortune. Improverished miners often found themselves unable to pay. The police, especially in Victoria, used irritating tactics in their attempts to collect it; they raided the diggings and chained to a log the miners who were unable to produce the required license. Much agitation ensued, in response to which the fee was cut to twenty shillings. But this reduction did not satisfy the miners, who wanted nothing less than the abolition of the whole license system. Since they had no vote in the Legislative Council, which was based upon a property franchise, they raised the cry of "no taxation without representation."

At Ballarat a reform league was organized whose platform borrowed from the People's Charter, which had agitated Britain fifteen years earlier, the following five planks: full and fair representation, manhood suffrage, abolition of the property qualification for members of the Legislative Council, payment of members, and short duration of parliamentary bodies. A great demonstration was held, at which thousands of miners burned their licenses and swore to pay no more fees. They erected a stockade on the Eureka lead and proclaimed a Republic of Victoria. The insurrection was quickly put down, the stockade being carried at the point of the bayonet. But the miners won their main point. The license system was replaced by the Miner's Right, costing one pound a year, and a small export duty on gold. All holders of a Miner's Right were given the franchise. No jury would convict those of the rebels who were brought to trial, and the prosecutions were abandoned.

In a few years the diggings on the surface everywhere played out. Thereafter mining became an enterprise for capitalists with machinery and miners working for wages. Thousands of the diggers and thousands of other new immigrants had to look elsewhere for work. Many would have liked to have taken up small farms but found all the good land already occupied, most of it by the estates of the big squatters. In Victoria a thousand squatters held among them over thirty million acres. In New South Wales one company had been permitted, as early as 1832, to take up well over a half million acres of the best land, and was also given two thousand acres on the Newcastle coal field and an almost complete monopoly of coal production for thirty-one years. Thus the great new population of vigorous men and women who had swarmed in during the gold rush found themselves a dispossessed proletariat in a land of great estates. They had come to Australia thinking it a land of opportunity, only to find the door of opportunity closed. It was this situation which gave its radical and dynamic character to Australian politics in the latter half of the nineteenth century and made Australia a leader among the world's democracies.

The growth of Australian population after 1861 was due to the continuance, during most of the period, of assisted immigration and a very healthy rate of natural increase. Industries of every kind developed. In many areas wheat farming, dairying, and fruitgrowing proved more profitable than sheep raising and led to the development of one-family farmers. Gold mining continued in the deep lodes and in newly discovered fields. Important deposits of silver, lead, zinc, copper, iron, coal, and other minerals were also discovered and worked, becoming the basis of important secondary industries. The great coastal cities grew rapidly as manufacturing, commercial, and cultural centers. At the turn of the century the population numbered three and three-quarter million, and since then it has doubled. Thus, the rate of increase has been rapid, but the total is still small in view of the country's resources and the teeming populations of her Asiatic neighbors to the north.

The national origins of the Australian people are very difficult to determine. More than sixty-five per cent are of English, Scottish, and Welsh extraction; nearly twenty-five per cent, Irish; and eight per cent are other European nationalities, chiefly German, with a recent influx of other elements, notably Italians and Greeks. Most of the Germans are descendants of people who emigrated in the mid-nineteenth century and for some decades thereafter. From the economic standpoint they have proved themselves excellent pioneers in Australia as in America, and for the most part have been thoroughly loyal to their adopted homeland in the two world wars. The Italians, most of whom are immigrants of the twentieth century, tend to congregate on the sugar-cane fields of North Queensland. The aboriginals number about 60,000 fullbloods and 20,000 half-castes; Asiatics and other non-Europeans about 29,000.

The "White Australia" policy, which excludes non-European races, is deeply rooted in the Australian concepts of democracy. The attempts that have been made to introduce Asiatic or Oceanic immigrants have usually been motivated by the desire for cheap labor and have been resisted as such. The object lesson provided by color problems in other parts of the world has been taken to heart. Motives less intelligent and less honorable have likewise played their part. The question certainly calls for fresh consideration in the light of the new world situation.

Australia today.— The six self-governing Australian colonies which had developed in the nineteenth century joined, on the first of January, 1901, in a federal union called the Commonwealth of Australia. The relation between the states and the federal government is virtually the same as in the United States. The structure of the governments themselves, however, in the Commonwealth and the states, is modeled on the British government. The prime minister of the Commonwealth and the state premiers are members of parliament and responsible solely to it. They and their ministers, who constitute the executive branch of government, can be dismissed at any time by a vote of no confidence in the lower house of the legislature. The judiciary also is not elected but appointed with tenure by the executive cabinet. Thus legislature, executive, and judiciary are not as completely separate as under the American Constitution; but the executive is directly, and the judiciary ultimately, under the control of the elected representatives of the people.

In each of the states the capital is the seaport established as the original nucleus of settlement. Being the points at which the necessary materials could most conveniently be assembled, these seaport capitals in the beautiful coastal fringe of Australia's most desirable areas have naturally become also the commercial and manufacturing centers of their respective states. In these centers the amenities of civilized life have developed most rapidly and fully. Long before connecting railways were built they were trading with one another by sea, and since nearly all interstate trade moves more cheaply by water, their commerce has not been seriously handicapped by the differences in railway gauge between several of the states.

Because Australian settlement is concentrated in this coastal fringe, the inland towns have never been able to compete with the seaboard cities as manufacturing and commercial centers. Moreover, because of its head start, the original seaport in each state continues to be pre-eminent. Urban life is therefore largely concentrated in the political capitals. Furthermore, the urban population far outnumbers the rural. The census of 1947 shows that less than 32 per cent of the total population live in rural areas, whereas 50 per cent live in the six capital cities, and 18 per cent in provincial towns. This process of urbanization, especially the movement into the capital cities, has been steadily increasing in recent decades. Sydney now has a population of nearly a million and a half; Melbourne, a million and a quarter; Brisbane and Adelaide, about 400,000 each; Perth, 273,000; and Hobart, nearly 77,000.

The causes of urban growth are the same in Australia as elsewhere. But the proportion of people engaged in rural industries is surprisingly small for a new country. The chief reason is that the leading rural industries—wheat growing, sheep raising, and cattle raising—require little labor. Wheat growing in Australia is a highly mechanized enterprise. The land and the climate lend themselves to labor-saving methods, as they do in the dairy industry also, since cattle can remain in the fields and eat the natural grasses all the year around. Thus primary production is carried on with a relatively small labor force, and Australia's growing population must find employment chiefly in the secondary industries of the towns. Wheat growing has already reached its limit of expansion, and sheep raising almost so. Cattle raising, on the other hand, can go much farther in the tropical north. Any considerable increase in Australia's rural population must therefore come chiefly as a result of further expansion of truck farming, fruit raising, and dairying. And such expansion in turn, because of the remoteness of overseas markets, depends largely on the growth of local markets through the development of secondary industries in the towns.

The urban Australian, however, lives a healthful outdoor life. His cities are well provided with parks and sea beaches, the climate is temperate the year around, and the law provides an abundance of holidays, with the result that there is a very general and vigorous participation in organized outdoor sports. Australian teams maintain a high reputation in international contests of tennis, cricket, Rugby football, and other games. The Australian death rate is, next to New Zealand's, the lowest in the world.

For the development of secondary industries Australia has excellent, though not vast, deposits of coal, iron, and many other minerals; and oil is available near by in the Dutch East Indies. Her steel mills not only met all her own needs for munitions-making during the war, but produced a surplus for export to England. Her munitions factories produced a wide range of artillery and small arms, tanks and armored cars, fighter planes and bombers, shells, mines, ships, and electrical equipment. Steel production, which had only just begun before the war, developed rapidly in the years of crisis. The country has, therefore, the necessary technical equipment and skills for a postwar industrial development to insure prosperity without too great dependence upon fluctuations of demands for her products overseas.

This expansion of secondary industries has not been achieved without cost. It has been done under the protection of tariffs which have certainly raised the cost of living for the community in general. Many of these industries, having a comparatively small market, cannot possibly be as efficient as those in larger countries, with the result that average production per man for the country as a whole is less, and labor costs and the cost of living higher. These higher costs have embarrassed most of the primary producing industries which have an export surplus. At Australian levels of costs and distance from world markets (chiefly Britain) they cannot compete with their rivals. These industries have therefore been granted export subsidies, which further add to the cost of living.

The result of these practices is that the national income in Australia has advanced less rapidly than it otherwise would have or than it has in comparable countries. Figures compiled in "international units" [1] (an economist's fiction) show that between 1901 and 1938 real income per head in New Zealand increased from 880 to 1,790, in Australia from 665 to 1,212. This is an increase of 82 per cent for Australia, 92 per cent for New Zealand. The absolute difference in income per head is attributable to differences in the economy of the two countries. New Zealand, far more than Australia, has concentrated on primary production without much attention to secondary industries. This has been a wise course since the country is too small to do much manufacturing for the home market and not well enough equipped to manufacture for export. Had Australia pursued the same policy she could probably have developed a greater income per head than she

[1] Colin Clark, *The Conditions of Economic Progress* (Macmillan, London, 1940).

has at present. But she could not have supported nearly so large a population as she does, and immigration would have had to be much less. Had it not been for the tariff burden, primary production might conceivably have been somewhat greater than it is, but this is dubious in view of the fact that the world market for these products was already glutted by 1929 and has recovered only on account of the destruction of war. Australia's slightly smaller advance in living standards as compared with New Zealand's must therefore be counted as the price to be paid for building up the population that is strategically necessary, and that is demanded by public opinion both inside the country and abroad.

Even so, Australia is a country with high standards of living. In 1937 real wages were calculated at 105 international units in Australia, 111 in New Zealand, 110 in Great Britain, and 133 in the United States. Similarly, comparative figures, in international units, for national income in the decade 1925–34 show Australia high in the scale, though not the highest:

United States	1,381
Canada	1,337
New Zealand	1,202
Great Britain	1,069
Australia	980
France	684
Germany	646

Concerning the quality of her soldiers little need be said. Their fighting ability, toughness, resourcefulness, and dash have been widely acclaimed. In part it is the open-air life of the Australian that accounts for these qualities; in part it is their participation in sport, and the generally wholesome conditions of life that prevail. But more important than these factors is something in the spirit of their country, the spirit of militant democracy. This may be ascribed to several factors: the freedom and individualism of the pioneer in the bush and the farmer battling with fickle natural forces; the vigorous unionism of the workers, their traditional attitude of "mateship" and loyalty in their struggle for economic security, their habitual assumption of equality, and rejection of all distinctions not based on merit; and deepest of all, the people's conviction that they have a heritage of freedom and opportunity worth fighting for, and that, in both the great crises of this century, it had to be fought for.

In both world wars Australia refused to conscript her manhood for service overseas. From a military standpoint this was foolish, and from the standpoint of a just distribution of burdens it was unfair. But when a vote on the question was taken in the first World War the soldiers in France, in need of reinforcements though they were, voted by only a very small margin in favor of conscription. In the country as a whole the proposal was turned down by an equally small margin with the help of the votes of the parents, sisters, and wives of thousands of volunteers serving in the forces overseas. At the root of this refusal to compel a man by law to do what was recognized as his duty was the feeling that where life itself is involved every man should make his own decision. Among the "diggers" in the trenches the feeling was widespread that they would prefer to bear a disproportionate burden themselves rather than compel a man to volunteer who lacked the "guts" to do so. Many of their people at home felt the same way. It was not sensible, but it was magnificent. It expressed the Australian's deep respect for the freedom of the individual and the inviolability of his personality, and his distaste for all regimentation that makes of a human being merely a means to an end. Whatever less honorable motives may have affected some voters, it was this sentiment that chiefly determined the issue.

Failure to impose conscription for overseas service can hardly be said to have weakened Australia's military effort in the second World War. Every man of military age was called up and trained for military service. Those who did not volunteer were from the start subject to conscription for defense of the homeland and, later, for operations in the Southwest Pacific. But ninety-five per cent of the men available volunteered for service anywhere in the world.

In the five years of war a total of nearly a million men entered the Australian armed forces. At their peak strength in 1943 they totaled 633,400. In proportion to population this is the equivalent of more than eleven million Americans under arms at one time. And it is certain that, for their personal and fighting qualities, there were no troops the American doughboy would rather have beside him in a tough place.

This broad picture of Australia and its people is followed, in subsequent chapters, by a brief review of some of their history, which will help us to see how they have tackled some of their problems in the past and prepare us to evaluate what they are thinking and doing about the questions of the present and future.

- 2 -

The Making of a Democracy

IN THE United States and in France democratic institutions were shaped in terms of a new ideology after the old order had been overthrown by revolution. In Australia they grew in typical British fashion by gradual changes in response to popular demand. Such growth was taking place in the American colonies prior to 1776, but a Tory government and a stubborn king were unwilling to let it advance fast enough. However, the lesson of the American revolution was well learned, and in Canada, Australia, and other colonies populated by British immigrants, self-governing institutions were more readily granted. Sometimes the London government was reluctant to move, but at other times it suggested political advances for which little or no demand had yet arisen in the colonies. Nevertheless, the growth was gradual, and the resulting institutions have the strength and weaknesses of political machinery thus developed. They are fairly well fitted to the temper and needs of the people, but they preserve some anachronisms that a revolution would certainly have swept away.

The early governors, from Phillip to Macquarie, were benevolent and capable for the most part, but their rule was autocratic. The country was primarily a jail, or at best a reformatory, and was governed with military discipline. The growth of free settlement during Macquarie's administration, however, made the earlier autocracy quite unsuitable. By 1821 the former jail had become a land of opportunity and of economic freedom. This called for political freedom, but because such a large proportion of the inhabitants were convicts and ex-convicts, and the economy of the country was dependent on convict labor, it was not thought wise, as yet, to place political control entirely in the hand of the local population. Moreover, such sudden and complete change was not in accord with the British temper. An act of the British parliament of 1823, creating a Legislative Council to act with the governor in an advisory capacity was the first step toward Australian self-government. At first this council consisted only of officials, but in 1825 three of its seven members were selected from the free colonists.

This arrangement, however, was far from satisfactory to those who wanted genuine self-government. It strengthened the hands of the class-conscious "exclusionists," who now had direct representation in the government. On the other hand, censorship was at this time removed from the press and the popular cause thus acquired a powerful new means of agitation. Popular papers took up the cause of convicts alleged to have been maltreated; they demanded trial by jury and a representative assembly. In response to these demands the London government passed another act in 1828 which created the machinery for introducing trial by jury, enlarged the Legislative Council to include more nonofficials, and gave it power to veto laws proposed by the governor. This satisfied most of the free colonists, who were by no means eager to put votes into the hands of the ex-convicts. But the agitation still went on.

In 1830 the Tories fell from power in England and the new government sent a liberal-minded governor, Sir Richard Bourke, to New South Wales. Bourke initiated the practice of publishing the proceedings of the Legislative Council and of placing before it for criticism the estimates of public expenditure. He also used his casting vote to secure passage of a bill allowing emancipists to act on juries. The government in England, however, refused to grant representative government until the transportation of convicts was discontinued in 1840. The way was then open for another forward step. An act in 1842 established a Legislative Council for New South Wales of which twenty-four of the thirty-six members were to be elected by the holders of a restricted property franchise. Laws passed by this Council had to receive the consent of the governor, and control over Crown (i. e., public) lands was withheld from it. Again the concessions fell far short of full responsible government, and the agitation persisted.

Control over Crown lands in particular was desired by the agitators, though this was the least legitimate of their demands. The London government quite rightly sought to prevent the small population then in Australia from taking possession of all the useful land and leaving nothing for later immigrants. It established, instead, the policy that public land could be sold at a pound an acre, the proceeds to assist immigration, public works, and the care of the aborigines. But at that time very little of the land in Australia, other than that close to the coastal settlements, seemed to be worth such a price. It required three acres to support a sheep and the squatters preferred, therefore, to lease the land, which they could do at little expense, and agitate for a reduction in its price. The London government deliberately kept the price up in order to conserve the land for closer settlement in the future. Those agitating most loudly for further powers of self-government wanted any such powers restricted to property owners. The Legislative Council, therefore, would represent only the property-owning class, who then would have the power to possess themselves cheaply of all the good lands of Australia, to the exclusion of the rest of the community and those who might come later on the scene.

The decisive step in granting self-government to the colonies was taken in 1850 when an act was passed creating in Victoria, Tasmania, and South Australia, Legislative Councils similar to that of New South Wales, and giving these Councils the right to amend their own constitutions. Control of Crown lands was still withheld, but politically the Australian colonies now had the power to make their own future.

In this task, however, they did not have a completely fresh start. They began with legislative bodies saddled with the incubus of a property franchise, a legacy from their evolutionary political development. The London government's act of 1850 did, however, reduce this load by one-half, starting the new self-determining Councils off by giving the franchise to all those who possessed freehold property to the value of one hundred pounds or a house worth ten pounds a year.

Constitution-making.— The right to reshape their own constitution, however, was not enough to satisfy those in New South Wales who had been agitating for full control of their affairs. The Crown lands, customs duties, and that part of the governor's expenditure called the Civil List were still withheld from colonial control. The Council, therefore, urged upon the London government its claim for full responsible government, meanwhile making no further move to amend its own constitution. The British Colonial Office at first resisted. But then in 1851, with the discovery of gold, the large influx of new immigrants submerged the ex-convict element of the population. In December, 1852, therefore, the British government declared that the time had come to place full powers of responsible government in the hands of the colonial legislatures and called upon them to draft suitable constitutions.

To draft its new constitution the Legislative Council in New South Wales appointed a select committee under the chairmanship of William Charles Wentworth, who, for many years, had been a most vigorous leader among those agitating for complete self-government. But Wentworth, who had been a radical in his youth, and who had sided with the emancipists against the exclusionists in the colonial class struggle, was now a man of considerable property and personal ambition. He emphatically stated that he had "no desire to sow the seeds of a future democracy." To the consternation of the radicals who had supported him in his past agitations, his committee brought forth the suggestion of a constitution modeled on the British, with a property franchise for the lower house and a colonial House of Lords.

Wentworth, however, had misjudged the temper of the people. His proposal was met with a storm of protests and a shower of bitter jests. Squatterdom was aspiring to be a "squattocracy," " a mushroom, a Brummagem, a bunyip aristocracy"—the bunyip being a mythical monster of the bush, stupid but fearsome, the theme of much Australian humor. Wentworth and his friends were thus forced to stifle their yearning for titles, and Australia was spared the creation of a hereditary ruling class.

The committee's proposals were revised. The upper house, called the Legislative Council, was changed to one consisting of persons nominated at first for five years by the Governor's Executive Council, and later for life by the government in power. They were to serve without payment, title, or any hereditary privileges. The lower house, called the House of Assembly, was to be elected by adult males having property worth one hundred pounds, or a salary of one hundred pounds a year, or paying rent of ten pounds a year, board and lodging of forty pounds, or lodging only of ten pounds. This involved a considerable broadening of the franchise, for a skilled workman could earn fifteen shillings a day, or over two hundred pounds a year. Legislation had to be passed by both houses, but the lower house alone had the right to initiate money bills. Having been passed by the New South Wales Legislative Council and the British parliament, this constitution received the assent of Queen Victoria in July, 1855.

The other states soon followed New South Wales in establishing bicameral legislatures on the British model with ministers responsible to their parliaments. All except South Australia required some property qualification for the electors of the lower house. South Australia, Victoria, Tasmania, and Western Australia, however, rejected the plan of a nominated Legislative Council. Instead, they established their upper houses with a narrower property franchise and a longer term of office, only a part retiring at one time as in the American Senate. Queensland, which was not separated from New South Wales until 1859, followed the example of the mother state in estabishing a nominated second chamber.

At that time, the election of the second chamber, although by a narrower franchise, seemed more democratic than the method of nomination. But in practice this has not proved to be the case. A nominated upper house which obstructs the popular will as expressed by the majority in the lower chamber can always be overpowered by new appointments. In Queensland, a Labor government in 1922 ended its troubles with the Legislative Council by appointing Labor supporters to vote it out of existence. This state has since carried on very successfully with a single-chambered legislature. In New South Wales, to prevent any subsequent Labor government from doing the same, an anti-Labor party in power in 1933 changed the Legislative Council from a nominated house to one wherein vacancies are filled by a combined vote of the two houses. Fifteen members of a house of sixty are elected every three years by proportional representation. Therefore, only a strong Labor majority in the larger and more popularly elected lower chamber can vote a majority of its own party into the upper house at any one election. The same legislation provides also that a deadlock between the two houses may be resolved by the submission of the issue to a referendum of the people. This provision would apply to any attempt to abolish the upper house, and since Australian experience has shown that the people are very reluctant to say "Yes" on any issue submitted to a referendum, no Labor government as yet has thought it worth while to attempt to eliminate the New South Wales Legislative Council in this way.

In the four other states, however, the Legislative Councils have never been controlled by the more popular party, even though the property franchises originally established have been considerably broadened. The upper houses have remained strongholds of conservatism, and some bitter fights have taken place between them and the more liberal governments controlling the lower houses. In Victoria, in 1865, 1867, and 1877, a series of deadlocks occurred which brought government administration almost to a standstill and the state to the verge of revolution. The Victorian Legislative Council had the highest property qualifications for its membership and franchise of any of the state legislatures, and in the period of the crises referred to, it was dominated by the wealthy class of squatters. The lower house, it was said, represented men; and the upper house, sheep. In 1865 the government wished to introduce a protective tariff. The squatters, being interested in maintaining free imports, resisted. The government therefore tacked the tariff measure onto a supply bill which the upper house could reject but not amend. It was rejected and the state was left without funds. The treasurer borrowed from the banks and carried on. In its appeal to the country the government won, and faced by the storm of adverse public opinion, the Council gave way. The deadlock in 1877 was over the question of payment of members of the legislature. Again the government of the day tacked the measure onto a supply bill and the Council threw it out. The dispute and consequent disorganization lasted long enough to cause a minor depression, but at length the Council gave way.

It is a strange anomaly that democratic communities like the Australian states should continue to tolerate such an anachronism as a property franchise for the second chamber. The explanation seems to lie in two facts. In the first place the conservatives in the Legislative Councils tend to give way when the public demand for a measure is really strong. They use the Councils to fight a delaying action, but they have had sufficient wisdom not to try to dam the stream of progress permanently. In the second place, a large bloc of public opinion looks upon the Councils as a barrier against extremism. Many people who are willing to elect the Labor Party nevertheless prefer to keep the undemocratic Legislative Councils in existence lest, at some future date, a body of extremists should obtain temporary control of the lower house and the ministerial benches and rush through legislation which the majority do not really want. Further, it would be no easy matter to force a change upon the elected Legislative Councils as they are now constituted. There are provisions in each of the states for the solution of deadlocks between the two houses, but none of these make it possible for a majority in the lower house to overcome a reasonably strong opposition party supported by a majority in the upper house.   Doubtless, the Councils would have to give way on a constitutional question if the clamor against them became sufficiently great, but hitherto they have avoided that danger by shrewdly judging the time to retreat strategically.

Liberalizing the constitution.— The original constitutions of the Australian states were made, as has been shown, by men of property, and were carefully designed to safeguard the interests and power of the propertied classes.   This was justified by the argument that the man of property "has a stake in the country," while the man who has none can be "here today and gone tomorrow."   Since migration between the Australian colonies has always been easy this latter point has been largely true of each particular colony or state, but it has never been true of the country as a whole.   And it ignores the fact that every man, no matter how poor, has a stake more important than property in the land in which he is born, or in which he earns his living and rears his family.

The people of Australia did not long rest content, however, with the constitutions established for them by propertied interests.   Little could be done about the Legislative Councils, but the lower houses, which determined the formation of an executive ministry and controlled the finances, were more amenable to change, since their property qualifications were not high enough to prevent liberal movements from obtaining a majority.

Australia in the period of the gold rush, and for some time afterward, was a land where work and wealth were fairly plentiful.   At the same time England was seething with political discontent.   The Chartists had, since 1838, been clamoring for the six points of "The People's Charter," including universal suffrage, vote by ballot, payment of members of parliament, and abolition of all property qualifications. By 1850 the Chartist movement in England was defeated and dead. But when gold was discovered in Australia the next year and self-government was offered to the colonies, it seemed to thousands of the disappointed Chartists that here was the opportunity to create the democracy that England had refused to give them. Thus it happened that among the new immigrants, as Wentworth pointed out with alarm, was "a very thick sprinkling of democrats, Chartists, socialists, red republicans, *et hoc genus omne*." Earning good wages in a young country hungry for labor and rich with gold and wool, these people overrode the property barrier to the franchise of the lower houses of the new state parliaments, and elected governments ready to put into operation many of the Chartist ideals.

Voting by secret ballot was introduced in Victoria and South Australia in 1856, in Tasmania and New South Wales in 1858. It became known in America as "the Australian ballot," and was adopted for elections to Congress in 1884. Manhood suffrage abolishing the property qualification for electors of the lower house was adopted by South Australia in 1856 in its first constitution, and by Victoria in 1857. Gradually the other colonies followed suit. Women's suffrage was adopted by all the states and the Commonwealth between 1894 and 1908, South Australia again taking the lead. Before the formation of the Commonwealth in 1901 all the six states had adopted, with regard to their lower houses, all the points of the People's Charter except annual parliaments. In this connection the compromise was made of an election at least every three years, since annual elections would not give sufficient time for a ministry to develop and execute its policy.

Unlocking the land.— The bitterest battles of nineteenth century political history in Australia were not fought over constitutional questions, however, but over access to the land and the introduction of a protective tariff. We have already seen how the Orders in Council of 1847 had given the squatters long leases and the sole right to purchase their land at one pound an acre. At that time they thought the price too high and agitated for the administration of Crown lands to be passed over to the colonial Legislative Councils where they could control the sale. With the advent of responsible government this was done. Further, with the great new influx of population, land went up in value and the squatters became more willing to exercise their right to buy at one pound an acre. The banks also were more willing to finance them in exercising this privilege. Many of them abused the privilege by "peacocking" or "picking the eyes" of their leasehold estates—that is, by buying the land around the sources of water supply in order to render useless the purchase of the remaining parts. Still there were enormous areas of good land held under lease and used only for sheep raising. This was especially the case in New South Wales and Victoria. Both states were importing grain from South Australia, where the Wakefield plan had placed a much larger number of settlers on agricultural holdings, and even from North and South America. Successful diggers were anxious to invest their fortunes in farms in the fertile plains of Victoria and New South Wales, but the squatters clung to their leases or themselves bought the freeholds to secure runs for their sheep. Thus the new population that had come during the gold-rush years and now wished to take up farming found no land on which to settle. Consequently by 1860 Australia was a country with an established landed gentry controlling great estates and a restless, land-hungry proletariat.

In New South Wales the land-seekers found a leader in the picturesque figure of John Robertson, a former squatter and world-rover, handsome, forceful, possessed of a keen sense of humor and a remarkable gift for profanity—in brief, a formidable Australian political fighter. In 1861, Robertson secured the passage of two acts by the legislature. These were not designed to recover land that had already been bought as freehold, but to give the small man a chance to make his selection from land still held on lease. One act reduced the term of lease to one year in the "settled" districts, and to five years in the "intermediate" and "unsettled" districts. The other permitted any person to select from forty to three hundred and twenty acres anywhere in the "settled" and "intermediate" districts whether already leased or not, and whether surveyed or not. Such selections were to be bought freehold when the land was surveyed at one pound an acre by paying twenty-five per cent down and the rest in installments. The selector was to reside on his land for at least three years.

The squatters had a legitimate grievance against this act. It enabled a selector to "pick the eyes" out of their leasehold estates and leave them without access to the sources of water supply for the flocks pastured on the remainder. Some selectors bought such districts with no intention of farming and merely forced the squatters to buy them out again at higher prices. The squatters sought to protect themselves, against both the blackmailer and the genuine farmer-selector, by buying the "eyes" of the land first and by putting dummies in possession, as alleged selectors, to fulfill the residence requirements and to keep the land from genuine agriculturalists.

Robertson's acts in New South Wales were followed by similar measures in Victoria. But in both states the squatters were able, to a great extent, to defeat the purpose of the acts, and to acquire their leasehold estates in freehold for themselves. They took advantage of loopholes in the acts. They practiced "peacocking" and "dummying" on a wide scale, and they perjured themselves in doing so to retain possession of their lands. In order to protect their investments in loans

on the squatters' flocks, the banks helped to finance these purchases in spite of the perjury involved. Respect for the law
fell to a low ebb. The moral effect was deplorable, and class
strife and bitterness were aggravated. Robertson's law,
which was intended to create in Australia a class of sturdy
yeomen cultivating the soil on family-sized farms, became "a
law which made perjury a commonplace in the lives of thousands of people." [1]

The resultant attitude toward the squatter and the law is
picturesquely recounted in Australia's only folk song, "Waltzing Matilda." This ballad tells the story of a "swagman,"
a jobless wanderer of the plains, who steals a sheep for food.
He is caught in the act by three mounted policemen and the
squatter "riding on his thoroughbred." But he cheats the
jailer by leaping into the billabong (a small lake) by which
he has camped, and is drowned. The sympathies of the bush-
men who sang and popularized the song (and, it must be admitted, of the average Australian today) were not with the
squatter and the forces of the law, but with the hungry land-
less man, who gleefully stole from the oppressor, risking and
losing his life in a bid for freedom.

From the other side of the contest, but admitting the
same grim fact of moral obliquity, may be quoted a rhyme of
the period by a squatter's mother:

> A was the Act, antecursor of strife,
> B was the Bill that brought it to life.
> C was the Court, overcrowded with law,
> D was the Dummy, the creature of straw. . . .
> G was the Grazier, whose cattle were poor,
> H was the Homestead, he sought to secure. . . .

[1] Sir Timothy Coghlan, *Labour and Industry in Australia* (Cambridge
University Press, Cambridge, 1918), 3: 1350.

O is the Oath that was sacred of yore,
P is the Perjury, shameful no more. [2]

In New South Wales twenty-three million acres were sold in twenty-three years under the terms of Robertson's acts and amending legislation. But at the end of that time only four hundred thousand acres of this land were under cultivation. Indeed the state had fewer acres under cultivation at the end of this period than when the acts designed to unlock the land for the small cultivator were first passed.

In Victoria the attempt was a little more successful. The holders of small farms rose from fourteen thousand to thirty thousand between 1860 and 1870. But they held only a fraction of the millions of acres sold for farming purposes. In both states these first attempts to open the land to small freehold farmers resulted in enabling the wealthy squatters to turn their leaseholds into freeholds at a fraction of the land's real worth and keep sheep grazing for the profit of the few while thousands of poorer men clamored for land to till.

For the greater success in the Victorian program of closer settlement there were two reasons. To begin with, most of the land in question was itself more suitable for agriculture under the conditions of the times than that in New South Wales. Moreover, an act of 1856 (Grant's Act) inserted clauses requiring that certain improvements be made on the land in the first three years of occupancy if the selector wished to complete the purchase.

There are three main reasons why the Australian attempt to settle small farmers on the land failed for the most part, while those being made at the same time in the United States were such a magnificent success. First is the difference in

[2] Robert D. Barton, *Reminiscences of an Australian Pioneer* (Angus and Robertson, Sydney, 1917), 18–19.

rainfall. Most of the Australian land which the small farmers tried to cultivate was not suitable for such purposes, using the methods of the day. Only since modern machinery, manures, and dry-farming methods have been applied has the growing of grain been economically successful in the greater part of the area concerned. Sheep raising in the sixties and seventies was financially more successful than wheat growing, and the pastoralist was able to buy out the farmer even after he had been forced to let him obtain his selection. In Australia, moreover, the pastoralists were the first settlers. On the American frontier the battle with the Indians prevented lonely settlers moving too far beyond the edges of civilization. Farms had to be close together for protection. In Australia the aboriginals offered little resistance. The squatter went where he wished, and the land was occupied in large holdings which were economically most successful. Finally, the American land acts were more wisely formulated in matters of required residence and improvements and in measures taken to prevent dummying.

After some twenty years of failure in their attempts to develop agriculture, success was eventually achieved. Australians learned how to farm their lands successfully in spite of the uncertain rainfall. Governments bought up the estates of squatters in the areas most suitable for agriculture and subdivided them on long terms of purchase. Taxes were laid on the unimproved value of this land, progressively rising with the size of the estate in order to discourage large holdings. Safeguards were introduced into the closer-settlement acts to prevent the abuses to which they had previously been subjected. Thus, as the nineteenth century drew to a close, agriculture was spreading over most of the lands on which, under existing conditions, farming was economically profitable. The remaining battles for the expansion of Australian agriculture are not political, but rather the economic problem of finding markets for produce, and the scientific problem of preventing erosion, utilizing water supplies, and making the soil as fertile as possible.

Protecting native industries.— The father of the Australian protective tariff was David Syme. In 1853 he went to Victoria as a young man, made a little money in the gold-fields, and with it bought a struggling Melbourne newspaper. He was a dour, silent Scot with a keen, skeptical intellect that thought its own way through the problems of his time, came to unorthodox conclusions, and then proceeded to defend them with extraordinary clarity and force. Syme was a democrat and a liberal. His sympathies were with the miners and the land-seekers, not with the squatters. The liberals and democrats of his day were free traders of the school of Adam Smith. The conservatives in Australian politics, being interested in cheap imports, were of the same opinion. But Syme's thinking convinced him that, although free trade suited the interests of England, it did not suit the needs of a young country like Australia.

So David Syme began his one-man campaign to introduce protective tariffs into Victoria. No country, he argued, could flourish without a manufacturing industry. It alone could provide employment for the thousands now turning away from the played-out alluvial gold fields. It alone could provide an outlet for the skill and intelligence, the art and science of a vigorous people. Without it Australia must sink into the intellectually backward condition of a merely pastoral and agricultural country, without any opportunity for the culture of the masses. But as long as free importation of manufactured goods continued native industries could never establish themselves. "By the system of naked competition," he wrote in his newspaper, the *Age,* "our manufacturers are prevented from even making a beginning in the work of opening up new sources of industry among us."

Soon Syme's brilliant and insistent harping on this theme began to convert some of his countrymen. The circulation of the *Age* increased. Importers, becoming alarmed, tried to stifle his voice by withdrawing advertisements from his paper. He replied by reducing its price from sixpence, to threepence, to twopence, and finally to a penny. Its circulation bounded and advertisers came back. Politicians, either genuinely convinced by his arguments or sensitive to the popular demand he had created, came over to his side. The election of 1864 returned a Protectionist majority to the Victorian House of Assembly. The struggle that ensued to force the adoption of a tariff bill upon the squatter-dominated upper house served effectively to increase Syme's popularity and power. So influential did he become that he dominated Victorian politics for the rest of his life. He could make or unmake a ministry almost with a stroke of his editorial pen. He demanded further protective tariffs, and he obtained them. In 1877 Victoria set up tariff barriers averaging twenty-five per cent on some imports and ranging as high as forty per cent on others.

Economists still debate the question of whether the protective tariff really helped or hindered the development of Victorian secondary industries. Certainly its initial success was noteworthy. In the first ten years of its operation the number of Victorian factories and the number of persons employed in them increased fourfold. But it failed to hold in the state the large numbers of its population initially attracted there by gold. From 1871 to 1881 Victoria lost population to New South Wales and the other states. From 1881 to 1890 she gained 114,000 compared to a gain of 162,000 in free-trade New South Wales. At the same time manufacturing industries in the older state advanced and overtook those of Victoria. These facts do not, however, indicate that the free-trade policy of the one state proved, in the long run, more favorable to secondary industry than the protectionist policy of the other. New South Wales, as a manufacturing state, has a great advantage over Victoria in the possession of abundant coal supplies. Victoria even today has to import most of the coal for her industry from New South Wales. When all the facts are taken into consideration it seems clear, therefore, that David Syme's policy enabled many secondary industries to establish and maintain themselves in Australia through a long period during which their existence otherwise would have been impossible.

The other states produced no such redoubtable fighter for tariffs and remained free trade for the most part. But the Victorian tariffs became a nuisance in intercolonial trade, bringing about many attempts at retaliation. Friction increased, cooperation became more difficult, and the need for a federation of the colonies more evident.

After the federation of the states into the Australian Commonwealth in 1901 protection of native industries became the accepted policy of the nation. Under the protection of the tariff Australia has gradually equipped herself with a fairly complete set of secondary industries. The two world wars, temporarily cutting off other sources of supply, have acted as quickening agents in the process. Especially is this true of World War II, during which the advance was remarkable, particularly in steel and engineering. In this postwar period further plans are rapidly being developed for the establishment of manufacturing concerns of all kinds. Both British and American firms are active in the establishment of branch factories in Australia for manufacturing their products. The government's aim, which is rapidly being achieved, is a balanced economy, capable of producing at home all the necessities of civilized life, and of trading surpluses abroad for luxuries and comforts more successfully produced in other lands. Such an economy is desired partly for reasons of strategic strength and independence, and partly as the necessary basis for a rapid expansion of the population by immigration. It has been pursued, not without cost to primary industries and to the general standard of living. But where the cost has weighed heavily on primary industries, they have been compensated by subsidies; and in spite of these costs the standard of living has remained one of the highest in the world.

Since 1921 Australia has had a tariff board composed of economists and representatives of industry and commerce. The particular job of this board has been to give advice on matters pertaining to the tariff and to inquire into the efficiency of industries receiving or seeking its support. It has sought to produce, at the minimum cost to all concerned, a scientific tariff which will support such industries as the country needs for its development and can maintain efficiently while discouraging all others. In this effort it has been eminently successful. Consequently, in recent years, there has been an increasing tendency for governments to follow the board's advice, thus removing tariff questions from party politics and from the influences of selfish pressure groups.

There is now no party in Australia that advocates a return to free trade, though some wish to lower duties on particular items. The tariff, it seems to be generally agreed, is the price the country must pay for supporting as large a population as it does, and for its opportunity to support more people. Without the tariff Australia would become a country of declining population, and the only compensation would be that its already inflated land values would further increase. Farmers and pastoralists would obtain cheaper goods, make greater profits, sell their land at higher prices, and their successors would find life (with the additional burden of debt on the land) no easier than it is now.

Formation of the Commonwealth.— In 1863 problems connected with the tariff and other matters of common interest led to the holding of an intercolonial conference. This proved to be but the first of a series of such meetings, and steadily the need for a closer political organization of the states manifested itself. In 1889 Sir Henry Parkes, premier of New South Wales, thrust the question of federation before the people of all the colonies in a remarkable speech calling for the appointment of a convention, representative of all the colonies, to draw up a constitution for " a great national government of all Australia."

The public response to Parkes's speech led to the appointment in 1891 of a National Convention, such as he had called for, which drew up a tentative federal constitution. But the way to federation was not to be plain sailing. The free traders in New South Wales believed that federation meant protection and so raised a variety of objections to the new constitution. The newly formed Labor Party suddenly acquired the balance of power in New South Wales and pressed so strongly for social reforms that federation was thrust into the background. Others opposed the movement on the ground that, once started, it would lead to complete unification and regimentation from a single capital city. In spite of the opposition and indifference, however, the movement gathered force as the scattered Australian colonial settlements acquired a sense of unity and a vision of nationhood. A second National Convention called in 1897 drafted a complete constitution. After further vicissitudes and amendments this was carried by referendum in all the colonies except Western Australia and was passed by the Imperial Parliament. At the last moment the people of Western Australia changed their minds and agreed to be included. The new constitution came into force on the first of January, 1901, and six Australian colonies became the six states of the Commonwealth of Australia.

In shaping their constitution the Australian statesmen and jurists took the American Constitution as their model for the relation of state and federal powers. The result is a federal system in which specific powers are vested in the Commonwealth government by the states, all residual powers remaining with the sovereign states. In other respects it follows the traditional British model on which the colonial governments themselves were shaped. There is a Governor-General to represent the Crown. He is nominally the head of the executive, but he has no vote and he selects as his prime minister the leader of the strongest party in the House of Representatives. The prime minister chooses his cabinet from other members of parliament and retains office only as long as his party holds a majority in the House.

As long as the ministry governs in accord with the constitution the governor cannot interfere. But he can call for the resignation of a prime minister and force an appeal to the electorate if he believes the government has exceeded or abused its power. There is also a High Court which, like the American Supreme Court, has the function of interpreting the constitution and can declare a Commonwealth law unconstitutional. Thus, there is a double check on any attempt to transform legitimate political power into dictatorship.

The Commonwealth Parliament, like the American Congress, consists of a House of Representatives and a Senate, both elected by universal adult suffrage. In the Senate, each of the six states was given six representatives, one half retiring at a time. In the House, representation was fixed in proportion to population, with no state to have less than five representatives in a house of seventy-five members. [3]

The Australian Constitution, like the American, provides for free trade between the states but gives the federal government power to impose tariffs and to legislate concerning trade and commerce with other countries and between the states.

---

[3] In 1948 the number of representatives in the House was increased to one hundred and twenty-two; and that of the Senate to sixty, ten from each state elected by proportional representation.

It also contains an important provision, not in the American Constitution, giving the Commonwealth government power to pass legislation for the settlement of industrial disputes extending beyond the borders of one state. This has been broadly interpreted by the court to mean that any demand made by a union on employers in more than one state is a dispute within the meaning of the clause. Such an interpretation has made possible the important development of the Commonwealth machinery for settlement of industrial disputes and, incidentally, for the regulation, on uniform principles, of conditions of employment throughout the country.

The Australian Constitution omits the American provision guaranteeing to the individual freedom to contract. The phrase "freedom of contract" was an industrial battle cry of the employers in the nineties, and the Australian delegates were well aware of the difficulties the clause had created for organized labor in the United States. Australian efforts to legislate concerning hours and wages have therefore not been hampered by this embarrassing safeguard of extreme individualism.

In their provisions for amendment the Australian constitution-makers also departed from the American model. They provided for two methods: first, by a voluntary transfer of powers by the state parliaments to the Commonwealth; and second, by a bill passed by the Commonwealth Parliament and endorsed in a referendum by a majority of votes in a majority of the states. These provisions were thought to make amendment a little easier than the American method, but that has not been the case. Of twenty-four different proposals for constitutional amendment submitted to referendums in nearly half a century of Commonwealth history only four have passed. Attempts to secure amendments by the voluntary transfer of powers by the state parliaments have been even less successful.

Attempts to enlarge commonwealth powers.— All the unsuccessful attempts to amend the constitution have sought to enlarge the powers of the Commonwealth government in the control of economic affairs. The most important and typical was that submitted by the Labor government in 1911. This amendment proposed to give the federal parliament power 1) to deal with trade and commerce generally, not merely with foreign and interstate trade; 2) to control and regulate corporations; 3) to legislate concerning labor and employment, not merely to create machinery for the settlement of disputes but, for example, to make general rulings for an industry, or for all industry, concerning wages, hours, and conditions of employment; 4) to deal with combinations and monopolies, including the power to declare an industry a monopoly and nationalize it.

The opposition declared that the proposals were but a first step to the unification and centralization of all government at the federal capital, to socialism, and to the regimentation of every aspect of life. The referendum was defeated by considerable majorities in five of the six states. Similar proposals were submitted again in 1913. They were carried in three states but failed by a small margin to carry a fourth. The aggregate vote was only a half of one per cent short of a majority, the closest Australians have ever come to voting for an increase of the central government's power over commerce and industry.

In 1926 an anti-Labor government sought by referendum to secure power to pass Commonwealth laws concerning the creation and control of corporations; to allow Commonwealth machinery to deal with all industrial disputes (not only with interstate disputes) and to regulate conditions of industrial employment; to invest state authorities with certain of its powers; to control trusts and combinations in restraint of trade, including trade unions; and to protect the interests of the public against interruption of essential services. Apart from the last point (which had to be voted on separately) Labor itself had previously advocated such extensions of power. But when proposed by an anti-Labor government, and especially in conjunction with the last proposal, the workers feared that the powers would be used against them. Therefore they joined with those who, on principle, opposed extension of federal powers (the states' rights group), and the referendum was again defeated.

In 1937 another anti-Labor government, fast growing unpopular with the people, asked for power to control air navigation and to make laws for the organized marketing of Australian products. There was some opposition to the latter proposal, and the electors again voted "No" on both.

In time of war the Commonwealth Parliament has adequate power to do whatever is necessary. Its defense power, as interpreted by the High Court, enabled it to invade at any point the sovereign powers of the states and the ordinary liberties of its citizens, even to the extent of conscripting labor, as was done in the recent war. But Australians are loath to extend any of these powers to times of peace. The most deeply rooted objection to the extension of Commonwealth power seems to be an aversion to submitting to governmental authority in general, a dislike of regimentation, and a fear of the abuse of power. Most authorities in Australia are agreed that some extensions of federal power in the economic sphere are needed to deal with the complex problems with which the country is now faced. But it will be no easy matter to get such measures adopted by referendum. The plain citizen asks himself, "What could the government do with such power?" His fears of possible abuses are played upon by interested parties, states' rights advocates, and conservatives generally. And he decides not to take the risk.

This situation is illustrated by the fate of the proposals for extension of Commonwealth power for the postwar period. In December, 1942, a convention of representatives of both government and opposition parties in the Commonwealth and of all six states met at Canberra and drew up a list of fourteen powers which should be conferred on the Commonwealth for the war period and five years thereafter to meet the problems of postwar reconstruction. Since all parties in all states had agreed upon these recommendations it was decided to seek their enactment by uniform legislation in the state parliaments, transferring the powers to the Commonwealth for the period stated. But the necessary bill was passed without amendment or qualification by only two states and was rejected outright by one. When, after this failure, the government attempted to secure the same result by referendum the proposals were defeated again.

The High Court, also, has shown a conservative tendency to place narrow interpretations on the federal government's power. It has declared unconstitutional a great deal of legislation for the pooling and marketing of primary produce where the overseas market was the most important factor involved. It even rejected the Commonwealth's right to provide free pharmaceutical benefits, a decision which threw the whole program of social services into jeopardy. To meet this situation the Labor government in September, 1946, submitted another referendum asking for federal authority to legislate for social services, organized marketing of primary products, and conditions of employment in industry. The people returned the Labor government to power with a large majority, but the only one of its referendum proposals passed was that for the social services.

In May, 1948, with world-wide inflation threatening the price structure, the government tried again. They asked for peacetime power to control prices, rents, and wages. Wartime controls, it was recognized, had been more successful in keeping prices down in Australia than in any other country at war. But once again the people voted "No." It is not without significance that the only extension of power on a controversial issue that the federal government has been able to obtain by constitutional amendment is that for the maintenance of its social services. It is evident that the further ambition of the Labor Party to secure powers in the federal parliament for the socialization of industry, or the nationalization of monopolies, will long be delayed.

During the war, however, a profound change in the relations of the Commonwealth and the states, which greatly increases federal power, occurred without any constitutional amendment. This was the introduction in 1942 of the uniform income tax plan, the legality of which has been confirmed by the High Court in terms which admit of its continuation in the postwar years. Before the war there were pronounced differences in the income taxes of the different states, Queensland being the highest (especially on high incomes) and Victoria the lowest. The social services of the states also varied in a way roughly proportional to their income taxes. As the war required the imposition of high income taxes by the Commonwealth government an anomaly soon appeared. A federal tax that, added to state taxation, would constitute a reasonable absorption of private income for war purposes in Victoria would result in a tax of more than one hundred per cent for the higher incomes in Queensland. Yet public opinion demanded that income taxes should be high enough to compel every individual to make his full measure of financial sacrifice to the common cause, and the Commonwealth constitution required that its taxes should be uniform in all the states.

It was found impossible to secure any agreement with the states to modify their income tax rates to approximately common levels.   Therefore, the Commonwealth government acted in the only way left and imposed its rates at the required levels, thereby forcing the states to abandon the income tax field, but at the same time offering to each an annual grant equal to the average of its income tax receipts in the previous two years, with the understanding that it refrain from imposing an income tax.   The states could do nothing but accept, and the measure has met with general approval.   It is almost entirely agreed that the uniform income tax has come to stay.

Farsighted Australians see in this change the final establishment of the supremacy of the Commonwealth over the states in the matter of determination of policy.   Income tax will remain so high that no state can afford to refuse its grant and raise its own income tax.   The states therefore depend on the Commonwealth for the major sources of their revenue, and the Commonwealth can attach what conditions it deems fit to its grants.

In this situation the states seem destined to become, for the most part, not the determiners of policy, but the local instruments for the administration of policies determined by the federal parliament.   Changes will be made in the basis of distribution of grants to remedy existing anomalies. Social services will be equalized throughout the Commonwealth by direction of the federal authority.   Actual administration will be decentralized and will continue to operate through the present agencies and with the local supervision of the states; but the Commonwealth will be able to plan common and uniform policies for the country as a whole.   States' rights enthusiasts bemoan this prospect as the death knell of the states.   Others welcome it as promising the blessings of planning without central, over-all regimentation.   Whether it works out that way will depend upon the wisdom with which Australians, through their federal representatives, utilize the power which it is now seen that the Commonwealth constitution actually provides.

- 3 -

The Rise of Labor

AUSTRALIAN political history in the nineteenth century tells the story of the development of a liberal democracy shaking off the trammels of class rule. It tells of the majority asserting their rights against the privileged classes to obtain control of the country. In the twentieth century, however, the emphasis and the alignment are changed. No longer is it the struggle of the majority against the few for equality of political rights and economic opportunity. Now it has become primarily the effort of an economically repressed minority to obtain a larger share in the material welfare of the country. The issue is not political equality and freedom, but economic justice and opportunity; not the majority against a privileged minority, but the rise of a still-repressed minority against the opposition of a powerful and privileged few and the indifference of the middle classes—an indifference swinging between the poles of an impatient resistance and a hesitant help.

The dynamic agent in this new movement was trade

unionism.   Labor unions obtained an early start in Australia and have grown to greater size and power there than in any other country in the world.   A report of the Bureau of Census and Statistics for 1914 (which may be taken as typical of most of the present century) shows that Australia had 106 members of trade unions for every thousand persons in the population.   At about the same time Great Britain had 86; Germany (1913), 74; New Zealand, 68; France (1912), 38; and the United States (1913), 27.   Even in 1941, after the rise of the Congress of Industrial Organizations (CIO), the United States had only 91, compared with Australia's 149.

One important reason for the strength of trade unionism in Australia is that it has, almost from its inception, embraced the unskilled workers as well as the skilled tradesmen.   The failure to do this before the organization of the CIO accounts for the smallness of the American figures in 1913. The early and strong participation of the masses of unskilled and semiskilled laborers has also been an important factor in shaping the policy of Australian trade unionism, making it not merely an attempt to improve the lot of the workers in specific trades, but a mass movement of the underprivileged classes using every means in their power to overcome their disadvantages.

The real beginning of the Australian trade union movement dates from the period of the gold rushes.   Before that time conditions had not been favorable for such a development.   The class of free employees was relatively small, most of those who were not convicts being eager to go on the land for themselves as squatters.   Assigned convicts formed the bulk of the laboring class.   Further, the lack of free political institutions put too much power into the hands of the employing class to give a trade union movement much chance.

Nevertheless a beginning was made.   There was a strike of newspaper employees in Sydney as early as 1829.   Benefit societies were formed in connection with various trades from 1831 onward to provide sick, funeral, and unemployment benefits. In 1828 the newly formed Legislative Council of New South Wales (nominated by the governor and possessing only advisory powers) had passed the Masters and Servants Act attaching a penalty of six months' imprisonment to any artisan or laborer who left his job in breach of contract of service. In 1840 a petition signed by Sydney working men secured a modification of this penalty to three months' imprisonment or a fine. The trade unions were not responsible for this action, but nevertheless, it may be put down as the first important successful action of organized labor in Australia in either the political or the industrial fields.

In England, during the same period, trade unionism had gone much further. Before the end of the eighteenth century, working-class organizations had made enough trouble for employers to bring about the passing of the Combination Acts of 1799 and 1800 which made it a criminal "conspiracy" to join a trade union or organize a strike. After much agitation these acts were repealed and replaced by two others in 1824 and 1825 which legalized combinations of workers to improve their conditions but still made it a "conspiracy" for such combinations to do anything "in restraint of trade"—a clause which could be stretched to cover many things.

The repeal of the Combination Acts was the signal for a vigorous trade-union movement in England. Its aims and methods were nothing less than revolutionary. An attempt was made to organize a general strike, but this failed, and in a multitude of little strikes the workers were badly beaten. The trade unionists then turned to political action. In 1846 they secured the repeal of the Corn Laws and thus launched Britain on her career of free trade and cheap food. They joined in the unsuccessful agitation for the People's Charter. Many who joined in these struggles were convicted of political crimes and sentenced to transportation to Australia. Others, as we have seen, when the Chartist movement had failed and gold was discovered in New South Wales, set out to try to build their material fortunes and establish their political ideals in the new land.

Direct action in prosperity.— Apart from a depression in the forties, which was a repercussion of conditions in Europe, Australia was prosperous before the gold rushes, and the free laborer and tradesman enjoyed good working conditions. During the gold rush period, 1851–60, conditions were also favorable. Even after the alluvial gold had played out and the rush was over, work was still plentiful because of the rapid development the country was undergoing. The good times lasted until 1890, and in this thirty years of steady prosperity trade unionism developed apace. There was both the need and the opportunity for it.

In 1861 the coal miners at Newcastle, New South Wales, formed a union which seems to have proved permanent. Its aims were legislation for better ventilation of the mines and an improved and uniform wage scale. In a strike in the same year the wives of the miners drove off strikebreakers with stones, and a settlement was achieved by compromise.

The chief objective of early union activity, however, was the eight-hour day. This was first secured by the stone-masons of Sydney and Melbourne, in 1855 and 1856, on the ground that the heat of the Australian sun was too strong for longer hours at such strenuous work as theirs. But they had to sacrifice part of their wages to obtain the concession. From then on workers everywhere agitated for the eight-hour day without wage cuts. To achieve this goal became the principal object for the formation of unions. To celebrate the victory of 1856 annual "Eight-Hour Processions" were held in all the principal cities. In these labor dramatized its grievances and its ideals, and the eight-hour day became the rallying point of the movement.

It was not until after 1870, however, that the Australian trade union movement really hit its stride. In the twenty years following, practically every industry of importance in the country was organized. The aims set forward by the gold miners of Bendigo in 1872 were typical. They included the eight-hour day, maintenance of wage rates, resistance to the admission of Chinese, and legislation to regulate conditions in the mining industry.

The Seamen's Union was formed in Sydney in 1874 in protest against extremely low pay and bad conditions. Most notable and most typically Australian, however, was the organization of unions among the shearers and other workers in the great and scattered pastoral industry. Here, industrial unionism took in the migratory worker and the settled employee, skilled and unskilled, and rapidly welded them into a vigorous fighting organization.

The opposition to Chinese labor played an important part in this early period. As early as 1848 Chinese workers had been employed as shepherds, a lonely and poorly paid job for which little other than assigned convict labor could be obtained. During the gold rush period they came in large numbers, and in the Victorian census of 1861 they formed eleven per cent of the population. Racial misunderstandings and clashes, in which the whites were chiefly to blame, were common in the gold fields. But when the rushes were over a more serious situation developed. The Chinese were looked upon by the employers as a source of cheap labor. Sometimes they were used as strikebreakers. Their low standard of living and willingness to work long hours constituted competition which the white man could not meet. Justifiable objections to them on economic grounds were supported by sheer race prejudice and ignorant misunderstanding. These were backed by the fear that the small stream of oriental immigration already started might turn into a flood which would swamp the working-class population and turn Australia into a land where rich landholders and mineowners fattened on the cheap labor of a repressed coolie class while the poor whites were squeezed between the upper and nether millstones. In the existing conditions (political, psychological, and economic) this was probably the only alternative to exclusion of the Oriental. The workers, therefore, fought strenuously for an exclusion policy, while the employers fought for cheap Chinese labor.

Most of the unions were at first organized on a local or state basis. But it was not long before they began to come together into organizations overstepping the boundaries of the colonies or states into which the country was politically divided. This was necessary because, in spite of political divisions, Australia was, in many respects, an economic unit.

The first Intercolonial Trade Union Congress was held at Sydney in 1879. Eight such conferences were held, in different states, before the federation of the Commonwealth took place in 1901. They manifested a growing sense of Australian nationalism and played a considerable part in paving the way for political federation. The first Congress concerned itself with the extension and consolidation of the eight-hour day, legalization of trade unions, workmen's compensation for injuries, cooperation, education, encouragement of local industries, resistance to Asiatic immigration and to assisted immigration generally as tending to flood the labor market, and other matters affecting working conditions. Among significant additions to the agenda of later conferences were payment of members of parliament and direct parliamentary representation of labor (second congress); conciliation and arbitration, property and land

taxes (fourth congress); one man—one vote, land nationalization (fifth congress); compulsory courts of arbitration
(sixth congress). These items show a progressively increasing concern with political matters. But it was the
seventh congress, held in 1891, that heralded the special concern with politics that came to characterize what was then
called the new unionism. Here the political problems and
proposals for the political organization of the working class
became, for the first time, the principal topics of discussion.
During the period before 1891 there was no such thing as a
Labor Party in politics, but labor nevertheless succeeded in
impressing its will on the other parties by means of the ballot
box, and even in electing some specially selected members to
the state parliaments to represent working-class interests.
Charles Jardine Don, who worked for eight-hour legislation
in the Victorian legislature in 1859, is credited with being
labor's first genuine representative in an Australian parliament. Angus Cameron, in New South Wales in 1876, was
the first man to have his election expenses defrayed by and
to receive a salary from union funds as a parliamentary
representative.

Among the most important political concerns of the
unions was the legalization of their status. When self-government was granted to the Australian states English law
was assumed to hold good until expressly changed by stat-
utes of the new colonial legislatures. Australian trade
unions thus commenced operations under the protection and
limitations of the English acts of 1824 and 1825 already
referred to. The English acts of 1871 and after, which
gave further protection to the rights of trade unions, did not
apply in Australia. Thus, in 1891, strike leaders were sentenced to imprisonment in Australia under the "conspiracy
in restraint of trade" clauses of the English act of 1825,
although that act had been repealed in England twenty years

earlier.　Therefore one of the early objectives of labor in the various colonial legislatures was to secure legalization of collective bargaining, security of their funds from embezzlement, and other rights afforded by English legislation in 1871 and after.　This was done by South Australia in 1876 and similar legislation was passed by the other states within the next few years.

In strikes during the years before 1890 labor was for the most part successful.　Wages were maintained at a level probably higher in purchasing power than at any other period of Australian history.　The eight-hour day became general.　The closed shop was won in many industries. National organization of practically all unions was achieved in an Intercolonial Trades and Labour Congress.　Miners, shearers, seamen, and others were organized on an intercolonial basis.　Craft and industrial unions worked together for the common cause.　State governments, composed almost exclusively of members of the employing class, were considerate of labor's demands.

But all these successes depended on continuing prosperity throughout the country.　Wool, hides, tallow, and metals, which were the country's principal exports, brought highly profitable prices overseas.　The land was constantly being improved and put to better use.　The population was increasing; factories were being built in the cities.　Labor was in strong demand; unemployment was low.　Profits were high.　Employers were impatient to get on with the job and, therefore, ready to make concessions.　It was an ideal situation for the application of the methods of direct action.　The unions were organized for that purpose, and they succeeded.

Direct action in adversity.— This picture of prosperity changed rapidly in 1890 and the years immediately following.　In that year there was a panic on the London money market. Prices of wool, metals, and other Australian exports fell sharply, causing a serious reduction of income in the pastoral and mining industries of the colonies. The resulting general loss of confidence also stopped much of the flow of British capital into private investment in Australia. Government investment at this time was a small factor. Land prices, especially in Victoria, had for many years been inflated by speculators and these artificial values now collapsed. This resulted in widespread and serious unemployment and many business and bank failures. And before the country could recover from these it was struck by one of the longest and worst dry periods in its history—the droughts of 1896–1902. The twelve years beginning with 1890 were indeed years of adversity.

The early years of this period constitute a turning point in the history of the Australian labor movement. They were marked by a series of great strikes in which the unions fought for the principle of collective bargaining, the union shop, and the union shed, and the employers fought for what they called freedom of contract.

The lines of battle were deliberately drawn—with the employers as well organized for the fray as the workers. For example, the chairman of the Steamship Owners' Association is quoted as saying, "All the owners throughout Australia have signed a bond to stand by one another, and do nothing unless a vote of all the members be taken. They are a combined and compact body, and I believe that never before has such an opportunity to test the relative strength of labor and capital arisen." [1] The "opportunity" was created by the fact that large numbers of unemployed were walking the streets of the cities, hungry enough to be used as strikebreakers, and that the usually individualistic employers, faced with

---

[1] *The Silver Age,* July 29, 1890. A newspaper in the mining center of Broken Hill.

adversity, were ready to combine to protect what was left of their investments and their profits.

The preliminary skirmish was fought in Queensland and ended well for the workers. The squatters had formed the Pastoralists' Union to try to enforce freedom of contract, that is, the right to bargain with employees independently of the union. The shearers refused to accept anything but union rates of pay. The pastoralists brought in nonunion labor but the wharf laborers and seamen refused to handle the wool thus shorn. A conference was held and the pastoralists gave way on the major issue of union pay.

In New South Wales, however, events took a different turn. There was similar trouble in the shearing sheds over the employers' demands for freedom of contract and employment of nonunion labor. There too, the wharf laborers and seamen refused to handle "black" wool. But there was no ready surrender of the employers. This dispute soon became linked with another that had started in Melbourne. The marine officers had formed a union and affiliated with the Melbourne Trades and Labour Council. The shipowners objected to any association of officers with the unions of the men they had to command. While this was being threshed out the Sydney seamen sought support of the new Marine Officers' Association. Officers, seamen, and shearers thus became joined in a widespread battle which was fought bitterly for two months.

The shearers bolstered their solidarity by forming great camps from which they refused to move except for union pay. In this way, they exerted great pressure on the half-hearted and frequently intimidated would-be strikebreakers. Nonunion labor was brought in under special police protection. There were riots at the wharves when "black" wool was brought in and put on ships by strikebreakers. A certain Colonel Price, in charge of troopers protecting this activity, earned notoriety by his order "Fire low, and lay 'em out!" The state governments, controlled by the pastoralists and other capitalists, combined with the employers to break the strikes with nonunion labor protected by special constables. The miners came out in sympathy with the maritime and shearers' unions. Funds to assist the strikers poured in from other unions, from the public, and from England. But it was a losing cause. With so many thousands unemployed and destitute it was exceedingly easy to hire strikebreakers and the governments were eager to prosecute every act that could be construed as intimidation or conspiracy.

Faced with exhaustion of their funds and an unlimited supply of nonunion labor, the leaders at length saw that the case was hopeless. They were forced to give way on every point. They could not even protect themselves or their followers from retaliation by the employers. Many of them were prosecuted under the old Masters and Servants Act for breach of contract of service. They were heavily fined and made to forfeit their wages. The Marine Officers' Union had to withdraw from the Trades Hall. Freedom of contract had to be recognized as the general rule.

This great victory led employers to make what amounted to a general and concerted attack on collective bargaining in the name of freedom of contract. The millers, for example, insisted on asking every applicant for employment whether he accepted the principle of freedom of contract. The pastoralists announced further reductions of wages for shearers in the season of 1891.

In spite of their earlier defeat the Queensland shearers again attempted to resist. But nonunion labor with the protection of special police and the military had created a situa-

tion in which their efforts were futile.   Many strikers were
sentenced to long terms of imprisonment for minor breaches
of the law.   The members of the executive of the union in
the great camp at Barcaldine were arrested, charged with conspiracy under the old English act of 1825, and sentenced to
three years' penal servitude.   This act of 1825 had been repealed in England in 1871.   In spite of the fact that Queensland legislation, based on the English Act of 1871, had been
passed in 1886, the Supreme Court of Queensland ruled that
the earlier English act was still in force in the colony.   The
very dubious legality of this decision reveals how intense was
the feeling among the colonial ruling classes at the time that
unionism must be curbed.

There was an equal intensity of feeling among the
workers who were gathered, ten thousand strong, in scattered camps.   In the principal camp at Barcaldine there were
over a thousand men, who, as a sign of their rebellion, flew
the blue flag emblazoned with the white stars of the Southern
Cross that had been flown at Eureka.   Henry Lawson, the
poet of Australian democracy, expressed their attitude in
spirited verses in the *Brisbane Worker,* the only newspaper
supporting the strikers.

> So we must fly a rebel flag,
>   As others did before us;
> And we must sing a rebel song,
>   And join a rebel chorus.
> We'll make the tyrants feel the sting
>   Of those that they would throttle.
> They needn't say the fault was ours,
>   If blood should stain the wattle!

But it was all a futile effort.   There was no repetition
of Eureka.   Any attempt at armed resistance would have

been worse than useless. The employers, backed by the state, were too strong; and they were determined to use every possible means to crush the unions.

Having defeated the shearers' and maritime unions, the employers carried the war into the greatest stronghold of unionism in Australia, the rich silver-lead mining regions at Broken Hill where they had previously been forced to concede not only the closed shop but also the checkoff (the practice whereby the company deducts the union dues from the employee's pay and hands them over to the union).

The miners at this time (June, 1892) were working under an agreement which provided that any cases of dispute be submitted to a Board of Arbitration presided over by either a chief justice or a judge of the Supreme Court of one of the Australian colonies. The companies, however, gave notice that this agreement would be terminated at the end of the month, that daily wages would remain unchanged, but that the mine managers should have absolute freedom of contract in engaging men for work not done by day laborers. The miners came out and established picket lines. In retaliation the companies brought in strikebreakers. There were frequent disturbances. Many of the miners were arrested and imprisoned for picketing and attacks on non-unionists. At length the state stepped in and arrested seven members of the miners' executive committee, charging them with "conspiring together to incite numbers of Her Majesty's subjects to riot, tumult and breaches of the peace [and] to prevent subjects of the Queen from following their lawful occupations." They were sentenced to terms of imprisonment varying from three months to two years.

After four months the strike was called off, the company reducing wages and extending hours. The union's membership fell to one-tenth of its prestrike figure. Most of the strikebreakers remained at the mines on the company's new terms, while a great number of the former miners took ship for the gold diggings newly discovered in Western Australia.

These are merely the most important of the great wave of strikes in the early nineties whereby Australian unionism tried, by means of direct action, to maintain its standard of wages and hours in a time of serious unemployment. It was a brave attempt; but it was a complete failure. When the city streets and the long bush trails swarmed with thousands hungrily seeking for the means of subsistence, the temptation to turn strikebreaker was too strong. Direct action could make gains for the worker in prosperous years when the employer could grant concessions and still make a profit, and when he must accept union labor or go out of production. But direct action failed the worker at the time he needed it most.

Further, the unions had found that the employers had an ally in the state, which not only protected the nonunionist strikebreaker against intimidation, but which, being controlled by class interests, could twist the law and direct its force against the workers' organizations. These facts, staring them in the face, started new processes of thought in Australian working-class circles. The state must be turned from an enemy into a friend. The new institutions of democracy, developed in the last few decades, must be turned to account in the economic struggles of the masses. The strike was not their only weapon; they also had the ballot box. What they had been unable to gain by the weapons of industrial war they might be able to win by the political weapons of peace.

Labor turns to politics.— As we have already seen political action was not altogether new to Australian labor. The Intercolonial Congresses had long concerned themselves with political questions and the unions had taken action to place representatives in the legislatures. But as yet there was no Labor Party. Political action was merely a sideline of union interests. The report of the New South Wales Labor Defence Committee, after the first great defeats, however, stated: "This, then, is over and above all others the greatest lesson of the strike, that our organization must become a means of education and constitutional power. . . . The rule that trade unionism must steer clear of politics, was a golden rule when there was so much work to be done within our present industrial environments. But that time, as we have said before, is drawing to an end, and ere we can radically improve the lot of the worker we must secure a substantial representation in Parliament."

Similar advice came in abundance from leaders of public opinion outside the ranks of the unions. There were plenty of sympathizers with the working-class cause who deplored both the attack made by the employers and the strikes and resulting violence with which the workers resisted. From the press, the pulpit, and the political platform such people urged that the new democratic machinery of universal manhood suffrage and payment of members of legislative bodies would give a constitutional and peaceful alternative to the strike as a means of securing economic justice.[2] Probably none of those who gave this advice, however, were prepared for the promptness and the success with which the unions followed it. The reports of the parliamentary committees of the various states to the Intercolonial Congress held in April of the same year showed preparation for vigorous political activity. The New South Wales committee took the lead by reporting that it had already drawn up the constitution and

[2] One notable utterance to this effect was that of Sir Charles Dilk, a delegate to the Labour Congress at Brussels in February, 1891. Another was that of the Liberal premier of South Australia, C. C. Kingston, in an address to the Trades and Labour Council of New South Wales only a month later.

platform of a Labor Electoral League and was planning to run a large number of candidates at the next election. This took place only a few months later and, of forty-five candidates nominated and pledged to its platform, the new Labor Party elected thirty-six. It had polled 31.5 per cent of the votes cast for successful candidates and held the balance of power in the new house between the opposing Free Trade and Protectionist Parties.

The platform of this successful new political Labor Party was designed to appeal not only to trade unionists, but to all democratic voters. It incorporated all the liberal ideas that activated the minds of democratic people of all classes in the community at that time and became a model for the political labor movements of all the states. It included the principles of one man-one vote, free and compulsory education, the universal eight-hour day, antisweating legislation, extension of employers' liability for accidents, repeal of the old Masters and Servants Act and other such legislation unfair to labor, taxation based on unimproved land values, a national bank, national irrigation projects and other government industrial enterprise, and "the federation of the Australian colonies upon a national as opposed to an imperial basis."

Apart from the achievement of one man-one vote very little progress in any of these measures was made by that parliament. The Party was wooed by promises from both sides, but it was itself split on the free trade issue which divided the other two parties. It therefore could not use its bargaining power to advantage. In an attempt to consolidate itself and reap the fruits of holding the balance of power, a caucus resolution was passed that members should vote as a unit the way the majority decided, and that the whole party vote should be given to whichever of the other parties would concede most of the measures in the Labor platform. This policy was to apply even to questions of tariff until these could be settled by a popular referendum. But conscientious convictions on the fiscal issue proved to be too strong to be suppressed in this way. The Party divided, one half supporting the ministry and the other the opposition. This division and ineffectiveness dampened Labor's political enthusiasm to the extent that in the remaining three elections before federation the Party retained a strength of only eighteen members pledged to its platform. Not until 1910 did the state of New South Wales elect its first Labor government.

In the other states political action similar to that of the older colony was taken. Victoria returned eight Labor candidates in 1892 and thirteen at the next two elections, but did not succeed in returning a Labor majority independent of other organized parties until 1945. In Queensland the Party had its greatest success. It became the official opposition in 1894 and formed its first government in 1915. Since then it has held power continuously except for the world-depression period of 1929 to 1932. In South Australia Labor early attained the balance of power, and the state had its first Labor premier in 1905. In Western Australia and Tasmania no effective strength was developed until after the formation of the Commonwealth in 1901, and not until 1911 and 1914 respectively, did these states return their first Labor majorities.

Labor's influence in the state parliaments, whether in power or in opposition, certainly led to a more rapid attainment of the liberal and democratic planks in its platform than would otherwise have been the case. It also did much to prevent the power of the state from being abused by use against the interests of the working class. It actively promoted the development of free and compulsory education, of public hospitals and other social services, of legislation to improve conditions in mines and factories, of the minimum wage, industrial conciliation and arbitration measures, the eight-hour day and later the forty-four-hour week, the abolition of plural voting, and the introduction of woman suffrage. In many of these reforms Labor had the active cooperation of liberals in the other parties, and most of them would probably have been achieved in due course without the formation of a political Labor Party. But it is certain that these reforms have gone further and faster in states such as Queensland and New South Wales, where Labor has been strong, than in states such as Victoria, where, because of the peculiar concentration of the working-class vote in a small number of electorates, it failed to obtain a majority until 1945.

Labor in the federal parliament.— In 1901, in the election of the first federal parliament, the Labor Party returned sixteen of the seventy-five members of the House of Representatives. The first measure introduced by the new parliament was a bill for the establishment of a civil service. Here Labor pressed for and won the adoption of the principle of an adequate minimum wage. Next came the Electoral Act in which the principle of adult suffrage was incorporated by a large majority. The only other important business dealt with in the first session was the establishment of a mildly protective tariff and the inauguration of the White Australia policy, which Labor had long advocated and which was adopted with very little opposition. On the protectionist policy the Labor members split, ten favoring the Protectionist majority and six supporting the Free Traders. The second session passed a bill for setting up the High Court, which is the Australian equivalent of the Supreme Court in the United States, and little else of importance.

In the second parliament, elected in 1903, Labor increased its representation to twenty-four. The government, led by Alfred Deakin (Liberal and Protectionist), had twenty-seven members and the Conservative and Free Trade opposition, twenty-four. This gave Labor the balance of power; and, with the tariff question now out of the way, they were able to maintain their unity and use their position more effectively. In the Senate Labor was even stronger, raising its representation to fifteen out of thirty-six seats, while the Deakin Government held only seven.

The Labor members flung their strength immediately into a fight to secure passage of a bill creating a Court of Conciliation and Arbitration for the settlement of industrial disputes. This bill had been introduced in the previous parliament but was withdrawn by the government when an amendment to include public servants of the states within its jurisdiction was carried. Meantime a great strike in the Victorian state-owned railways, in which the men had been badly beaten by threats of severe antiunion legislation, had brought this question to the fore. The Labor members were convinced that they must seek the protection of arbitration and law for the workers' standard of living, and that these benefits were as much needed by government servants as by any others. They therefore demanded that the bill be brought forward again. Once more they introduced and carried the amendment to include civil service workers. Prime Minister Deakin, whose ministry had opposed the amendment, was thus forced to resign, and the Labor leader, J. C. Watson, was called on to form a ministry.

It is significant that the victory which first brought a Labor government into office in the national legislature was won by the Party's support of industrial arbitration. For this, in spite of certain extremist opposition, has ever since been one of the most basic, most cherished, and most distinctive tenets of the Australian labor movement. The Labor Party, however, was not allowed to win the credit for putting the measure on the statute book, since the new government was given only a brief four months' tenure of office before the opposition combined against it. Labor now became the official opposition. The new government again brought in the bill, made some minor changes, and passed it. Thus the Court started its career with the blessing of all parties.

This injection of the power of the federal government into the industrial arena as peacemaker and lawmaker was made possible by the clause in the federal constitution which gave the government the right to legislate for the settlement of industrial disputes extending beyond the borders of one state. It made provision for the formation of associations of employers and employees and their registration with the Court. Any such association may appeal to the Court for the settlement of a dispute, even before it has led to a stoppage of work. And since both the workers and their employers can organize on a national basis no difficulty is found in giving a dispute an interstate character and thus bringing it within the jurisdiction of the Court. The individual states also have established courts of a similar character, but a decision of the High Court states that a federal award takes precedence over that of a state court. The state courts serve a useful function in matters of purely local concern, but the advantage of a federal award is that it puts competing employers in different states upon the same basis by requiring them all to pay wages determined by the one authority. That authority, however, has decided that wages in different states, and in different places within the same state, should vary according to differences in the local cost of living.

In Australia's third parliament Labor returned twenty-five members. The Liberal group, however, led by Alfred Deakin, was reduced to eighteen. Labor refused a coalition with the Liberals but agreed to support them in office provided they would introduce legislation in accordance with the Labor program. In this way they forced the passage of a bill for the payment of old-age pensions, provision for which had been made in the constitution. In return they supported (for the most part very willingly) a measure raising the tariff.

Soon, however, many members of the party became restive at supporting a minority party in power, and Deakin was voted out of office. Andrew Fisher, who had succeeded J. C. Watson as leader of the Labor Party, now became prime minister, but was not allowed to remain in office long. The anti-Labor parties reluctantly composed their differences and a Fusion Government took office with Deakin as prime minister once more.

The new ministry occupied itself with defense measures. The issue for some time had been between those on the one hand who advocated contributions to the British navy and the raising of a professional army, and on the other hand those who wanted an Australian-owned and manned fleet and compulsory training of a citizen army. Labor had for several years advocated the latter, and public opinion had been steadily moving in the same direction. The government, sensing this drift of opinion, decided to conform, and the new Australian defense agencies thus took shape as national forces rather than as adjuncts to the imperial power of Britain.

To fight the election of 1910 Deakin's followers, most of whom had previously been proud to call themselves "Conservatives," took the name of the Liberal Party. The country, however, which wanted genuine liberalism, was not deceived. Fisher proposed as the Labor platform a graded tax on unimproved land values (with an exemption of five thousand pounds), a Commonwealth Bank, the taking over of the note issue from private banks by the federal treasury, and an amendment to give the federal parliament power to legislate on all industrial matters. In most if not all of this program the majority of the electors saw more true liberalism than in that of the Fusion Government. They elected the full slate of Labor senators and returned forty-two Labor representatives to the House of Representatives.

When parliament met, Prime Minister Fisher proceeded to place the legislation of the party platform on the statute book. In spite of the prophecies that the new notes would soon be valueless, the function of issuing paper currency was taken over from the private banks. And in spite of the warnings that it would ruin the wool industry, the graduated tax on unimproved land values in holdings of over five thousand pounds was passed. It commenced at threepence on the pound and rose to sixpence (i.e., two and one-half per cent) on estates worth over seventy-five thousand pounds. One of its chief purposes was to cause the breaking up of large estates into small farms. In this it had only small success, but both measures brought in a considerable revenue from sources that could well afford it and none of the dire effects prophesied were ever in any way visible.

Against similar opposition the Commonwealth Bank was also established. It was Labor's first installment of socialism and was strongly criticized as such. But in subsequent decades its value has been abundantly demonstrated, especially as it has increasingly developed the functions of a central bank, and it is now a universally accepted part of the financial machinery of the Commonwealth.

In the final session of this parliament, with revenue abounding from land tax and customs duties, the prime minister brought in another piece of legislation not in the pre-election platform. This was an act for the payment of a maternity allowance of five pounds to every mother to help in the expense connected with childbirth. It was a piece of humanitarian legislation of which Fisher was very proud.

That plank in the platform which proposed to extend the powers of the federal parliament to deal with industrial matters, however, was not so successful. since the referendum needed to accomplish this extension of federal jurisdiction had been soundly defeated. [3]

When election time came around again in 1913 Fisher appealed for support on the strength of his record. His only new proposal of importance was for a further extension of socialism in the establishment of a Commonwealth line of overseas steamers to minimize freight charges on Australian exports and imports. This aroused little enthusiasm. The opposition promised to maintain the tariff and the pensions system but to abolish preference to unionists in government employment, a practice adopted by the Labor government. There was little interest in the election. As usual in such situations the working classes did not turn out in full strength to the polls. Labor came back to the House with a minority of one.

Joseph Cook, new leader of the anti-Labor parties, took office but soon found it impossible to conduct the government with so narrow a margin and without a majority in the Senate. He decided to challenge Labor on a decisive issue and brought in a bill to prohibit preference to trade unionists in government work. This was rejected by the Labor majority in the Senate. Both houses were therefore dissolved in a fresh appeal to the electors. This was July 30, 1914. During the election campaign, war broke out. While the crisis was developing Fisher pledged his party, in the event of war, to the support of the Mother Country "to the last man and the last shilling." No one expected that the other side would do less, but Fisher's early and emphatic announcement certainly helped his cause. Labor was returned with the comfortable majority of forty-two seats in the House and almost swamped the Senate by taking thirty-two of the thirty-six seats. It became Fisher's task to organize the country for war.

[3] See page 50.

Preoccupation with the war set aside for a time any consideration of further social legislation. The "Anzacs," so called from the initial letters of "Australian and New Zealand Army Corps," which was the first force raised, won glory at Gallipoli; and five Australian divisions, subsequently formed, added to these honors by their deeds in France, as did the Light Horse in Palestine.

Toward the end of the year 1915 Fisher was made High Commissioner for Australia to Great Britain, and William Morris Hughes became prime minister. He was a dynamic Welshman, a former schoolteacher who had become a fighting leader of the Sydney Waterside Workers' Union, had entered politics, studied law, and served as attorney general in the Labor government. He was also an ardent believer in the Allied cause in the war. In the difficult days of 1916, when enlistments to reinforce and increase the volunteer armies sent overseas began to fall off, he and many other leaders of the Labor Party became convinced that the time had come to introduce conscription for overseas service, a measure for which the press and the opposition had been calling for some time.

This proposal, however, ran against the deep convictions of many of his colleagues and of the majority of the working class. Compulsory training for military service and conscription for home defense were a recognized part of the Labor program. But the average Australian of the working classes did not clearly grasp the significance of the war in Europe. It was good and noble and generous, they believed, for volunteers to go and fight for the Mother Country, but they could not see the need or the right to compel any man to fight in such a war who did not feel the call to do so of his own free will. Further, labor had always been anti-Imperialist, and many were more or less convinced that the war was merely a struggle of rival imperialisms, in which the working class, as such, had no real concern. Added to these was a large body of citizens of Irish extraction (mostly city workers and trade unionists) whose sympathies were more with rebellious Ireland than with Britain.

Thus the Labor Party in parliament found itself divided on the conscription issue while a revolt against the proposal was rapidly brewing in the working-class constituencies. The upshot was a compromise. The question was to be put to a referendum in which both sides should be free to express their opinions. The referendum battle was fought bitterly. The rank and file of the Party proved to be strongly anticonscriptionist. In New South Wales the supporters of conscription, including the Labor premier of the state, W. A. Holman, were expelled from the Party. The referendum proposal was defeated by a narrow margin. But the split in the party had gone too deep to be healed.

When the Labor caucus met again after the poll a vote of no confidence in the leadership of Prime Minister Hughes was passed. He and twenty-four others (including half the members of the cabinet) then withdrew from the Party. They formed a new ministry and were supported in office for a time by the former opposition. Subsequently the two groups combined to form what was called the National Party with W. M. Hughes still as prime minister.

Labor had defeated the conscription proposals, but it had done so with the support of a great many people who were not prepared to vote for its political proposals. Further, Hughes and his National Party had, by their support of conscription, won the favor of many who had formerly voted Labor. This was shown when election time came around again in 1917. The Nationalists swept the Senate and returned forty members to the House of Representatives. Encouraged by this they made another, but still unsuccessful attempt to carry a referendum on conscription. It was defeated by a larger majority than before.

Twelve years elapsed before the Labor Party recovered from the split over conscription. It had lost its ablest leaders and had to develop new talent. The trade-union arm of the movement was also torn by strife between militant members of the Industrial Workers of the World (IWW), who fomented strikes as a matter of revolutionary principle, and the moderate union leaders. The resulting industrial strife further alienated the sympathy of the floating vote from the political Labor Party.

Hughes and those who had gone with him into the ranks of the Nationalists, however, were not able to liberalize the policies of their colleagues. They became the mere front for the conservative and reactionary forces of the day. Hughes was allowed to retain the office of prime minister until 1922, when he was dropped in favor of S. M. Bruce at the insistence of Country Party supporters of the government. The prosperity of Australia increased greatly between 1918 and 1929, but in matters of social legislation the country stood still.

- 4 -

The Battle with Depression

IN THE decade following the first World War the government of the Commonwealth was in the hands of the conservative parties. This was generally true also of all the states except Queensland. The Labor Party had lost so much of its able leadership in the split over the conscription issue that it made little appeal to the floating vote. Further, Australians generally were convinced that their country had already been made "the working man's paradise." They claimed, rightly enough, that wealth was more evenly distributed in Australia and New Zealand than in other comparable countries, and they pointed with pride to the fact that, after New Zealand's, theirs was the lowest death rate in the world. They also argued strenuously, but not quite accurately, that the general standard of living of their working classes was higher even than that in the United States and Canada. In these circumstances little enthusiasm could be aroused for further measures of social advancement.

Actually, the workers' standard of living had really suffered considerably through increases in the cost of living for which there had been no adequate compensation in rates of pay. Militant unionists, inspired by the theories of the IWW imported from America, sought to remedy this situation by strikes which broke agreements established by the Arbitration Court. This action further alienated the sympathies of the middle classes. To the general public labor seemed to be pressing mere sectional interests. The country was concerned with programs of economic expansion designed to benefit the community as a whole, and these seemed to be best left in the hands of the "businessmen's governments" of the conservative parties.

The policy adopted was twofold: first, the raising of tariffs to encourage the growth of secondary industries; and second, schemes for the extension of land settlement. Both were accompanied by a policy of assisted immigration under an agreement with Great Britain whereby selected immigrants were enabled to undertake the five weeks' journey to Australia at a cost no greater to them than the one week's journey to Canada or the United States, the balance being paid by the British and Australian governments. With this assistance the net immigration to the Commonwealth in the decade 1920–1930 amounted to over three hundred thousand persons. This, added to a fairly healthy natural increase, enabled Australia to boast that it had the fastest growing population in the world.

The protectionist tariff, which had first been established in 1908 by the Deakin Liberal Government with Labor support, was greatly increased by the Hughes Nationalist (non-Labor) Government in 1921. In the same year the Tariff Board was set up. At this time support for tariff increases was almost unanimous. Labor saw in them a protection for the workers' standard of living and a means of increasing employment. The manufacturing and most of the commercial interests were naturally enthusiastic. Primary producers were opposed, but their voices were lost in the chorus of approval. Soon they too began to ask for and receive protection and subsidies.

The Tariff Board, in its earlier years, acted on the widespread Australian assumption that the protection of infant industries must promote prosperity. After a few years, however, a closer examination of the cost of this process showed that inefficient secondary industries were unduly raising the cost of living and hindering rather than aiding the progress of the country. Under the system established by the Arbitration Court wages had been raised to meet the increased cost of living, and labor therefore did not complain. But the farmers producing for export found themselves squeezed between rigid or falling prices for their products and rising costs of everything they used. In 1925, and again in 1927, therefore, the Tariff Board issued warnings that a halt must be called to the spiral which was raising the price of everything except products which had to be sold overseas. In 1929 an expert committee appointed by the prime minister reported that one-quarter of the country's production, which enjoyed tariff protection, was costing the community twenty-four per cent in excess of the cost of imported goods, raising the general price level by ten per cent. This report did not, as we shall see, prevent the resort to still higher tariffs in the effort to overcome the depression of the thirties, but it did create a tendency, after the return of more normal times, to rely more and more on the board's advice in matters of protection. Questions on tariff policy are increasingly being removed from the arena of party politics and placed before an impartial and expert tribunal which periodically assesses the effect of tariff schedules on the national economy as a whole. However, this stage of political wisdom was reached only after the bitter years of the great depression had taught the dangers of wholesale protectionism.

The schemes for land settlement included the purchase and subdivision of large estates, the construction of irrigation works, and the building of roads and railways to open up new land of marginal quality which recent developments in farming methods, instruments, and fertilizers had shown to have possibilities for wheat production. Many of these schemes, especially the irrigation projects, have proved valuable additions to the productive resources of the country. They were semisocialistic in character but were carried out, for the most part, by conservative governments who saw that the resources of the country could be developed in no other way. However, many mistakes were made. In closer-settlement schemes the prices paid for land were often too high and the blocks allotted to settlers too small. Wheat farming was pressed forward into arid areas where the farmers were impoverished in dry seasons when drought wasted their crops and wind-erosion wasted the soil. The dried fruits produced in the irrigation settlements could not compete in price on the English market with the products of Mediterranean countries and had to be heavily subsidized to save the settlers' investments and preserve the productive value of the government's capital expenditure in irrigation works.

To finance these schemes and other public works the Commonwealth and state governments borrowed money from abroad, chiefly in London. From 1919 to 1928 the external debt rose from £347,000,000 to £570,000,000 and the internal debt, from £358,000,000 to £524,000,000. This involved an overseas interest bill of about four pounds a person, nearly one week's wages for a man on the basic wage. In the five years immediately before the depression, Australia was spending on public works, not all of a reproductive or developmental character, thirty million pounds a year borrowed overseas.

Even in these years of so-called boom, however, there was a considerable amount of unemployment. The figures of trade unions show nearly eight and one-half per cent as the average between 1919 and 1928. This compares with somewhat under six per cent in the years before the first World War. Such a high degree of unemployment in a young country undergoing a developmental boom and spending large sums of borrowed money has puzzled economists. The explanation, however, lies in the fact that Australia, with her large external trade, was merely a part of the total economy of the British Commonwealth, within which there was a free flow of capital and a fairly free flow of goods. Unemployment within this great economic unit was unevenly distributed, being heaviest in Wales and northern England. The system as a whole was not geared to maintain full employment anywhere, except in certain small areas, hence Australia's two and a half per cent increase in unemployment after the first World War (as compared with before) was simply her share of the general economic decline in the economic unit of which she was a part.

In 1927, the increase in the overseas debt and the difficulties which some of the states experienced in financing their part of the expansion program led to the formulation of a very important financial agreement between the Commonwealth and the states. By this agreement the Commonwealth took over the public debts of the six states; it contributed seven and a half million pounds a year to the payment of interest on these debts and established a sinking fund (from joint contributions) by which such debts were to be liquidated.

The agreement also established an Australian Loan Council consisting of a representative from the Commonwealth and from each of the states, which was given the power to control the borrowing of all the seven governments concerned. On this council the states have one vote each and the Commonwealth two, plus the casting vote. Thus the Commonwealth and any two of the six states form a majority.   The Loan Council, which has now become an established feature of Australian government, is a unique institution in a federal system.   Its purpose is to increase the credit of the states, enabling them to borrow at lower rates of interest, and also to restrain them from unwise borrowing programs.   The financial contributions of the Commonwealth to the states also mean that the wealthy manufacturing communities contribute to the support of the poorer states from which they draw part of their wealth.   To give the Commonwealth power to make such an agreement required an alteration of the constitution.   But with the unanimous support of all parties the amendment passed successfully over the hurdle of the necessary referendum.

The financial crisis.—   Australian overseas borrowing came to a sudden end in 1927–28 when loans of fifty-four million pounds were raised.   The average over this and the previous five years had been thirty million pounds.   London financiers then came to the conclusion that this continuous increase of public debt was unsound.   A loan raised in January, 1929, left eighty-four per cent in the hands of the underwriters, and London decided to underwrite no more.   Australia thus found herself with thirty million pounds of her income suddenly cut off and the great body of unemployed who had formerly been engaged in the public works on which the loans were spent were now without employment.

At the same time the prices of wool and wheat, the principal exports of the country, began to fall off drastically, the first shock being at the Sydney wool sales in August, 1929 —a prelude to the catastrophic slump on the New York Stock Exchange which followed soon after.   Between January, 1931, and 1932 the world price of wool fell fifty per cent and that of wheat sixty per cent.   The price of manufactured goods, which formed the bulk of Australia's imports, fell slowly and relatively little.   The huge external interest bill was a fixed quantity. The country's exports, therefore, (chiefly wool and wheat) were no longer sufficient to pay for its imports; and no loans were available to make up the balance. By the middle of 1930 it became evident that Australia was heading toward insolvency and something drastic had to be done.

In October, 1929, a Labor government had come into power in the Commonwealth parliament for the first time since the split on the conscription issue in 1917. The election had been fought on a proposal by the previous government to abolish the federal Arbitration Court and hand industrial arbitration over to the states. Since this would have meant that a state paying low wages would have an industrial advantage over its neighbors, and thus tend to drag all wages down, the proposal was interpreted as an attack on the workers' standard of living. The Labor Party won forty-six of the seventy-five seats in the House of Representatives, but was still in the minority in the Senate. The new government under J. H. Scullin therefore controlled the administration, but the opposition was in a position to block any legislation.

Labor could not have come back into power under more difficult circumstances. The people looked to the party to preserve the threatened standard of living. But that standard was being undermined by forces which neither the Labor politicians nor their opponents knew how to control.

In an effort to restore the balance of trade the government urged the farmers to grow more wheat in order to combat the fall in price by increasing the quantity for export. In response to this patriotic appeal, and backed by the promise of a guaranteed price of four shillings, which would yield a fair profit above costs, the farmers responded by increasing the acreage by more than twenty per cent in 1930–31. They reaped a good crop which, flung upon the already glutted world wheat market, further depressed the price. The government was unable to fulfill its price guarantee because the Senate turned down its wheat marketing bill. The farmers found that their patriotic effort had plunged them further into debt because the price did not pay for costs of production. But instead of blaming the Senate for refusing to guarantee a price far above world prices they blamed the government for urging them to grow more wheat and making them promises which could not be fulfilled. Thus Labor lost the support of the farmers.

Had the Labor legislators been sufficiently astute and bold to take up the challenge on behalf of the farmer and ask for a double dissolution on this issue they might well have gained a clear majority in both houses. They would then have been in a position to deal with the problem of deflation in their own way; or if they had lost they would have left the unpleasant task to their opponents and escaped the impossible situation of holding responsibility without power in a time of crisis. Instead they accepted defeat at the hands of the Senate and tried to hold back the avalanche with their hands tied.

In Labor circles generally it was believed that the existing unemployment had been caused by the high rate of immigration in the previous ten years and by an excessive volume of imports. If more of the goods now imported could be made in Australia and immigration were stopped, there would soon, it was argued, be work for all. So the Labor government's first efforts to mend the situation took the form of putting an end to assisted immigration and of setting up new and prohibitive tariffs. The tariff proved an inadequate means of reducing the volume of imports and created expensive trade barriers which it has subsequently been difficult to remove. The immigration restriction was generally approved, for few people then understood the truth that the immigrant creates more jobs than he takes and that opportunities for employment tend to be greater with a fast growing population than with one that is slow.

The ablest man in the Labor government, and probably the most farsighted in Australian politics at the time, was E. G. Theodore, the Commonwealth treasurer. He appears to have seen from the beginning that the simplest way to remedy a general depression is not by ruthless deflation but by increasing government expenditure. In April and May of 1930 he brought in two bills designed to make the Commonwealth Bank a central bank under government control with powers to assist the government in a policy of reflation.

The Commonwealth Bank had been established by the Fisher Labor Government in 1911 as a people's bank, a government trading enterprise to compete with private banks, not as a central bank. Starting without capital it accumulated profits of four and one-half million pounds in the first thirteen years. During this period it was administered, free from political interference, by a governor on seven years' appointment. In 1924 a conservative government changed the control of the bank to that of a board consisting of the governor, the secretary of the Treasury, and six representatives of big business and finance. The bank was also given control of the note issue and the functions of a clearing house for the trading banks. The new board pursued a policy of limiting the bank's ordinary banking operations to prevent it from becoming a competitor of the private banks.

Theodore's bills in 1930 were designed to give it all the normal functions of a central bank and bring it under almost complete government control by stipulating that four of the nine directors be civil servants; the bills also empowered the bank to make unsecured advances to the government without limit and to buy municipal securities of the capital cities. This policy, obviously, would have enabled the government, through the bank, to finance a program of expansion of public works and agricultural subsidies sufficient to restore the purchasing power of the community. Such a program would, just as obviously, have further strained the exchange position and driven Australia off the gold standard. The Senate saw in these proposals nothing but the danger of a spiral of uncontrolled inflation and rejected both bills. The Labor government thus found its program stymied at every point except on immigration and the tariff. But still it did not resign.

The experts take a hand.—— The conservative parties found support for their position in the influential figure of Sir Otto Niemeyer, who had been sent out by the Bank of England to investigate the financial position of Australia, a debtor country in difficulties and applying for further assistance. He advised a Senate committee that the Commonwealth Bank should be free from political control and should have a limit placed on its advances to governments. He pointed out to a conference of state premiers that Australian credit in London was the lowest of all the Dominions, lower even than that of India. He criticized the lavish government spending of the twenties, the high wage rates, and the protection of uneconomic industries. He pointed to the difficulty the Commonwealth Bank was having in maintaining parity with the English pound and warned that "rising exchange rates prejudice the whole fabric of government finance." He thus supported the bank board, which had taken the position that "it could not possibly desire to advise any action which would savour of Australia departing from the gold standard." [1]

The six state premiers and the Commonwealth prime minister to whom Sir Otto read this lecture in August, 1930, were so impressed by his authority as an economist and finan-

[1] D. B. Copland and E. O. G. Shann, *The Crisis in Australian Finance, 1929–1931* (Angus and Robertson, Sydney, 1938), 6, 24.

cier that they all (three of them Labor Party leaders) signed an agreement that they would balance their budgets in the financial year 1930–31; that they would raise no more overseas loans until existing short-term debts in London had been funded; and that they would undertake no further public works that could not be expected to pay for themselves. This meant drastic reductions in expenditure, further unemployment, and heavy taxation. Labor supporters throughout the country were amazed and angry that the leaders of three Labor governments should have consented to such proposals. Conservatives rejoiced at what seemed to them a victory for sound common sense.

In October an election took place in New South Wales. William Lang, leader of the Labor opposition, fought the election on the issue of repudiating the agreement of the Premiers' Conference and won a resounding victory. In the same month the caucus of the Labor members of the federal parliament passed two resolutions which became notorious. One required the Commonwealth Bank to create sufficient credit to finance the needs of the Commonwealth government, including twenty million pounds for public works. The other resolved to introduce legislation compelling London bondholders whose loans were falling due to hold their securities for a further year at the usual rate of interest. Both of these resolutions were futile gestures for, without control of the Senate they could not pass such legislation or compel the bank board to change its policy. The second resolution was not only foolish but dangerous. It made the holders of Australian bonds everywhere fear for their security and morally shocked the good people of the country to whom the thought of failing to fulfill their financial obligations to the letter was abhorrent.

All the governments, except that of Premier Lang in New South Wales, made honest attempts to keep the agreement to balance their budgets, but none of them really succeeded.   The Loan Council had to allow them to borrow from the trading banks for temporary purposes.

Australian economists, though inclined to be cautious, did not agree with the rigid financial orthodoxy of Sir Otto Niemeyer and the Commonwealth Bank Board.   At the meeting of the Australian Association for the Advancement of Science in June, 1930, the economists in attendance issued a statement pointing out that the fall in prices of exports and the cessation of loans from abroad entailed a serious loss of national income.   They urged that measures should be taken to distribute this loss over all classes of the community by reductions in both profits and wages and that taxes on income from property should be increased to help balance the budgets.   They criticized the existing system of wage fixation according to the cost of living as too mechanical and based on inadequate figures.   They objected to the increased tariff.   But they supported unemployment-relief plans and opposed the complete cessation of overseas borrowing.   Very significantly, they threw away the fetish of the gold standard and declared that the exchange should be left free to find its own level.   But they advised against any exploitation of the note issue.

Four months later, three leading economists (D. B. Copland, L. F. Giblin, and E. C. Dyason) issued another joint statement.   They estimated that Australia had lost one-fifth of its national income owing to the repercussions of the fall in the prices of its exports and the cessation of external borrowing.   They then made specific suggestions for the distribution of this loss equitably through the community. These involved a reduction of real wages by ten per cent and the imposing of a graduated supertax averaging ten per cent on income from property.   But they urged the Commonwealth Bank to liberalize its loan policies and declared that the price of sterling exchange should be fixed at a premium of at least twenty per cent on the Australian pound. The recommendation to lower the exchange value of Australian currency was, of course, to give the hard-hit exporter of primary products the advantage of the premium and to discourage unnecessary imports. In January, 1931, the assembled economists issued a third manifesto along similar lines but added a recommendation to reduce interest rates and cut public expenditure. The effect of these manifestoes was seen in the same month. With specific reference to their arguments as justification the Commonwealth Bank agreed to let the exchange find its own level, and the Commonwealth Arbitration Court announced a ten per cent cut of the basic minimum wage. This, as a matter of course, was followed by a similar reduction of all other wage scales fixed by the Commonwealth Court, with the state tribunals, for the most part, making the same reductions.

The exchange fell immediately to a thirty per cent premium on the English pound sterling. This was a shock to financial orthodoxy and to Australian pride, but it was not long before it was made respectable by the Bank of England's following suit, leaving only the dollar clinging to the old gold parity. The Australian primary producer then had a great advantage over his rivals in the United States, Canada, and Argentina. Until President Roosevelt took the dollar off the gold standard American farmers had to take a heavy discount on all the exports they sold on the London market and in other countries with currencies based on sterling. The Australian, on the other hand, received a handsome premium on the price of his wheat, wool, butter, fruit, and other products, an advantage which proved to be an important factor in Australian recovery.

Reducing basic wages was an honest mistake made by people who were still under the spell of classical economic theories. Labor argued in vain that it meant a further disastrous decline in the purchasing power of the community. The Court replied that it meant merely that the employee would receive a little less purchasing power and his hard-pressed employer would retain a little more. Few concerned seem to have grasped the point that money received by the employee would for the greater part be spent on consumer goods and thus give further employment, while, in the existing circumstances, much of the money retained by the employer would not be expended but would be used to reduce debts or saved for investment in better times—in either case it would be withdrawn from circulation, causing further unemployment. Economists and businessmen were still under the illusion that the best way to stimulate a demand for labor, as for anything else, was to reduce its price. And it was on this theory that the Court acted.

The basic wage had already fallen ten per cent with the fall in the statistical figures on the cost of living to which it was tied. The new cut was a cut in real wages designed to reduce the workers' standard of living, which, it was believed, had been fixed at a figure the economy of the country could no longer support.

The battle of the plans.— In February, 1931, a month after the great drop in the exchange and the lowering of the basic wage, the premiers met again and found themselves presented with three alternative plans. The first was that of a committee appointed by the Loan Council consisting of treasury officials advised by three very conservative economists, Professors Brigden, Hytten, and Shann. They criticized the high exchange rate, recommended severe economies, and said that interest rates could not be cut until confidence was restored. The second plan was presented by E. G. Theodore, the Labor government's treasurer. He recommended government economies but pointed out that these alone could not restore financial equilibrium. He urged a generous credit policy by the banks, reduction of interest rates on deposits and overdrafts, new internal loans for farm relief and public works, and letting the exchange find its natural level.

This latter plan depended on the cooperation of the banks, which was not forthcoming, as they were still convinced that further deflation was necessary. The new Labor premier of New South Wales, William Lang, anticipating this opposition, offered a more radical plan which shocked most of the country as appearing to be financially dishonest. No more interest should be paid to British bondholders, he urged, until they reduced their interest to three per cent. Interest on all government loans in Australia should also be reduced to three per cent. And the gold standard should be finally abandoned for a "goods standard"—by which he probably meant that the exchange should be allowed to fluctuate with the price of major Australian exports.

The government would not accept the plan of the Loan Council's committee. The banks would not support Theodore's plan. Everybody except a Labor minority was shocked by Lang's plan. But he, nevertheless, decided to put it into operation in New South Wales insofar as he was able. He stopped paying interest on the state's overseas debt; and the Commonwealth government, to save the national good name, paid it for him. His actions split the Labor party once more and undermined the confidence of a great body of its supporters.

Since the banks would not lend him the money to stem the tide of deflation Treasurer Theodore brought in a bill to issue eighteen million pounds in fiduciary currency, and another to remove the requirement for a gold backing to the note issue and to ship Australia's gold (to the value of fifteen million pounds) to London to pay off maturing loans. The ugly word "inflation," savoring of the recent and all too serious object lessons provided by Germany, France, and Russia, was now added to the still uglier word "repudiation" as terms with which to stigmatize the Labor Party.   Confident that the government had lost the support of the country, the Senate rejected both bills.   The Commonwealth Bank declared that it would limit government borrowing to a figure which, at the existing rate, would be reached by June, 1931.

In the face of this situation the Loan Council early in May appointed a subcommittee to draw up yet another plan, advised this time by a committee of economists, including some less conservative members, notably Professors Copland and Giblin.   This committee drew up a plan which was presented to a new Premiers' Conference at the end of the month.   It was adopted and became known as the Premiers' Plan.

The Premiers' Plan was probably the most remarkable exercise in planned economy that had ever been carried through by any democracy up to that time.   And it was distinctly the product of a "brains trust."   The ideas applied showed cautious adherence to traditional economic ideas in some respects and bold departure in others.   The keynote of the whole was the ethical concept of equality of sacrifice applied to a situation where it was believed considerable sacrifice was necessary.

The Commonwealth basic wage, it was pointed out, had been reduced to twenty per cent below the predepression level, and the national income had fallen by about the same percentage.   Equality of sacrifice therefore required a twenty per cent cut all around.   All wages, salaries, and pensions should be cut by this amount.   Opposition to cutting pensions was met by the argument that there had been a fifteen per cent drop in the price level already and, with all around cuts, the drop would go further.   To match this sacrifice by the wage and salary earners interest rates on government bonds were to be reduced by twenty-two and a half per cent and interest on private loans by similar or somewhat smaller amounts. This, it was pointed out, could be done only by a great patriotic movement winning the consent of all bond-holders and money lenders. Some additional taxation was also recommended. To balance its budget the government was to be allowed to borrow about fourteen million pounds, but currency inflation was to be avoided.

There were loud howls over the suggestion to reduce interest rates. One of the leading conservative politicians, R. G. Menzies, who was later to become prime minister, branded the proposal as a theft. Some financiers spoke of it as a breach of public honor and a breaking of contracts. But these were in a decided minority. The banks and great financial houses publicly endorsed the plan and loyally carried through their part. The necessary legislation passed both houses. The loan raised to convert all government bonds to the lower rate of interest was a magnificent success. Only three per cent of the bondholders refused to convert volun-tarily and these were forced to do so by special legislation. Rents were reduced by about twenty per cent, either volun-tarily or by special acts of the state parliaments. A con-cession was made to old-age and invalid pensioners, who had their pensions reduced only twelve and a half per cent.

Recovery.— The adoption of the Premiers' Plan made everybody feel better. The sacrifice was being equitably shared and the country was going to pay its debts honorably to its overseas creditors. Government budgets were still running deficits but they were not large enough to create alarm. Imports had fallen off so drastically, as a result of the exchange premium, import restrictions, and prohibitive tariffs, that the bank was able to peg the exchange rate for sterling at a premium of twenty-five per cent. Nevertheless the expected recovery did not take place. Unemployment rose from 27.6 per cent in the second quarter of 1931 when the Plan was adopted to 30 per cent in the second quarter of 1932, and then very gradually declined. The measures adopted had been equitable to everybody but the thousands who were left still out of work.

Australia at this time had no national system of unemployment insurance. Britain, Germany, and many other countries were far ahead of her in this. Moreover, the Commonwealth persistently refused to undertake the care of the unemployed. This responsibility was left to the states which had adopted various measures to meet the need. So far as loan funds were available this relief took the form of public works in which arrangements were often made to distribute the work so that the unemployed could all get a few days' work each week. The unions successfully resisted attempts to pay a lower wage to those on relief work. In the earlier days of the depression those in need were cared for by rationed government issues of food or small money doles, the latter especially for rent. No one was actually allowed to go short of food. Gradually, the doles of food and cash were replaced by plans for part-time work on the basic wage. But as the basic wage itself represented only a minimum of decent civilized existence, the thousands who were forced to subsist on much less than this suffered considerable hardship.

Acceptance of the Premiers' Plan deepened the split in the Labor Party and in November, 1931, the federal supporters of Premier Lang of New South Wales voted against the government on a no-confidence motion. Parliament was dissolved. The election resulted in a resounding defeat for Labor. In the old parliament they had held 40 seats. They came back with 18, and their opponents with 57.

Premier Lang, having wrecked the federal Labor government, then proceeded to wreck his own. He again defaulted in his payment of interest on his state's overseas debt.

The federal government, now in the hands of his political opponents, again paid the debt and instituted proceedings against him for the violation of the financial agreement made between the states and the Commonwealth. Under the terms of this agreement the federal government seized the state taxes. Nevertheless, Lang, fighting to the finish, ordered state officials to continue to carry out state business. The governor of New South Wales, as representative of the Crown, dismissed the premier from office for breaking the law. Lang appealed to the people, but was badly defeated at the ensuing election in June, 1932.

At a Premiers' Conference in the same month some relaxation of the deflationary features of the Plan were decided upon. It was agreed that the states should be allowed deficits of nine million pounds, and that the Commonwealth should set up a three-year plan of unemployment-relief works amounting to fifteen million pounds, and a public works program of six million pounds. Further, in both 1931 and 1932 bounties were given to wheatgrowers. These bounties, with the assistance of the exchange and of Great Britain's departure from the gold standard, restored Australian agriculture to solvency. In July, 1933, the federal budget showed a surplus of three and one half million pounds, and in September of the same year Australia was able to convert 6 per cent and $5\frac{3}{4}$ per cent loans maturing in London at the modest rate of $3\frac{3}{4}$ per cent. The financial crisis was over, but twenty-five per cent of the normal working population was still unemployed.

Further recovery was very slow. Economists whose advice had been taken in the formation of the Premiers' Plan now began to perceive the error in the policy of deflation and advised a bolder policy of government borrowing and spending to stimulate recovery. But politicians who had defeated their opponents by criticizing all such projects as dangerously inflationary did not have the courage to change their policies. They therefore continued the policy of balanced budgets and strict economy. At the outbreak of war ten per cent of the workers were still unemployed. The Labor Party was so badly shaken that it remained in the doldrums for nearly a decade. Not until it had developed new and able leadership could it again make itself felt. Fortunately it was able to do this before the outbreak of the second World War.

In retrospect it can be seen that the measures taken to overcome the depression were, in the main, orthodox and deflationary. The new economic analysis with which J. M. Keynes startled the financial world in 1936 had not been written at that time.[2] The preliminary presentation of the new theory in Keynes's earlier work and in that of J. A. Hobson was as yet not sufficiently convincing for cautious men to feel justified in risking a country's solvency to follow it. European inflation was too recent a memory to allow departures from financial orthodoxy without fear. One cannot, therefore, blame the economists for not having advised a bolder and better way out. The interesting and important thing is to find that they did, for ethical reasons, make small departures from financial orthodoxy and found them economically justified.

As a revelation of the Australian spirit the story of the crisis has real significance. In Premier Lang and his following we see the radical wing of Australian politics. It is not doctrinaire, but experimental. Its motivation is an impulsive concern for the underdog and a longstanding antipathy for the power of money. In their concern for the social ends they conceive to be just, the radicals are sometimes inclined to ignore well-established rights. But they form a minority, and the majority are concerned with both the ends and the

[2] J. M. Keynes, *The General Theory of Employment, Interest and Money* (Macmillan, New York, 1936).

means. They are anxious to establish what they conceive to be social justice and are ready to assert their own rights and interests. However, they will not allow a small group to assert private rights at the expense of the community as a whole—as is seen in the brushing aside of the objections of the small group of bondholders who refused to convert their holdings at the lower rate of interest. And what is more, they have a remarkable capacity for cohesion in a common cause.

Individually they do not do much thinking but look for advice to leaders in whose character and intelligence they believe they can trust. History must give E. G. Theodore his due as the wisest man in the crisis. But one reason for his failure to win acceptance for his monetary proposals was that he was suspected by many, at the time, of complicity in certain political scandals. In Australia the vote of the white-collar worker holds the balance of power. He is ready to ally himself with the manual worker to promote a more equitable distribution of wealth, but he tends to look at both sides of every political question. He is not doctrinaire. He judges policies and politicians by what he sees of the results they achieve. And he likes to see that everybody gets a fair deal.

- 5 -

Arbitration and Labor Relations

IF THERE is one social institution more than any other that is distinctive of the democracies of Australia and New Zealand, it is their courts for the settlement of industrial disputes. Half a century has now elapsed since the system was first adopted in New Zealand in 1895. The setting up of wages boards for the same purpose followed in Victoria in 1896. But the first industrial court of law, as distinct from the wages boards, was set up in New South Wales in 1901. And in 1904 the Commonwealth Court of Conciliation and Arbitration was established. The constitution limited the jurisdiction of this Court, however, to disputes extending beyond the borders of any one state. The states therefore have established their own legal tribunals to deal with questions lying outside the jurisdiction of the Commonwealth Court. Victoria and Tasmania keep to wages boards for this purpose, while the other states have established special courts.

Both parties can claim credit for the establishment of the system. The pioneers were Liberals rather than representatives of the trade-union movement itself. But after the failure of direct action in the nineties, industrial arbitration became a Labor objective. Opposition from the employers' side was met by a stronger movement in favor of the idea. Thus the final enactment of the necessary legislation had strong support on both sides, though most doubters and opponents admittedly were in the ranks of the employers.

It was a bold experiment in methods of social control. In the words of Justice H. B. Higgins, second and most distinguished president of the Commonwealth Court, and one of the greatest jurists to practice in the field, it created "a new province for law and order." The field of relations between employer and employee has, in all classical conceptions of the state, been one of free bargaining, the state merely setting up the rules and defending rights of contract. But the practice of industrial arbitration brings courts, judges, and the law into this field to decide questions of wages, hours, and conditions of employment. The judges of such courts do not merely have to decide whether a law has been obeyed or broken, they have to make laws and decide questions of economic justice.

It was prophesied, on the one hand, that government decisions concerning wages and working conditions would necessarily be followed by the use of compulsion to force men to accept work on the agreed conditions. On the other hand, employers feared that the government's power to take decisions concerning wages and hours out of their hands would prove to be the opening wedge to increasing state interference in the management of private business. It is hardly necessary to say that neither of these fears has been realized. There has, of course, been a further growth of government regulation of business and industrial concerns in Australia as elsewhere, but so far are the employers from believing that this is because of the Arbitration Courts that they are now the strongest supporters of the system.

The chief objects of the Commonwealth Court, as set out in the act, are: 1) to promote good will in industry by conciliation and arbitration; 2) to provide for the exercise of the jurisdiction of the Court by conciliation with a view to amicable agreement between the parties; 3) in default of amicable agreement between the parties, to provide for the exercise of the jurisdiction of the Court by equitable award; 4) to facilitate and encourage the organization of representative bodies of employers and employees and the submission of industrial disputes to the Court by such organizations, and to permit representative bodies of employers and employees to be declared organizations for the purposes of the act; 5) to provide for the making and enforcement of industrial agreements between employers and employees in relation to industrial disputes.

Thus it will be seen that the first objective of the Court is conciliation rather than arbitration. If the parties can agree, their agreement will be embodied in an award. Therefore, the system can be called compulsory arbitration only in the sense that either party may summon the other before the Court, and that if an award is made it binds both the employer and the union. It does not bind any individual, however, even though he is a member of a union that has received an award, to accept work under that award. The award states the minimum wage, the maximum hours, and the working conditions that the employer may offer. If an employee is not satisfied with what is thus offered, he may decline or bargain for more, but the employees as a group are bound not to bargain collectively for more and not to strike against an award.

A strike was defined in the original act as "the total or partial *cessation* of work by employees acting in combination as a means of enforcing compliance with the demands made by them or other employees on employers." Further, no award is made if the employees are already on strike. Thus those working who are given an award are bound as a body, though not as individuals, to accept it. The union is under no compulsion to apply for an award, but having applied, it must accept the verdict. And if either party, union or employer, applies for an award, the judge must set a time to hear the case and summon the parties before him.

Principles of operation.— The principles upon which the decisions of the Court are made are of great importance in revealing the spirit in which the problem of industrial relations is approached. Their significance is emphasized by Justice Higgins' statement that they have been recognized and accepted as guiding principles not only by the judges, but by both sides in the cases which he has had to adjudicate. He presented them clearly in an article published in 1915:

1) Industrial peace is impossible unless the employee has secured to him wages sufficient for the essentials of existence. This must be sufficient for "the normal needs of the average employee, regarded as a human being living in a civilized community." It must be sufficient to support a family of average size, which is taken by the courts to be a man, wife, and three children.

2) In addition to the basic wage there must be a secondary wage for some employees as remuneration for the special gifts or qualifications (that is, for skill, knowledge, or physical strength) necessary for the execution of their duties. This secondary wage preserves, as far as possible, traditional margins between the unskilled laborer and the skilled artisan.

3) After ascertaining the proper wage scales the Court must consider the capacity of the industry as

a whole (not of any particular employer) to pay these wages. This should not be allowed to affect the basic wage (that amount which is socially and humanly necessary) but may, if the industry is in difficult circumstances, be allowed to justify a reduction in the secondary wage or margins for skill. On the other hand, wages are not increased simply because a particular employer or industry is making good profits.

4) The rate paid to an employee must be that recognized for the highest of the duties he is called on to perform; thus, if he has to do some laboring work and some plumbing he must be paid a plumber's wage.

5) The Court does not offer extra pay for work simply because it is laborious, dirty, or otherwise disagreeable. Workers may bargain individually for such considerations. If conditions are unhealthy they should be remedied. The Court does not encourage the idea that such conditions may be justified if extra pay is given. Workers who suffer by reason of their work receive "workers' compensation" but not extra pay awarded by the Court to encourage them to take such work.

6) Higher rates are paid for casual labor because of loss of time.

7) Exceptions to the minimum rate may be made for aged, slow, or infirm workers, but not for "improvers," a class of workers used to beat down the wages and to reduce the opportunities of skilled tradesmen.

8) Allowance is made for any marked difference in the cost of living in different localities.

9) The basic wage for a woman is based on her own

cost of living, not on that of keeping a family, since the average woman worker does not have that to do.[1] In general, basic wage rates for women have averaged about fifty-four per cent of those of men. But if women are employed to do work normally regarded as men's they must be paid the same wages. 10) The standard working week is set at forty-eight hours.[2]

11) The Court does not dictate to employers how they should manage their business, or what tests should be applied to candidates for employment. It leaves them free to choose employees on their merits and assign duties as they see fit so long as they do not create industrial disputes.

12) Under some conditions the Court assigns piecework rates based upon a careful calculation of what an average worker can do in a day and how much he should be paid for a day's work. [3]

13) The Court does not award "preference to unionists" (the union shop) unless the employer shows himself inclined to give preference to nonunionists. Most Australian employers prefer unionists because the presence of nonunionists causes dissatisfaction and disturbance among the employees. The feeling for unionism is so strong that the unions have no trouble in persuading employees to join.[4]

[1] It is implied that society must make some other provision for those dependents who have not male breadwinners.

[2] In later years it was reduced to forty-four, and on January 1, 1948, to forty.

[3] It is calculated that the average pieceworker should be able to earn about ten per cent more than a timeworker.

[4] H. B. Higgins, "A New Province for Law and Order," *Harvard Law Review*, November, 1915. The clause defining a strike was repealed, however, in the act of 1930.

The basic wage.— Though the Commonwealth Court was established in December, 1904, it was not until 1907 that it was faced with the problem of determining the basic wage. This, however, was the first question brought before Justice Higgins when he became president of the Court. The government had passed legislation combining a tariff on certain machinery with an attempt to raise the rates of pay in protected industries. It provided for an excise tax on certain goods manufactured under protection of the tariff which was to be remitted if those goods were produced under conditions asserted to be "fair and reasonable" by the president of the Court. Application was made by a Melbourne harvester-manufacturing company to determine whether its rates met this standard. The Court, therefore, had to decide what constituted a fair and reasonable standard of living for men of the laboring class in Melbourne.

There were no scientifically collected figures on the cost of living available at that time, nor had modern calculations of nutritional needs and food values yet been made. The Court, therefore, did its best by a rough and ready approach to the problem. It called for evidence from housewives and others regarding the cost of living, inquired into rents and other expenses, forming a judgment admittedly approximate. This approximation fixed the fair and reasonable wage for an unskilled laborer at seven shillings a day, or two pounds and two shillings a week, which at the exchange then current equaled slightly over ten dollars in the United States. This, it must be remembered, was in 1907.

At that time a laborer's wages in Melbourne averaged only five or six shillings a day. The newly declared fair and reasonable wage therefore represented an increase of over twenty-five per cent. In future cases coming before the Court the basic wage of forty-two shillings a week became the standard on which awards were based. It was questioned by the employers as too high in the first such case, but not subsequently. As applications poured in and cases were heard wages were raised to the new level. State courts and wages boards began to base their decisions on the new standard. Many employers voluntarily and by agreement among themselves raised their employees' pay in accordance with the award.

The government's legislation tying remission of an excise tax to the payment of standard rates of wages was declared unconstitutional by the High Court, but the need of such legislation had passed by. The new Arbitration Court, by its awards, brought about the same effect, and over a much broader field. Workers in all industries, not merely those enjoying the protection of the tariff, were guaranteed a fair and reasonable daily wage.

By 1911 it had become evident that a steady increase in prices had lowered the purchasing power of the basic wage. The president of the Court therefore asked the Commonwealth statistician to collect figures to give an exact measure of changes in the cost of living. This was done and the figures, based on the prices of food and rent only, were made available in 1913. They showed a steady rise in prices from 1901 onward, the rise between 1907 and 1911 amounting to ten per cent. The Court therefore adopted the practice, as new applications came in, of granting increases in accordance with advances in the cost of living. The basic wage, as thus adjusted, was known as the "Harvester Equivalent."

During the first World War there was a rapid increase in prices, especially in clothing, which had not been assessed in the statistician's figures. There were therefore complaints against the system on two grounds: first, that the rise in the cost of living was actually much greater than the Harvester Equivalent recognized; and second, that the wage awarded steadily lost its value during the period of the award as living costs rose. To compensate for these disadvantages Justice Powers, in 1921, added three shillings a week to the Harvester Equivalent, a sum known thereafter as the "Powers three shillings."

In the same year the Court began the practice of including in awards a provision for the automatic adjustment of wage rates with changes in the statistician's figures for the cost of living. From 1923 onward these adjustments were made quarterly, and the "Powers three shillings" had to be regarded as compensation only for increases in the cost of living not adequately provided for in the statistician's figures, not as compensation for a lag in wages behind rising costs. Some have claimed that it represented a real increase in the purchasing power of the basic wage. If so, it did no more than partially compensate for losses due to rising costs before it was granted. There can be no doubt that, for most of the period prior to 1923, the workers received less than the Harvester Equivalent, especially during the years of rapidly rising costs after the beginning of the first World War.

Changes in the basic wage.— During the depression of 1929 to 1934 the basic wage was reduced ten per cent. This action involved the adoption of a new principle in determining the rate of wages—"the ability of industry to pay." Justice Higgins had laid down the principle that the basic wage should be fixed by consideration of needs alone; therefore, only the secondary wage (margins for extra skills) should be varied by consideration of the difficulty industry might have in paying the fixed rates. But in 1930, on the ground of the disability of industry in general, the Court lowered the basic wage while leaving the proportional margins for skill intact.

In 1934 the Court decided to review the whole question of the basic wage in the light of its new philosophy. Conditions had improved and, considering both human needs and the ability of industry to pay, it fixed a new basic wage of three pounds, four shillings, at Melbourne, with variations elsewhere according to the cost of living. It also reaffirmed the adoption of a new "All-Items" price index (first adopted in 1933) for determining the cost of living; this index included clothing as well as other expenses and was truly a fairer estimate than the former one. Finally the Court restored the ten per cent cut applying to margins for skill. This increase was equivalent to a restoration of the Harvester Equivalent minus the "Powers three shillings," and left the worker where he was in 1907, but a little worse off than in 1921. In 1937, however, again on the ground of the increased ability of industry to pay, the basic wage was raised yet another five shillings. During the war further additions of from one to six shillings, called "war loadings," were added for workers in many industries connected with the war. The higher standard of wages set during the war has been maintained in postwar adjustments made by the Court. With increases in the cost of living the basic wage in Melbourne had risen to £6/5/0 in April, 1949. This amounts to $20.12 in American currency, but in purchasing power it is probably equivalent to $35.

The argument concerning the ability of industry to pay, used during the depression to justify reductions, is now used as a powerful argument for further increases, since it is surely obvious that, with all the advances made in technology, industry must be able to pay much higher real wages than in 1907. The depression, as can now be shown, was not due to the inability of industry to pay high wages, but to the accumulation of surplus savings on the part of those who received its profits. This, indeed, was recognized by the Court in its statement of its reasons for raising the wage in 1937. Any sign of general depression, therefore, becomes an argument for increasing wages rather than decreasing them.

Surprise has sometimes been expressed that Australian workers have not protested more strongly against a basic wage that remained static (or declined) for the 30 years from 1907 to 1937. One of the reasons is the depression of 1929, which stayed the demand for increased wages just as it was accumulating force. Another is the fact that concessions have been won in the reduction of hours from 48 to 44 and in 1948 to 40 a week, and that political action has won for the people the advantage of important social services. But the chief reason is that, from 1917 to 1941, apart from the depression period when economic forces placed them on the defensive, they have been faced by anti-Labor governments in power in the Commonwealth—governments which believed that labor in Australia was too highly paid for the prosperity and progress of the Commonwealth. Against this opposition political action was stymied, and direct action, though tried, proved worse than futile.

Boards of reference and conciliation commissioners.— One of the most valuable subsidiary provisions of the Commonwealth Act has been that for the appointment of boards of reference, to which can be assigned the function of determining questions concerning the application of an award. Such a board consists of employers and employees with a neutral chairman. Where piecework rates are fixed, a board of reference is always needed. In an act passed in 1904 the operation of these boards was said to apply to "any *specified* matters or things which under the award or order may require from time to time to be dealt with by the board." The High Court interpreted this (in a majority decision) to mean that the award must make clear beforehand the specific grievances with which the board may deal. Since it is impossible to foresee many types of grievance this gravely limited the usefulness of the provision. But it was not until 1928 that this defect was remedied and boards were allowed to deal with any matter affecting the good relations of the parties concerned.

Justice Higgins, in pleading for extension of the powers of these boards, pointed out that one ground of dissatisfaction among the workers is that they have no voice in the regulation of the conditions under which they work; their opinions as to the possibility of remedying hardships in their lot have no hearing, except in a protest backed by the threat of a strike or an appeal to the Court. Where shop committees and local boards have been provided for this purpose, they have proved their value in the creation of contentment and efficiency. The boards of reference, given sufficiently broad powers, could, he argued, function in the same way. This sound advice long went unheeded by the legislature, but was at length adopted in the act of 1928. The act contained much to which the workers violently objected; but this particular provision was retained when a Labor government again amended the act in 1930.

Conciliation as well as arbitration was envisaged as a function of the Court from the beginning, but judges became so busy with the latter function that they had little time for the former. An amendment of 1926, however, made provision for the appointment of a special Conciliation Commissioner, who was not a judge of the Court. It was found that he was able to deal with many troubles by bringing the parties together for discussion, securing agreement which made it unnecessary to bring the matter to the Court, or which could be brought to the Court simply for registration. Because of this success the act of 1928 provided for conciliation committees to consist of equal representation from both sides with a paid, neutral chairman. These committees were empowered to foresee friction and to take action to remove its causes before a dispute arose as well as to deal with actual disputes. Agreements arrived at could be filed in the Court, and if no agreement could be obtained a majority (probably decided by the casting vote of the chairman) could make a recommendation to the Court.

Little use was made of these committees, however, employers tending to avail themselves of the opportunity to delay the hearing of a complaint (and a possible requirement to remedy it) by refusing to appoint representatives to such committees and leaving the matter until the Court could attend to it. In the Labor government's amending act of 1930, however, provision was made that these committees must be appointed if any party to a dispute made application for them. This decision made the committee closely resemble the wages boards which have long operated with great success in the state of Victoria. On a technicality the legislation was declared unconstitutional by the High Court. Nevertheless, this technical difficulty could be removed in an amending act and the trade unions urged legislation to this effect.

The act of 1930 also increased the number and enlarged the powers of the conciliation commissioners, enabling them to make an award binding on the parties in a dispute and to disallow an agreement if they considered it inimical to the interests of the public. The powers of the conciliation commissioner, however, still fell short of those of a judge. He could not change the basic wage or standard hours, or deal with questions involving an interpretation of the law, or impose penalties for the breach of an award. Notwithstanding these limitations, the commissioners could greatly facilitate the work of the Court and avoid delays, and the unions continued to urge a further extension of their numbers and powers.

Defects in the system.— One defect, which has caused considerable trouble in the working of the system, is inherent in the constitutional division of power between the Commonwealth and the states. The federal Court's power is limited to industrial disputes extending beyond the limits of any one state. However, most Australian unions have an interstate organization and can therefore present their demands to employers in more than one state, thus bringing their case within the jurisdiction of the Commonwealth Court. For example, the state tribunal of New South Wales in 1910 refused to raise wage rates in shoe factories above those paid by competitors in Victoria, though the justice of the claim was recognized, whereas the federal (i.e., Commonwealth) Court, when appealed to on behalf of employees in both states, was able to raise rates all around.

The overlapping jurisdictions of federal and state courts have caused considerable difficulty, though the High Court has decided that an award of the federal Court takes precedence over that of a state. The most serious constitutional limitation, however, is that which prevents the Court from making a "common rule." The constitution gives the federal government power to legislate only for the settlement of industrial disputes. The High Court therefore decided that the Arbitration Court cannot, having decided a certain dispute, make a common rule that this decision shall apply to all persons engaged in the industry, whether parties to the dispute or not: for example, to a new firm established after the award is made, or to any firm not cited before the court as a party to the dispute, or to one that employed only non-unionists.

This was a serious blow at the outset of the Court's activity, but it has in large part been overcome. In the first place, the unions have organized so vigorously that the non-union shop has been practically forced out of existence. In the second place, thorough preparation of the case before presentation makes possible the citing of every existing employer in the industry, though this has added to the expense of the proceedings. Finally, the High Court has decided that the mere fact that an employer is paying a lower wage, or otherwise not fulfilling the conditions of an award already made (even if he was not a party to that dispute or was not engaged in the industry at the time), constitutes a dispute between the union and that employer. The union has, therefore, only to cite such an employer before the Court, and he is ordered to comply with the conditions of the award. Thus, indirectly, an award of the Court is almost as effective as a common rule. This result was achieved only in 1935, however, after many years of litigation.

Much litigation was also required before it was finally decided by the High Court, in 1920, that employees of state railways could have their cases reviewed by the Commonwealth Court. This was a matter of great importance in Australia, because so many public utilities and other industrial undertakings are state owned, and a state tribunal might hesitate to make a decision against its own government. The Commonwealth Court is a neutral court of appeal for state employees. In the case of Commonwealth government employees there is, of course, no higher neutral tribunal to appeal to. The federal government, however, has, from the inception of the Court, made a practice of leaving to it the responsibility of determining wages and conditions for federal civil servants.

The most serious difficulty faced by the Court, however, does not stem from any defects in the constitution or in its own structure, but from the defects in human nature with which it has to deal, and from the fact that the judges, too, are human. Inevitably, the judges are affected both by their human sympathies or prejudices and by their own ideological backgrounds. They reflect the economic philosophy prevalent in their day and, as we have already seen, this has sometimes led to mistakes. They try to be impartial, but it is not always easy for a learned gentleman of the upper class to appreciate fully the point of view, the feelings, and the limitations of people whose experience of life is so different from his own. On the whole, however, the judges do this much more successfully than the employers.

The chief difficulty in the human situation is the tradition of antagonism existing between employer and employee. Some commentators on the Australian system of industrial arbitration, observing this antagonism, have attributed it to the courts themselves, as institutions which necessarily place employer and employee in the position of opposing litigants. But this is to ignore Australian history, which from its beginnings has been a story of class struggle. The emancipists strove with the "pure merinos"; the migrant worker (such as the swagman in "Waltzing Matilda") strove with the squatter; the miners and landseekers strove with the squatters; the unions of the nineties fought bitterly with the employers; the Labor Party turned Australian politics into a class struggle before the dawn of the twentieth century. The Arbitration Courts have not added to that struggle. They have, as the Communists who revel in the struggle well know, modified and softened it. But it still exists.

Failure to stop strikes.— Because of this deep historic tension in Australian society, the system of arbitration and conciliation has not succeeded in eliminating strikes. Every union official knows that it has prevented a great many, but it cannot prevent all. Men grow impatient under grievances the courts cannot or will not remedy. Some union leaders, for personal or ideological reasons, encourage militancy. Unions go on strike even when working under awards. Rarely are the strikers then successful, and often they or their leaders have been subjected to penalties. Sometimes they go to the Court with their minds made up that if they do not get what they want by arbitration they will try direct action.

Some union leaders, especially members of the Industrial Workers of the World or of the Communist Party, stir up strife in defiance of the courts in order to break the system. Others do so because they believe that a show of militancy will influence the judges to grant their demands, lest the award fail to keep the peace.

When the Court has been too busy to hear their pleas, some unions have gone on strike in an effort to force an immediate hearing for their cases. Occasionally, embarrassed governments, faced with a widespread delay in essential services, especially in wartime, have intervened with the Court to arrange for it to give an immediate hearing. In particular, Prime Minister Hughes did this during the first World War. He even took some cases out of the jurisdiction of the Court and created special tribunals to hear them and to grant demands which the Court, in fair administration of its own principles, could not have awarded. Justice Higgins emphatically pointed out that such action undermined the whole structure on which the arbitration system had been built—that of an impartial decision in all cases in accord with known and accepted general principles. He resigned in protest at this practice, and his protest has served to limit the resort to such measures. Moreover, the operation of these tribunals has, as he prophesied, been opportunist, though it has not had the widespread disintegrating effect upon the system that he feared.

The great majority of Australian unions, however, work loyally with the Court. The flour mill employees, for example, have not had a strike or stoppage in all Australia since 1909 and conditions in the industry are above average for the workers. This is due to a conciliatory and cooperative attitude on the part of both employers and employees. The most outstanding success of the system, however, is in the great pastoral industry. This industry before the advent of the Court was in constant and bitter turmoil. But since its regulation was undertaken by the Court peace has been almost continuous, and the conditions for all classes of workers in the industry have been vastly improved. The shearers, one-time leaders in the threat of a working-class revolution, have come to be numbered among the staunchest adherents of the practice of law and order in industrial relations.

Another example of the success of the system is provided by the silver-lead miners of Broken Hill. This area, up to the inception of the Arbitration Court, had an extremely turbulent industrial history. It is still a center of strong and radical working-class opinion. But it has, in the past twenty years, developed a spirit of cooperation between employer and employee which is probably the best in Australia. This has been effected through the Barrier Industrial Council, an organization which coordinates the work and policies of all the unions concerned with mining operations. The council regards itself as responsible for seeing that the workers have good working conditions and that they keep their agreements. It has succeeded in making a distinctive arrangement with the mining companies based on the dual principle of the needs of the workers and the ability of the industry to pay higher wages. Under this agreement all workers receive Arbitration Court award rates. But when the price of lead goes above a certain figure, at which the mines can make more than normal profits, the miners receive a bonus on their wages. This arrangement removes from the miners the sense of being exploited for high profits in good times and cast out as useless in bad, and, in the recent years of high lead prices, it has proved a bonanza to the workers in the industry as well as a means of securing peace and employee cooperation for the employers.

In contrast we may turn to what, for many decades, has been Australia's most turbulent industry—coal mining. This industry has, except for certain brief periods, refused to accept the jurisdiction of the Court. From the beginning both employers and employees were opposed to it. The employers have lived to regret their stand. The miners themselves, having very genuine grievances, especially in the depression years, and being animated by a tradition of direct action and class struggle, have retained the conviction that more is to be gained by industrial warfare than by an arbitrated peace.

But the troubles in the coal industry are not to be regarded as an example of the failure of industrial arbitration in Australia. They are rather an example of one field where, even in Australia, the method has never been genuinely tried. Prior to 1939, so far as there had been any attempt at regulation at all, it had been done almost entirely by state agencies and special tribunals, the opportunist decisions of the latter aggravating an already difficult situation. The real trouble lies in a long history of unsympathetic attitudes upon the part of the owners, in the incapacity of an unorganized and overexpanded industry to create satisfactory conditions, and in the bitterness ingrained in the miners by accidents, occupational disease, unemployment, and the difficult nature of their work. Arbitration cannot bring peace where the grievances are caused by the nature of an industry and its lack of adequate organization. It has therefore come to be recognized that only a very thorough reorganization of the industry under some form of government control or ownership can create conditions which will be reasonably satisfying to the miners.

The attempt is often made to assess the value of various methods of dealing with labor problems by comparing statistics of time lost through strikes in various countries. These have for some time been collected by the International Labour Office. In 1926 the *International Labour Review* published the following comparison of days lost per 1,000 of population. [5]

Great Britain	819	New South Wales	661
Sweden	795	West Australia	461
Australia	411	South Australia	270
Italy	352	Victoria	234
France	259	Queensland	223
Canada	194	Tasmania	121
New Zealand	84		

From these figures hasty conclusions have been drawn lauding the New Zealand system, in which arbitration is combined with and supplemented by conciliation committees, and suggesting that arbitration of itself is comparatively ineffective. However, in New South Wales, the state (as distinct from the Commonwealth) has developed a wide-ranging system of conciliation committees. The state of Queensland has not; it relies on an arbitration court. Yet Queensland has a much better strike record than New South Wales. Similarly, the fact that Australia, as a whole, has a much better record than Great Britain cannot, of itself, be taken as proof of the value of the arbitration system, for Canada, without such a system, shows a better record than Australia.

It is obvious, therefore, that international and even inter-state comparisons are of little value in attempting to decide whether the machinery for settling industrial disputes (or the lack of it) is better in one country than another. In different countries, and in different parts of the same country, and at different times in the same place, the economic and psychological conditions are different. In different types of industry there are similar types of differences. In short,

[5] *The International Labour Review* (International Labour Office, Geneva, 1926), vol. XIII, p. 646.

a multitude of causes—historical, economic, and ideological —determine the militancy of trade unionism and the resistance of the employers.

The value of machinery for improvement of labor relations can therefore be tested only by actual experience of its working, and must be judged by the opinions of those most intimately concerned in it who have had actual experience in trying to settle labor problems in a variety of ways. In Australia many ways have been tried, from free collective bargaining to compulsory arbitration and conciliation. Also, in Australia the unions are strong and militant, and the employers equally well organized. For these reasons the Australian verdict is important. And that verdict is emphatically that the system as a whole is sound, though capable of improvement; that it should certainly be retained, but that experimentation for its improvement should be continued.

Only the Communists, who find the Court a barrier to their attempts to press the class war to what they regard as its inevitable conclusion, now advocate that the whole system be scrapped. Their attitude is emphatic. In 1942 the president of the Australian Communist Party stated that, "the Communists regard the State-controlled Arbitration System as a pernicious, anti-working class institution, whose object is to keep the workers shackled to the capitalist State, i. e., eternally wage slaves. . . . Arbitration is detrimental to the development of the class-struggle and class-consciousness and of that genuine and fundamental solidarity and perfected organization necessary to the revolutionary struggle for Socialism." [6]

Communism in Australia is not strong in the political field. Its few candidates make an extremely poor showing

[6] L. L. Sharkey, *Communist Theory and Practice of Trade Unionism* (Sydney, 1942). Pamphlet published by the Communist Party of Australia.

at election times even in strong working-class constituencies. It has never elected a member to the federal parliament and only one, in Queensland, to a state parliament. But, as in America, its members have won places of influence and control in many important trade unions. Where they cannot secure influential positions in a union, as in the Australian Workers' Union (AWU), the largest in Australia, they try to form rival unions of their own to disrupt those working with the courts. They failed in a recent attempt to do this in the pastoral industry, but they did succeed in causing a strike which delayed the hearing of a case before the Court. Their policy in this respect has been frankly stated by a leading Communist of the Ironworkers' Union. "We campaign for strikes, with the result that we can say we have been surprisingly successful, when we remember that our Union has deliberately and in a planned way, been involved in more strikes than other unions in the past few years. These strikes were not just the sporadic strikes which are typical of the coalfield; they were planned strikes, because we made strikes our business." [7]

It may therefore be said with confidence that the system of Arbitration Courts as a means of settling industrial disputes has worked extremely well in Australia. It has done more for the improvement of industrial conditions than the unions, in spite of their strength, have ever been able to achieve by direct action and independent collective bargaining. It has raised wages, though not always as much as it should; it has shortened hours and improved conditions. It has been a powerful factor for industrial peace. Apart from the chronic unrest of the coal miners, who have not accepted arbitration in principle, and the influence of political ideologies, such as those of the IWW and the Communist Party, which seek to promote class war rather than peace, there have

[7] E. E. Thornton, *Trade Unions and the War* (Current Book Distributors, Sydney, 1942).

been very few strikes to mar the record of the Commonwealth Court. This does not mean that the unions are not usually justified in the causes for which they go on strike. More often than not their grievances are real and just. It means rather that, apart from Communist influence, they nearly always consider it better to wait until those grievances can be remedied through the courts than to endure the sacrifices of industrial strife.

Rival proposals for reform and the act of 1947.— Both the trade unions as a whole and the organizations of employers definitely and strongly support the continuance of the system of compulsory conciliation and arbitration, but they have opposed ideas for its improvement. In 1946 both sides urged reform on the government. The one sought to strengthen the element of compulsion in the Commonwealth act, the other that of conciliation.

The Australian Council of Employers' Federations wished to see the existing Commonwealth act amended to allow the appointment of as many conciliation commissioners as the judges thought necessary to assist them in their work. This, they felt, would give permanence to what had already been done as a special war measure and would meet the complaint of employees concerning delays in securing access to the Court. But the Employers' Council would have had the commissioners follow precedents established by the Court, and it did not wish to have independent chairmen heading conciliation committees in which representatives of both sides would be brought face to face. It preferred to keep the employee at arm's length and deal with him only through the official person of a judge or commissioner.

The Australian Council of Trade Unions, on the other hand, wished to have the actual function of conciliation and arbitration taken out of the hands of judges and placed in those of conciliation commissioners and conciliation committees, the commissioners and chairmen of the committees to be, not lawyers, but men experienced in industry generally, or in the particular industry concerned. They wanted the Court to become merely a Court of Record, with a registrar, and presided over by a judge of the High Court. The appointment of the commissioners they would leave, not to the judges, but to the Governor-General in Council, that is, to the prime minister's Cabinet, according to the methods of the civil service. The conciliation commissioners, each in his particular industry or area, would then appoint conciliation committees, consisting of representatives chosen by both parties and with himself as chairman, to adjudicate all disputes. Decisions of the committees would be registered with the Court and would have the force of awards. They would even be empowered to amend the basic wage as long as they did not reduce it below a level having purchasing power equal to that of 1928.

Employers' objections to proposals of this kind questioned the possibility of obtaining really independent conciliation commissioners if they had to be chosen from persons experienced in industry instead of from professional life, such as lawyers. Probably with more justification, employers also questioned the advisability of allowing such committees to raise wages and make other decisions which would not be coordinated by the authority of a judge who takes a broader view than that of one industry or area. It is possible for employers and employees in a protected industry to boost wages and costs to the detriment of the public; and this would be made too easy with the committees as proposed.

The other chief ground of difference between the two sets of proposals concerned the use of compulsion and penalties. The unions sought to limit penalties to fifty pounds for an employer and to ten pounds for an employee. But they insisted that a strike or lockout should not be deemed a breach of an award. They agreed, however, that an organization (whether of employees or employers) should live up to certain requirements if it is to retain registration with, and right of appeal to, the Court. They agreed that no officer of an organization should incite any member to refrain from entering into agreements that are in accord with awards; that an organization should have proper rules and abide by them; that it should offer reasonable facilities for the admission of new members; should have its accounts properly kept and audited, should obey orders under the act, and should be in no way tyrannical. But the only penalty they would admit for conviction of any infraction was deregistration from the list of organizations with a right of appeal to the Court and loss of the benefit of its protection in accord with any of its awards.

The employers, on the other hand, wished to make strikes illegal for all unions working under Court awards. And they would define a strike not merely as a cessation of work in combined action to enforce demands, but would also include a combined refusal to accept work in an attempt to enforce variation from conditions fixed in a Court award. They would attach a penalty of twenty pounds to the action of any union official who advocated a strike or go-slow policy and would provide that the Court might (and, in case of a second conviction, must) prohibit such a person from remaining, or in future becoming, an officer of the union. To the publication of incitements to strike they would attach a penalty of one hundred pounds, and to participation in the boycott of a strikebreaker working in accordance with an award, a penalty of twenty pounds. In addition they wished to provide that a union must take a secret ballot, conducted by the registrar of the Court, before declaring a strike, the penalty, one hundred pounds for each person engaging in, or inciting to, such a strike.

The result of the proposals and counterproposals of 1946 was the amendment to the Conciliation and Arbitration Act in May, 1947, which adopted most of the trade unions' proposals. This bill, as was stated by H. V. Evatt in introducing it, opens a new chapter in the history of Australia's attempts to regulate the relations of employer and employee. It is a frank turning away from the past method of settling disputes by judicial decisions, made according to the procedures of courts of law, to that of conciliation in face-to-face conferences, with the law in the background. The new emphasis is on informality as opposed to the more conventional legal procedures, expedition as opposed to the law's delays, but with the law bringing the parties together, defining some of the basic principles on which decisions are to be made, and providing for their enforcement. This, the new act seeks to achieve by transferring most of the arbitral functions of the Court to conciliation commissioners, but leaving to the Court the function of deciding the basic wage, standard hours, annual leave, and minimal rates for women. The matters left to the Court thus provide a common nation-wide basis for the decisions of the conciliators, while leaving them free to deal quickly with the wide range of other matters concerned in industrial relations in accordance with the exigencies of the local situation and the industry concerned. Decisions of the conciliators have the force of law.[8]

In the matter of award enforcement, the mild penal clauses of the previous act have been retained. The employers' proposal to require a secret ballot before declaring a strike has not been adopted. In the light of the American experience of this requirement under the Smith-Connally Act, perhaps this last is not surprising. It has been found here that the employees always vote to strike, thus strengthening the hands

[8] In its first year of operation the new act has been remarkably success-ful. According to a statement made by the federal Minister for Labor in September, 1948, the loss of man hours through industrial disputes since the act went into operation has been reduced almost to nil.

of their union organizers and putting the taxpayer to the expense of paying for a ballot which, from his standpoint, is worse than useless. Australian employers, however, have hoped that, with the arbitration system as an ever present alternative to the strike, the experience would prove to be different. The experiment might well be worth trying.

In refusing to adopt the penal clauses of the employer's proposals the government is probably wise. The attempt to enforce industrial peace by penalties on strikes and on incitements to strike when employees are working under an award of the courts has never been popular in Australia. Especially under the proposed extended definition of a strike, such an attempt would arouse bitter resentment from all ranks of unionists. It would definitely alienate them from the Court and strengthen the Communist plea that unions should not appeal to the Court but rely on direct action. There was great resentment over the much milder attempts to impose penalties for strikes included in the amendments to the act of 1928, and these were removed by a Labor government in 1930. The infliction of heavy fines upon the striking Timberworkers' and Waterside Unions in 1928 produced more strife than peace; and feeling was further embittered when the government failed to prosecute the coal owners who, in defiance of a Court award in 1929, locked their men out. The militancy of which employers complain today is due largely to the bitterness created at that time and in the depression which followed.

It is understandable that employers should feel that the operation of compulsory arbitration is one-sided. They are usually compelled by law to keep the terms of an award, but the employees are not compelled to offer themselves for work upon those terms. Under the penal clauses of the Australian arbitration acts unions have been fined, and their officials have been fined and even imprisoned. But to fine or imprison a union official for fighting for the workers' cause is to make him a martyr and a hero. One official, once thus treated, is now a cabinet minister, and another is a senator. If union members could not, by law, honor such a fighter by retaining him as a union official, then their loyalty and solidarity would almost certainly put him into parliament, or failing that, they would remain loyal to their champions and abandon the Court.

It seems, therefore, that compulsory conciliation and arbitration can be made to work only if the compulsion is almost entirely on one side—that of the employers. The only compulsion that can safely be placed upon employees is that of deregistration of the union and withdrawal of the protection of the Court and the benefits of its awards. An arbitration system must be viewed as a method of persuading unions to avoid the strike weapon and seek peaceful means of remedying their grievances; and such persuasion cannot be made effective if it is accompanied by threats making the union feel that in approaching the Court it surrenders the privilege of fighting for what it believes to be its rights if they cannot be obtained peacefully. The employer must accept the fact that the compulsion is one-sided. He, however, has one protection, in that he knows that whatever conditions he is compelled to grant to his employees, his competitors must grant the same. Under the alternative system of free collective bargaining he may be forced to pay higher rates than a competitor who has more docile employees. Further, the Court or conciliator is usually able to dissuade a union from pressing unreasonable demands, thus saving the employer the expense of resisting a strike.

Wage policy and increased production.— One of the most serious defects in the Australian arbitration system, however, has not been touched by the recent reforms, although it is recognized by many of the more perceiving minds that have studied the problem. It lies in the practice of tying the basic wage to the cost of living. Labor has demanded this as a defense against rising costs, for, throughout most of the period of the Court's existence, living costs have been on the upgrade. Employers, on the other hand, have urged that the basic wage should take account of the capacity of industry to pay. They, however, tend to interpret this in a merely negative way as meaning that when times are bad (in general, or in a particular industry) wages should be lowered. Economists, however, have frequently pointed to the positive implications of the phrase "the capacity of industry to pay." For thirty years after the Harvester award, real wages in Australia remained at almost a dead level or declined. Surely with all the technological advances in that time, industry must have developed a capacity to pay higher real wages than at the beginning of the period.

Output per man increased greatly in those thirty years. Real wages of skilled and unskilled workers did not. Where did the increased product go? It cannot be accounted for as having gone to the capitalist in higher interest rates and higher rates of profit, for these, taken together, are certainly not higher. Much of it, undoubtedly, was absorbed by increased taxation and thus distributed in various services to the community. Much of it went to an increase in the proportion of better-paid jobs, including an increase in the proportion of skilled manual workers, white-collar workers, professional, and semiprofessional men. Thus the employed class benefited by an increase in the numbers in its upper brackets; but the lot of those in the lower brackets has not been improved. How, then, can this state of affairs be remedied?

Furthermore, another difficulty, and a serious one, manifests itself. When the cost of living falls the worker's wages are reduced. He therefore has no incentive to do anything to reduce the cost of living, for its reduction leaves him no better off. Indeed he is apt to find himself put into financial difficulties by it, for if he is buying a house or purchasing something on time payment, or paying insurance, his payments due remain the same though his income is decreased. He therefore has no real economic interest in increasing production per man and thus reducing living costs, or even in preventing moderate inflation. He is protected against rising costs, but he finds himself no better off, or worse off, when costs go down.

It is generally recognized that the greatest need of industry in Australia today is to get the worker interested in increased production. Here, therefore, is the first step that should be taken. He should be assured that, if he does increase production and thus reduce costs, when these are reflected in a lowering of the cost of living which benefits everyone else, he (the worker) will not be deprived of that benefit by a cut in his wages. If wages are guaranteed to remain fixed while the cost of living is steadily forced down by increasing production per man (and at the same time financial policies and other factors that increase living costs are avoided), then it should be possible to secure the essential co-operation of the worker in a combined effort of the community to achieve that goal. Thus the low-paid worker would share equally with everyone else in the benefits of technological improvements, and providing full employment can also be guaranteed, his opposition to these, too, would be removed.

It may be taken as axiomatic that continued technological improvements will force the costs of production downward. The only reason why this process does not always have the effect of continuously lowering the cost of living in terms of money is that it is so often counteracted by hidden taxes, monopoly profits, credit expansion, and other kinds of

financial inflation.   Both the world wars have involved considerable financial inflation; and the world-wide process of
capitalistic expansion prior to 1914 was, during most of the
period, inflationary.   There is no guarantee that inflationary
policies will not be pursued in the future also.   The worker
must therefore be guaranteed against the effects of inflation
upon his standard of living.   He must be assured that if
the cost of living goes up his wages will be raised to meet
it.   But in order to interest him in fighting inflation, cutting
costs, and increasing production, he must be assured that
when the cost of living goes down his wages will remain the
same, and he will be allowed to reap the benefit.   Why, it
may be asked, should everyone but the wage earner be allowed
to share in the benefit of a decrease in the cost of living?

If this method for fixing the basic wage is adopted it
will be necessary to guard against the effects of minor fluctuations in the cost of living index.   These fluctuations may be
due to purely temporary causes and, if the wage is not reduced again when the temporary cause of higher costs ceases
to operate, a purely inflationary boost will be given to the
wage structure.   To obviate this, a provision could be made
that no wage increase need immediately be allowed for any
quarter's increase in the cost of living index if the Court
thought such an increase merely temporary and if it did not
raise the index above the highest point of the past year.
If this were done, the worker would be guarded against the
effects of inflation, and yet would tend to obtain his proper
share in the benefit of every decrease in the cost of living
arising out of increased production per man.   Until some
such change is made it will probably prove impossible to
secure the genuine interest of the Australian worker in the
problem of increasing the efficiency of industry.

The objective of raising the purchasing power of the
basic wage can, of course, be achieved, at least temporarily

and within certain limits, by the simple action of the Court granting an increase in wages based on a calculation of the increased capacity of industry in general to pay. This should certainly be done periodically if inflationary financial practices continue to prevent that lowering of living costs which should naturally follow upon improved technology. But it is very difficult to assess this increased capacity to pay accurately; and the results of fixing the wage structure too high or too low are both detrimental to industry. A wage level fixed too high will destroy the weaker industries of a country; and one fixed too low will result in too high a level of profits, savings that outrun opportunity for investment, and consequent depression. The safe policy is therefore to start with wages that are certainly not too high, guard carefully against unemployment and inflationary finance, allow increasing production to force costs down, and, by keeping the monetary wage fixed while living costs fall, continuously raise real wages. Providing monopoly profits, excessive salaries, and other means of inflation are also avoided, this policy would maintain wages at the highest figure industry can pay.

- 6 -

The Social Service State

IN THE palmy days before 1929 it was true in Australia, as it was in America, that an energetic and capable person could usually earn an adequate wage. Bad times came occasionally, but they were comparatively short-lived. And the working classes, by reason of the demand for labor and the strength of their industrial and political organizations, were much better off than those in Britain and Europe. Nor did they suffer from the existence of sweated industries in the way their counterparts in America did. Hence, comfortable people repeated over and over again, until almost everyone believed it, that "Australia is the workingman's paradise." There were some slums and some destitute poor; but it was firmly believed that in such a land of opportunity, poverty, apart from that induced by some infirmity or the death of a breadwinner, must be attributed to personal defects.

Therefore, prior to 1929 Australia had very few social services. In Britain, Lloyd George had introduced his national insurance scheme with its unemployment pay and sick benefits. Australians looked on complacently and assured each other that nothing of that kind was needed in their favored land. "If a man is worth his salt he can always get a job here. If there is no work in the towns he can go trapping rabbits, or he can make 'tucker'[1] fossicking for gold. Or he can get a job on a farm. Farmers are always looking for help, both for men and women, so long as they don't want too high wages."

Queensland alone, of all the states, followed the British example in the establishment of a system of unemployment insurance. It was introduced by a Labor government in 1923 to cover all persons over eighteen years of age working under state awards. It was financed by equal contributions from the employer, employee, and the government, but benefits under the scheme were very small. There were extra allowances for a wife and children but the sums were barely sufficient to provide food, leaving nothing for other expenses, and were payable only for a maximum period of fifteen weeks. During the depression a great deal of special relief had to be provided for those outside the fund and for those whose period of unemployment outran their right to receive benefit. This was done in all the states by relief work and relief in kind.

Neither Queensland, nor the Commonwealth, nor any other state attempted to emulate Britain in the adoption of the medical features of Lloyd George's social insurance scheme. Australia, thus, for a quarter of a century, lagged behind the more advanced democracies in the provision of social services. The depression found her unequipped to

[1] Australian slang for food.

meet the needs of dire poverty. One state had a meager
scheme of unemployment insurance. The Commonwealth
provided old-age pensions of a reasonable amount for men at
sixty-five and women at sixty. It also offered a maternity
allowance of five pounds to help meet the expenses of childbirth. All the states were equipped with public hospitals in
the chief centers of population which gave free care, or
charged fees proportional to the income of the patient.
There were also various homes, asylums, orphanages, and
other provisions for the unfortunate and indigent, supported
by both state funds and public charity. There was relief
in kind for the needy. There were excellent measures for
caring for children who needed it by a supervised system of
boarding them out to foster parents. In general the country
was up-to-date in its provision for social casualties. Moreover, it had a system of free and compulsory education up to
the age of fourteen, with free, or heavily subsidized, high
school education beyond that age. But there was little inclination even to recognize the existence of undeserved poverty among the able-bodied working classes.

Yet such undeserved poverty certainly existed even
before 1929, and had steadily created large slum areas in the
cities. The depression, for the first time, forced home upon
the general community a widespread recognition of these
conditions. The census of 1933, taken when the financial
crisis was definitely over and the country again on the upgrade, showed that unemployment was still high and relief
measures were inadequate. Thoughtful people studied the
figures with care and pointed to facts which rendered further
complacency impossible. At a time when the basic wage
was still subject to depression-time reductions and thus represented something less than a decent minimum standard of
living, it was revealed that nearly two-thirds of the adult

male breadwinners of the country were receiving much less than this minimum. The basic wage was £3/4/2. But the census revealed that more than half the workers earned less than that amount:

Percentage of Workers	Earnings per Week
31.6	less than £1
47.4	less than £2
59.9	less than £3
72.4	less than £4
83.0	less than £5

This meant that fifty per cent of the families of the country were in serious want. A few years later (1936) a Slum Abolition and Rehousing Board established in Victoria made a survey of housing within five miles of the General Post Office in Melbourne. Out of 83,000 houses in the area it picked 7,000 of the worst-looking for closer inspection, with the following results. Two thousand were without a bathroom, 3,000 without a washhouse, 5,500 had no sink in the kitchen, and 6,000 were considered unfit for human habitation.

These 7,000 houses were inhabited by 25,000 people (including 11,000 children) whose total income averaged £2/10/4 a family. These Melbourne conditions may be taken as typical of Australian cities, Sydney being much worse, and the smaller capitals rather better.

Studies of malnutrition among children also revealed disturbing conditions. In 1936 an examination of 18,180 children in Western Australia showed 26.7 per cent undernourishment in the metropolitan area and 32 per cent in the country. A survey a year later in Melbourne showed the striking difference in the physique of children in the inner and poorer suburbs compared with those in the better residential areas.

Facts such as these gradually aroused the public conscience.   In all the states organizations were formed to press for further reforms.   Protests from the working-class organizations became louder and stronger.   More and more frequently churches began to voice the demand that the paradox of poverty in the midst of plenty be ended.   Educators and public spirited citizens of influence added their voices to the growing demand.   At length the governments responded, and the movement for new social services got slowly under way.

Child endowment.— The first step was not insurance against unemployment and sickness, but a measure to supplement the inadequate wage structure at its weakest point by a system of child endowment.   This was introduced by a non-Labor government in the federal parliament in 1941, but it had had some interesting antecedents.

The movement for child endowment had its origin in the report in 1919 of a Royal Commission to enquire into the adequacy of the basic wage.   The rise in living costs during the war years had created a great deal of discontent with the working of the Harvester Equivalent; and Prime Minister Hughes appointed a Royal Commission under the chairmanship of A. B. Piddington to determine, by a thorough inquiry, "the actual cost of living at the present time according to reasonable standards of comfort . . . for a man, wife and three children."   The commission took the phrase "reasonable standards of comfort" at its face value. It was a more generous phrase than Justice Higgins' "normal needs of the average employee, regarded as a human being living in a civilized society."   The commission found that a "reasonable standard of comfort" for a family of five required an income of £5/16 a week. The Harvester Equivalent at that time was only £4/18/3.

The difference was so great that the prime minister asked the Commonwealth statistician to report on the feasability of raising the basic wage to this level. In reply, figures concerning the national income were brought forth which showed that the whole produced wealth of the country, including the employers' profits, would not suffice to pay such a wage to all adult males with proportionate wages for female workers. The commission's findings were therefore set aside as not in accord with practical realities. But unions nevertheless frequently demanded that the findings be put into effect, and the whole affair added to the prevailing discontent with the basic wage.

Out of this otherwise abortive commission, however, there came a suggestion that in later years bore fruit. The chairman, A. B. Piddington, pointed out that a man and wife need roughly seven-tenths of the family income and the children one-tenth each. If, therefore, the basic wage were calculated on the needs of man and wife only, it could be fixed at four pounds. Then a family endowment of twelve shillings per child could be added, the fund to be raised by some form of taxation. This plan he showed to be within the resources of the national income. The suggestion was too radical to take immediate effect, but it did set people thinking.

The basic wage, as fixed by the Harvester award, had been a roughly made approximation of what was considered, in 1907, a reasonable standard of living for an unskilled laborer with a wife and three children. Time had proved it to be inadequate for that purpose; and this became increasingly evident as the years passed and other classes of the community acquired new comforts and luxuries. But industry could not afford to pay every laborer a wage really adequate for such a family; and it was not necessary that it should, for the average laborer did not possess such a family. He made the basic wage serve his needs because he had only one or two children, or none. In the meantime, the large family endured privation or depended upon charity. But why should industry be expected to pay for nonexistent children? And why should large families be compelled to live in want while single and childless men had more than they needed? The remedy was plain. The basic wage should be recognized as inadequate for a family of three and the large family should be endowed from the public purse.

Credit for the introduction of the first system of child endowment goes to Premier Lang's Labor Government in New South Wales in 1927. Their plan made a grant of five shillings a week for each dependent child in the family for all families whose income was below the basic wage plus thirteen pounds (five shillings a week) for the previous year. This was changed by the same government two years later to exclude payment for the first child, thus assuming that the basic wage was sufficient to support man, wife, and one child. Allowances under this act were paid until the child reached the age of fourteen and were continued to sixteen if the child was incapacitated from earning. There was a provision, however, that the endowment should not raise the family income above the basic wage plus thirteen pounds a year for each child above one. Claims under this act numbered from 41,000 to 72,000 each year and cost the state, on an average, over one and a half million pounds a year, or about twelve shillings per head.

In 1940, in the days of the so-called "phoney" war, the unions applied for an increase in the basic wage on the ground of the increased prosperity of industry. The judges, who did not believe the war was "phoney," refused the application but promised to consider it again in June, 1941. Just before they gave their decision the Commonwealth government, led by R. G. Menzies, an able conservative, announced its intention of introducing a child endowment scheme. This, it was declared, was a first installment of the social reconstruction which would issue from the war. The Melbourne *Argus* praised this policy and said its aim was "to ameliorate the lot of many persons who are at present being penalized for performing what is a valuable national service, and to encourage the more adequate population of a continent which is at present woefully underpopulated." [2] There can be no doubt that part of the motive was also to meet the criticism of the inadequacy of the basic wage and forestall a general increase in wages.

This measure was passed in 1941 and the endowment was fixed at five shillings a week for each child after the first. This was not sufficient to provide for the keep of a child, the cost of which the Royal Commission had calculated at one-tenth of the income of a family on a fair minimum wage. The Labor government raised the amount first to seven shillings and six pence, and then in 1948 to ten shillings. Even with these increases, however, it still falls short of one-tenth of the basic wage. But even at the lower figure it has proved a great help to large families on low incomes and, since there is no means test attached to receipt of it, it has been welcomed by all classes of the community. The large Labor minority in parliament supported the measure as an installment of their own program, though declaring themselves not satisfied with either the amount or the method of financing it.

The scheme was estimated to cost between twelve and thirteen million pounds a year. Of this sum two million pounds were to be provided by removing the income tax ex-

[2] The Melbourne *Argus,* March 28, 1941.

emption on all children after the first (these being eligible
for the endowment); nine millions were to come from a
special payroll tax of two and one-half per cent; and the
remainder from the consolidated revenue. Thus far the
payroll tax has left very little to be met in the last way.

Just before the federal elections of September, 1946,
the Liberal Party, led by R. G. Menzies, surprised the Labor
government by announcing as its policy the extension of
the endowment to include the first child, the money to be
found by adding to the payroll tax. Within the Liberal
Party there was much criticism of this move as being incon-
sistent with its policy of economy and tax reduction. It is
to be noted, however, that it was definitely intimated that the
burden was not to fall on the income tax, which the Liberals
felt should be reduced. The motive was humanitarian to a
degree, especially on the part of Dame Enid Lyons, the Liberals' leading woman politician. It was also an astute political move, stealing the Labor Party's thunder by revealing
a concern for extension of the social services. But there was,
finally, an economic motive, for it would have meant that,
in the future, the basic wage would have to be considered as
necessary to meet the needs of only husband and wife, with
a little margin for the cost of children above the amount
of the endowment. The proposal would carry the dual
conception that the state is responsible for the welfare of
the child and that industry should not be charged with the
burden of paying wages for the support of nonexisting children. The trade unions urged the adoption of the proposal
as part of their long-established policy, but the Labor government was reluctant to accept it until it could be financed
without taxation of a kind that would further raise the cost
of living, as would an increase in the payroll tax.

Social security.— In 1938 R. G. Casey, Commonwealth
treasurer in a non-Labor government, secured the passage
of a carefully planned scheme of social security, the National

Health and Pensions Insurance Act. This measure was
never put into operation. It faced difficulties at the outset
in opposition from the medical profession and other sources.
Before these could be overcome war broke out and the act
was shelved. The Labor government which came into power
in 1941 was not satisfied with the scheme and replaced it by
one of its own. But it is well worthwhile to compare the two
schemes in some detail in order to bring out the likenesses
in the attitude of the two major parties to the question.

The 1938 scheme was designed to include all employed
manual workers and all other employees earning not more
than seven pounds a week. This left out a considerable
number of people—for example, employers and independent
workers—but the government announced that it had in preparation a supplementary plan to include these. In the
meantime the existing pensions would be continued for their
benefit.

The scheme was one of compulsory insurance in which
the employer and employee were each to pay equal contributions and the government to add a certain sum. In a time
of unemployment the employee's contribution was waived
and he was given "free insurance." The benefits consisted
of old-age pensions, widows' and orphans' pensions, sickness
and disability benefits for time lost through these causes, and
free medical attendance and treatment provided by doctors
of the patient's own choice at a fixed annual fee for each
patient. There was no provision, however, for unemployment arising from causes other than sickness or disability.

There was a dual motivation for the introduction of the
scheme. The humanitarian motive was certainly present in
the plans for widows' and orphans' pensions, sickness and
disability benefits, and medical attention. But a financial
concern over the increasing cost of pensions was present in
the plan to place these on a contributory basis instead of paying the whole out of general taxation. This was plainly

stated in the treasurer's speech on the second reading of the bill. "In view of the impending liability of the existing pensions schemes, I say quite frankly that unless something is done to put these schemes on a contributory basis, no Government of the future, however well-intentioned, could embark upon any worth-while extension of our social services without seriously threatening the whole financial fabric of the Commonwealth."

The first argument for placing all social security benefits upon a contributory basis was therefore the financial one. It removed some part of the burden from the general revenue to the shoulders of those who received the benefits. The act contained a provision that wage tribunals, in fixing wages in relation to the cost of living, should not take into account the cost of national insurance contributions without also considering the benefits received. This was to prevent the cost to the employee from being handed on to the employer. There was not, however, nor could there be, any provision to prevent the employer from handing the cost of his contribution on to the public in increased prices. Competition would prevent this only in the case of the export industries, and then only to a limited extent.

Actually, however, the scheme did not provide for any great saving to the Treasury by making pensions in part contributory. The contributions were fixed at a figure which paid for the new benefits and made only a small contribution toward the existing old-age and invalid pensions. What the sponsors of the scheme probably considered more important was not the actual saving in the existing pension bill, but the establishment of the principle that all social security schemes should be financed by plans to which the beneficiaries themselves made contributions, thus creating a sense of responsibility and preventing the growth of the system to lengths which might be deemed extravagant.

Also, it was argued, there is a distinct moral advantage in an insurance scheme which distributes its benefits as a right for which people have paid instead of as a piece of state charity. In the latter there must always be a means test to limit the benefits to those in need. Such a test may deprive many deserving people of benefits while conferring them on others who have wasted their substance and opportunity. But in an insurance scheme the benefits are received as a right for which the recipient has paid the required dues and which he can accept without injury to his self-respect.

Critics of the contributory scheme pointed out that it exacted payments from people who were in receipt only of the basic wage or less, and that this wage was calculated as barely sufficient to meet civilized human standards of decency without any such deductions. The argument that the self-respect of the citizen is undermined when he is made a recipient of state grants was countered by the assertion that it is no disgrace to be poor and in need of such grants, that pensions and other benefits of a social security scheme are merely a recognition of the inadequacy of the wage system to which the masses of the people are subjected, that the worker pays for his benefits through the profit the employer makes on his labor, and that he pays his just share of the taxes which, in a noncontributory scheme, provide the benefits. His income tax is not as large, but his share of the hidden, indirect taxes is proportionately much heavier.

From the standpoint of finance, also, the contributory scheme was criticized. Like almost all insurance schemes this one was designed to accumulate an initial surplus which would earn interest and help meet the larger payments which would come with the increasing age of the beneficiaries. But success in this connection, it has been pointed out, depends on the maintenance of the estimated rate of interest (three and a half per cent) and on there being no need to increase pensions in later years to meet rising costs of living. Further, the accumulated surplus would either have to be used to reduce the public debt, which might prove disadvantageously deflationary, or it would have to be borrowed and spent, thus adding to the public debt; and the temptation to a government to borrow and use it unnecessarily would be very strong.   In any case, the withdrawal of large sums of money from circulation and its accumulation in enforced savings is apt to add to the problem of maintaining employment.   The idea that the savings of the present decade can be set aside and used in thirty or forty years' time is true only so far as individuals are concerned.   The nation as a whole can use from day to day only the goods it produces from day to day.   Each generation must care for its own aged and indigent; it cannot feed them on the paper money or bonds accumulated by the past generation.   Finally, there is an objection to contributory schemes on the ground of the great bookkeeping expense involved.

For reasons such as these the Labor government headed by John Curtin, which came into power in 1941, decided that its own social security proposals should be financed by special taxation rather than by a contributory insurance scheme. In the next few years, while the war was still in progress, a series of acts was passed designed to make a reality of the ideal, "freedom from want," which had been written into the Atlantic Charter.   These included raising the old-age and invalid pensions to meet increases in the cost of living, a large increase in the maternity bonus, a fifty per cent increase in the child endowment plan, the introduction of widow's pensions, unemployment and sickness benefits, free hospital care for all persons in all public hospitals, free pharmaceutical supplies, rent subsidies, and subsidies for university education.   Opposition from the medical profession has delayed the introduction of a scheme of free medical service.

After much negotiation a bill was passed in December, 1948, which provides for the payment of fifty per cent of the fee for medical, dental, and similar services according to a prescribed scale of charges. Patients are left free to choose their own practitioner, and no doctor or dentist is compelled to participate in the scheme. Provision is also made for the establishment of health centers staffed by specialists on a salary basis, as well as for specialists at hospitals, and for salaried medical practitioners to serve sparsely populated areas. To overcome the shortage of personnel, assistance is to be given to medical schools to expand their training programs, and scholarships will be provided for students in training and for specialization and research. Operation of this plan has been faced with difficulties, however, due to the opposition of the profession to details of its administration.

On page 148 a table is presented comparing the benefits offered under the National Insurance Bill of Great Britain (1946), which incorporates many of the Beveridge proposals, with those prevailing in New Zealand and Australia in the same year. The figures for the British plan are given in sterling which is at a premium of twenty-five per cent on the Australian or New Zealand pound, so that these figures should be increased by twenty per cent to give an exact comparison in terms of money. Living costs in all three countries are much lower than in the United States, but a fair idea of the purchasing power in Australia of the benefits listed may be obtained by remembering that the basic wage in the six capital cities in 1946 was £4/16/. The Australian pound exchanges for about $3.22, but its purchasing power in Australia was, in January, 1946, equivalent to between five and six dollars in the United States at that time before prices were decontrolled. The invalidity, sickness, and unemployment allowances are worked out for a man, wife, and two children; the widowhood for a widow with two children.

SOCIAL SECURITY BENEFITS
(For man, wife, and two children where applicable)

	AUSTRALIA	NEW ZEALAND	GREAT BRITAIN
Unemployment	£2/17/6 per week	£5 per week	£2/ 9/6 per week
Sickness	2/17/6 per week	5 per week	2/ 9/6 per week
Invalidity	3/—/– per week	5 per week	2/16/– per week
Old Age	3/ 5/– per week	4 per week	2/12/– per week
Widowhood	2/ 5/– per week	3 per week	1/18/6 per week
Child Endowment	7/6 per week (Each child after first)	10s per week (Each child)	/5 per week (Each child after first)
Maternity	15/—/– first child 16/—/– second and third child 17/10/– all others	Free hospital and medical services	£4 grant. In addition £1/16/– weekly for 13 weeks if wife was working. £4 attendance allowance if not working.
Medical and Health	Free public hospitals or 6s per day subsidy for those who prefer private hospitals Comprehensive plan for medical and pharmaceutical service in preparation.	Free medical, hospital, X-ray, pharmaceutical, and massage services.	Comprehensive national health service planned to replace that of prewar days.
Funeral	Actual expenses up to £10 for old-age and invalid pensioners only.		£20 grant for adults, less for children.
Rent Subsidy	For persons on basic wage in government houses, a rebate of rent over 1/5 of income.		

Paying the piper.— The British scheme is one of contributory insurance in which schedules of payments are fixed for employees, employers, the self-employed, and the non-employed, with contributions also from the national Exchequer. The New Zealand scheme is financed primarily by a special social security contribution of one shilling on the pound on all incomes and an annual registration fee of one pound for males over twenty, and five shillings for females over sixteen and males aged sixteen to twenty. Any balance required is appropriated by parliament for general revenue. In Australia the social services are financed by a National Welfare Fund maintained: 1) by a special "Social Services Contribution" levied on individual incomes in addition to ordinary income tax [this "contribution" is fixed on a graduated scale with a maximum of one shilling, sixpence on the pound]; 2) by the payroll tax enacted for child endowment; and 3) by supplementation from the general revenue.

This plan is plainly a compromise between a contributory and a noncontributory scheme. It avoids keeping records of individual contributions but nevertheless imposes an individual contribution upon every person whose income is able to bear it. For a person without dependents the Social Service Contribution begins with an income of £104 a year; and for a person with one dependent, £156, which is £95 below the basic wage. But exemptions for children are such that less than one per cent of the total comes from families with one or more children and from those whose income is less than £300. According to tax regulations in 1945–46, ordinary income tax was not paid by a person receiving less than £200. For man and wife the tax commenced at £266, and for man, wife, and one child, at £318. It will thus be seen that everybody is made to feel that he is paying a fair share of the cost of social services, but that the cost is nevertheless made to rest most heavily on the shoulders best able to bear it.

Australians, like other people, complain about their income taxes, and with some justification. During the war Australian income taxes were made exceedingly severe. The following table was given publicity by the Victorian Taxpayers' Association in June, 1946, to show that Australian income taxes were at that time the highest in the world. The figures are stated in terms of Australian currency and refer to tax on earned income.

	TAX ON £470 UNMARRIED	TAX ON £625 MARRIED	TAX ON £1,560 MARRIED
Australia	£116	£149	£575
U. S. A.	62	63	264
Britain	91	120	500
France	58	84	234
Russia	78	118	334
China	94	125	313

No allowance is made here for differences in living costs. The table therefore compares the tax of an Australian with that of an American having about forty per cent less real income. It should also be noted that the Australian figures include the social security contribution, while those for other countries do not. But even when these allowances are made, the claim that the Australian income tax at that time held the world's record probably still holds good.

The effect of such taxation on the incentive to earn and in the redistribution of wealth can be better gauged from the figures in the next table (page 151), the first three columns of which were supplied by the South Australian Taxpayers' Association. They show figures for 1944-45, when the income tax was at its wartime maximum. They are calculated for a person without dependents and include the social security contribution. It will be seen that at the wartime rates, the incentive to earn was reduced toward the vanishing point when an income reached £5,000. A man with an earned income of this amount retained only £1,469 after paying his

AUSTRALIAN INCOME TAX, 1944–1945

INCOME	TAX	RATE PER £ ON LAST £100	INCOME RETAINED FROM LAST £100
		s. d.	
£ 300	£ 55/ –/–	6/ 7	£67/ 1/8
400	95/ 8/–	8/ –	60/ –/–
500	136/13/–	8/ –	60/ –/–
600	178/15/–	8/ 5	57/18/4
800	265/ 8/–	8/ 8	56/13/4
1,000	355/ 8/–	9/ –	55/ –/–
1,500	618/19/–	11/ 7	42/ 1/8
2,000	951/ 5/–	14/ 7	27/ 1/8
3,000	1,747/ 2/–	17/ –	15/ –/–
4,000	2,622/ 2/–	17/10	10/16/8
5,000	3,530/ 8/–	18/ 5	7/18/4

taxes, a sum which was equivalent in purchasing power to about $7,500 in America. If he earned another $100 he retained only $8 of it after paying the additional tax. If part of his income was from property instead of from personal exertion his tax was still higher, rising to a maximum of 97.5 per cent. It will thus be seen that Australian wartime taxation went far beyond President Roosevelt's proposal to limit incomes to a maximum of $25,000 "for the duration."

No attempt has been made, however, to maintain these exceedingly high rates now that the war is over. A reduction of 12.5 per cent for all categories was made at the beginning of 1946, and this was followed in June of the same year by cuts ranging from 18 per cent on low incomes to 7 per cent in the higher brackets. In succeeding years further reductions have been made, the chief benefit in every case being given to the low-income groups. The following table indicates just how far this program has gone since 1945. It again shows the tax on earned income for a person without dependents, and includes the social security contribution.

AUSTRALIAN INCOME TAX

INCOME	TAX 1948–49	TAX 1949–50
£ 300	£ 18/ 5/–	£ 13/ 2/–
400	34/14/–	23/15/–
600	74/14/–	53/10/–
800	124/14/–	91/10/–
1,000	184/14/–	137/10/–
1,500	368/ 1/–	283/ 7/–
2,000	593/ –/–	470/17/–
3,000	1,122/ 3/–	929/ 3/–
4,000	1,726/ 7/–	1,470/17/–
5,000	2,405/10/–	2,095/17/–

These reductions were made in response to protests that the heavy taxation of the war years, if continued in peacetime, would destroy incentive. During the war there were other incentives to maximum effort, but in time of peace it is necessary that the profit motive be restored if production is to be maintained. There have been reports of professional men who would work only a few days each week because two-thirds or more of the additional income they would earn would be taken in taxation; of businessmen who would not risk their capital for higher returns because most of the additional profit would go to taxes; and of coal miners who, contented with the thirteen or fourteen pounds they could earn in a normal week, refused to work overtime to produce more coal because so much of their increased earnings would go to taxation.

However, apart from the disinclination of a few well-paid workers to work overtime and of a few high-salaried professional men to work fulltime, the country does not seem to have suffered from any diminution of incentive. It may well be that some people sought safe investments at low interest who would otherwise have preferred greater risks and more profit. But the Capital Issues Control Commission, whose function it was, under special wartime powers, to review and control new investments in the national interest, reported that its only difficulty was to hold back a flood of money seeking investment in new enterprises of all kinds until labor and materials were available. The eagerness to invest still threatens inflation, so if high taxation somewhat diminishes that eagerness its influence is salutary. Wartime developments have created the basis for such a great expansion of secondary industries, and the owners of capital are so keen to seize these opportunities, that Australia will be faced with labor shortages rather than unemployment for a number of years to come.

One reason, however, why the effect is not so great as might be expected is that the tax on public companies is still low enough for them to make good profits and provide their directors with a desire to expand. The wartime excess profits tax was abolished at the end of 1947, leaving a flat six shillings on the pound, plus a surtax of one shilling on income in excess of five thousand pounds and a further two shillings on

net undistributed income.   In the case of private companies
(those held by not more than seven families) undistributed
income is treated as the income of the shareholders who would
have been entitled to it had it been distributed.   It will thus
be seen that public companies have an incentive to expand
their activities if these promise to be profitable, for the company can show a profit and distribute dividends even though
its more wealthy shareholders find those dividends largely
absorbed by taxation when calculated in their individual incomes.

The prospect for further large reductions in taxation,
however, is not bright.   The prime reason for this, of course,
is the cost of war debts, pensions, and the rehabilitation of
ex-servicemen.   But other reasons lie in the policies to which
both parties are now committed.   In the first place, all parties
are convinced that the expenditure for defense must be
greater in the near future than it has been in the past during
peacetime.   In addition, it is recognized that money is required to improve the capital equipment and amenities of the
country to accommodate a flow of immigration, and much
of this must at first be tax supported.   Moreover, the standard of social services now being demanded by the people
calls for further advances.   The four chief features of their
demands are the health service contemplated in the legislation of December, 1948, the need for an adequate housing
program and for improvement in the educational system, and
the abolition of the means tests.

The problem of the means tests.—   The question of the
means tests is one of the greatest political importance.   Under existing regulations the recipients of the old-age, invalids',
and widows' pensions, as well as of unemployment and sickness benefits, have been subject to a means test.   The sched-
ule in force in 1945–46 prescribed that old-age and invalids'
pensions should be reduced by the amount of income in excess

of 12/6 a week (25/– for a married couple) an applicant has from other sources. They are also reduced if the applicant holds property (other than a home) worth fifty-nine pounds. And no pension at all could be claimed by a person with property to the value of four hundred pounds (excluding a home) or an income of £2/5 weekly. Very similar conditions held true for the receipt of widows' pensions. And the unemployment and sickness benefits were reduced by the amount of any income over one pound a week. But when the social service contribution was introduced there arose a general demand for the withdrawal of the means test. Everyone pays for the pensions and everyone, it is contended, no matter what his financial status, should be allowed to receive them.

Abolition of the means test would remove all stigma from the receipt of a pension. It would also remove a certain obvious unfairness that even discourages thrift. With a means test in force the person who has saved a little money, or maintained an endowment insurance policy, or contributed to a pension scheme organized by his employers is deprived of much or all the pension benefits, while another person, with the same income, who has lived up to the limit of his means receives full pension benefits. Those who are paying contributions to employee's pension schemes feel particularly aggrieved. The pensions they will receive may be less or little more than the government's old-age pension. Yet they have paid special contributions for them in addition to the general social service contribution. In spite of these payments, in retirement they may be no better off (or very little better) than old-age pensioners who have paid nothing but their taxes.

For these reasons the Liberal and Country Parties (the present political combination opposed to Labor) have endorsed the plea for the abolition of the means test, at the same time urging that the entire cost of the pensions be placed upon the basis of a contributory insurance scheme. Prior to the elections of September, 1946, the caucus of the Labor Party in the federal parliament, not to be politically outdone, urged on the government the abolition of the means test, but rejected the plan for a contributory insurance scheme. Neither side can afford to ignore the protest against the means test, for it comes most strongly from precisely that lower middle class whose votes, turning now to the left and now to the right, sway election results.

The federal Labor government, however, though recognizing the fairness of the claim and its political implications, was embarrassed by the problem of financing the increased cost while the expenses of repatriating and demobilizing its armed forces were not yet over; and considering its other plans of social and national importance, it declined to promise this new boon. It pledged itself only to a progressive reduction of the means tests as finances permit.

A first installment of this reduction was announced in June, 1946. The new arrangement raised the allowed income from 12/6 to one pound, allowing a married couple with an income of two pounds a week from some other source to receive full pension, thus increasing their total income to £5/5 a week, nine shillings above the basic wage. The reduction of the pension for property other than a house was retained, but the allowed amount at which an applicant could still claim some pension was raised from £400 to £650. Similar modifications were made in the means test for widows' pensions. These concessions brought about 95,000 new people into the pension field and increased the partial pensions of 50,000 others. It cost the Treasury an additional £4,500,000, raising the total bill for social services during 1946–47 to £68,300,000. The social service contribution in the same year was estimated to bring in £51,000,000 and the payroll tax £11,000,000, leaving £6,300,000 for which other provision had to be made.

It was estimated in 1946 that complete abolition of the means tests would add a further £41,500,000 to the budget, which would have made impossible any reduction of taxation. The new plan raised the roll of old-age pensioners to 355,000, but still left 363,000 people of pensionable age (women over sixty and men over sixty-five) not receiving pensions. Most of these, it is fairly safe to assume, have not applied for pensions because either they or their husbands are still earning their normal incomes.

It would seem ridiculous to offer pensions to persons who have not retired and have no need to do so. With the increasing age of the population it is wise to encourage old people to take some light work, both for their own mental and physical health and for the benefit of national production. In a country with a high employment policy in operation there is no need to consider the retirement of older people as a means of making work for the younger. A pension plan, therefore, which allows possession of a house and an earned income of over two-fifths of the basic wage, and adds to it a pension that raises the total income of a married couple to nine shillings above that wage, would seem, therefore, to be adequate, so far as its income provisions are concerned, to meet all the more important arguments of those who urge abolition of the means test .

The provision which reduces the pension progressively for owners of any property (other than a home) valued above fifty-nine pounds and abolishes it at six hundred and fifty pounds is more dubious. This is subject to the ethical objection that it is unfair to the person who has saved a little money. The aged person who has saved a few hundred pounds in addition to buying his home should not be penalized for having done so or encouraged to expend such savings unnecessarily in the last few years before becoming eligible for a pension. The property qualification should, therefore, either be abolished altogether or raised to a figure at which the savings of the ordinary middle-class family man would not affect his eligibility for full pension. This would remove the stigma from the application for a pension and overcome the ethical objection to the means test.

There is a good case for allowing the cost of abolishing or lowering the property qualification to be laid upon the general income tax, for its benefits would accrue to the class who pay most of that tax. It would not be impossible either, as taxes are further reduced, to increase the social service contribution as the old-age pension bill rises with the increasing age of the population. This contribution rests lightly on the shoulders of those with low incomes. In 1946, seventy-six per cent of it came from those with an income of over three hundred pounds, and less than one per cent from families with one or more children and an income of less than three hundred pounds. Its maximum, even on the highest incomes, was only seven and one-half per cent. As financed at present, therefore, the social services constitute a real and important addition to the resources of the lower income classes, and the present defects in the system can be remedied without undue burden on any class. If the means test were completely abolished and the whole cost laid on a contributory system the financial benefit to the lower income class would disappear.

Political pressure for a scheme of universal pensions without a means test is, however, so strong that it cannot be long delayed. [3] The only important question lies in how it will be financed. Both parties have declared in favor

[3] The means test was further liberalized by the budget of September, 1948, and increases were made in pensions and child endowment to meet the increase in the cost of living.

of the principle, and Labor is evidently anxious both to secure credit for its introduction and to establish it in accord with its own financial principles. Prime Minister Chifley announced in February, 1948, that such a scheme was in preparation and it may be expected, therefore, that it will be placed upon the statute books by one party or the other in the not too distant future.

Education.— Rhodes scholars from Australia and New Zealand have especially fine records at Oxford. This is not because they are more intelligent than the others, but because the whole education system of the countries from which they come is designed to produce at the top the sort of minds that can win distinction in examinations. They are very efficient in what they set out to do. But one who has seen what education is doing for all classes of the community in the United States and some other countries is inclined to say, "These things ought ye to have done, but not to have left the other undone."

Thoughtful Australians are beginning to recognize the shortcomings of an education system of which, in the past, they have been very proud. Thus the Vice-Chancellor of the University of Melbourne concluded a plea for broader policies and greater freedom by saying: "It is worth while considering the Americans who are now amongst us. They have convinced me that you can educate men into a genuinely democratic attitude towards their community. They are as different from the Americans with whom I talked in France in 1918 as chalk from cheese. It is at least significant that in the 25 years that have elapsed since the last war they have faced squarely up to the problem of educating a whole community for a modern world, they have gone some way towards the creation of a real equality of educational opportunity and they have not counted the cost. They have, as they are the first to admit, made many mistakes, but they are on the high road.   They hold out to us our main hope of a decent world." [4]

The virtues of the Australian education system are those given it by the genuine liberalism of political and intellectual leadership in the half century before the first World War.   Its deficiencies are due to the conservatism and penny-pinching which prevailed between the two great conflicts. During these years expenditure per pupil on primary and secondary education in Australia has been allowed to become definitely the lowest in the British Commonwealth—which means very far below American levels.   Yet, in the decade before 1915, Australia had one of the finest systems of general education in the world.

"Free, compulsory and secular" education was established in the four largest Australian states before 1880 and shortly thereafter in the other two.   It was organized on a state-wide, not a local, basis.   This has brought a state-supported school with a qualified teacher to every community where six to ten pupils can be mustered, and at the same time, it has provided an effective system of correspondence instruction for those still more isolated, thus reducing illiteracy to the vanishing point.   The system has produced a body of trained teachers in every state who may be transferred freely throughout the state, giving service and gaining experience in both city and country.   Moreover, they are free from political interference, assured of their tenure and of promotions in accordance with their academic qualifications and marks earned for teaching skill, and they are paid salaries which arbitration courts consider equal to those of people in equivalent walks of life.

If the function of primary schools is to give a grounding in the three "R's," if that of the secondary schools is to

[4] J. D. G. Medley, *Education for Democracy* (Australian Council for Educational Research, Melbourne, 1943), 13.

prepare students for the university, and that of a university is to train people for professional and academic life, then the Australian education system must be recognized as extremely proficient. Here it is relevant for me to speak from personal experience. My two boys have spent at least a year in school in each of the states of Indiana, Kentucky, Wisconsin, South Australia, and Victoria. The Australian period came at the end of grade school (primary) and the beginning of high school. Their emphatic testimony is that they were worked harder and learned more in the Australian schools than in the American, though the American were much better equipped. My own experience with students as a teacher at the university level in both countries is the same. In the matter of efficiency of organization America has much to learn from Australia.

In the extension of education at the higher levels to all strata of the community, in the cultivation of a spirit of social democracy, in the awakening of interest, curiosity, and the critical faculties in minds not naturally very alert, in the freedom of the teacher to deal with individual differences and to experiment, and in the freedom of the pupil to discover and pursue his own interests, in all these, American schools and colleges have made real achievements which the Australian have only begun to attempt. To do these things requires smaller classes, better libraries, facilities for extra-curricular activities, and less emphasis on examination results. Those who have held the purse strings of Australian education in the last twenty-five years have been too much interested in securing persons who can perform efficient services, and in obtaining these results at the least possible cost, to provide any of these necessities. The spirit of the average Australian child has thus, for a quarter of a century, been sacrificed to the ideal of low taxation and balanced budgets.

The most serious deficiency has been at the secondary school level. Education has been compulsory only up to the age of fourteen years, though in 1943 New South Wales raised this to fifteen years and the other states are preparing to follow suit. All the states maintain high schools, technical, commercial, agricultural, and other types of schools for children over fourteen, and there are numerous private and denominational schools catering to those of high school years. But the private schools charge fees that are beyond the means of most parents. In some states fees, though small, are charged even for state high schools. The free secondary schools are not sufficiently numerous, and most of them are too academic. Their curriculums and home-work schedules are too demanding to enable the pupils to earn a little money after school hours as so many do in America. And the majority of parents cannot afford to keep their children at school after the age of fourteen years. The result is that only thirty-two per cent of Australian children between fourteen and seventeen years of age are in school. This compares with eighty per cent in the United States. At the university or college level the comparison is even more striking. In Australia, in any one year, about one person in five hundred and eighty-three is attending a university (or college); while in America about one person in ninety is in some institution of higher learning, though not all of these are of standard university level.

There are three main reasons for this failure to attain a wide spread of higher education. One is that the years between the two world wars, which have been the years of greatest advance in this respect in the United States, were the years when Australia was in a stage of political inertia. The reaction against the rise of a socialistic Labor party, divided and defeated over the conscription issue, had destroyed genuine liberalism and placed conservatism in the saddle. Second is the persistence of an academic tradition derived from the British ruling class. It is expressed through the British-trained faculties of the universities, who, by their control over university entrance examinations, largely determine the school curriculum. In spite of some notable exceptions this university influence has been, in general, academic and professional in its outlook. Finally, there is the influence of the private preparatory schools, which call themselves "colleges."

These "colleges" are a very important part of the Australian education system. They are modeled, more or less, on the English public school and try to cultivate its spirit of school loyalty and its code of conduct. Some of them are privately endowed, but for the most part they are maintained by their fees. Some of their pupils are boarders but the majority are day students only. The fees charged are lower than those of the English public schools, and consequently the teachers are poorly paid. In a pamphlet published by the Australian Council for Educational Research we find the following statement concerning them: "We can say fairly confidently that the general standard of formal education is higher in state schools, while at a number of the big private schools, the brightest pupils are likely to have a type of education in their later years which allows them to develop in a freer and more interesting way than most of their contemporaries in state schools. It is certain that there are some valuable things in the educational methods of some private schools which the state schools lack; it is also certain that in many, even in those which may be making interesting experiments in some departments, there is a good deal of incompetent teaching." [5]

In America 6.5 per cent of secondary school pupils attend private preparatory schools, in New Zealand 14.1 per cent, in England 25.4 per cent, in Australia 33 per cent.

[5] J. A. La Nauze, *Education for Some* (Australian Council for Educational Research, Melbourne, 1943).

There are two main reasons for this high percentage of private school pupils. One is the slowness of the Australian government to provide high schools. The other is the social prestige of going to a private school. Mercifully, the Australian private schools do not have a special accent to preserve, as do the English, or the class division created by the old school tie and a special manner of speech would be complete—and class consciousness is all too strong as it is in Australia. The Australian accent badly needs improving, but the development of a public school accent would be too high a social price to pay for such an aesthetic boon. Even without the help of an accent every Australian middle-class family knows that there is a social and economic advantage to be gained from sending its boys and girls to a "college" instead of to a state high school. At "college" they will meet the sons and daughters of the "best families"; the girls will have better marriage possibilities by gaining entry into the right social circles; and the boys will have better business and professional opportunities both because they will make contacts that will be useful in later life and because many employers have a partiality for boys from their old school.

When the midde-class people of the community are paring the family budget to send their children to private schools, they are not likely to be enthusiastic about paying extra taxes to provide improved secondary education, conducted by better-paid teachers, for other people's children, who may thus acquire advantages which will enable them to compete with their own children. Therefore, those elements in the community which, in America, are keenest to create the finest possible high school for the town are, in Australia, often only lukewarm or worse toward the expansion of free secondary education.

In spite of these difficulties, however, secondary education in Australia has developed, and the way is being paved to create genuine equality of educational opportunity from kindergarten to university. The latest move in this direction, and significant of more to follow, is the subsidizing of students at the university. This was begun as a war measure in 1943 when one thousand six hundred and forty-three students received subsidies. It is being continued as part of the government's peacetime program, with increasing numbers of students and extension to all faculties. The maximum assistance allowed is £153 plus fees, but this sum is reduced in cases where the parents have sufficient income to bear part of the cost.

An analysis of the occupations of the parents of students assisted in 1944 showed a considerable number of laborers and other manual workers. The selection, however, is made on the basis of examination results at the university entrance level. It presupposes, therefore, four or five years of secondary school, and as there is as yet no assistance other than the family endowment, which ceases at sixteen, to help support a child in high school, not many young people from the lower income groups really have an opportunity to avail themselves of the assistance offered at the university level. The present scheme therefore needs to be supplemented by a plan to increase the child endowment for older children still at school, and to extend financial aid up to eighteen years of age for young people who can profit by continued schooling.

It will be seen, therefore, that Australia requires a greatly increased budget for education. To raise the school-leaving age and reduce the size of classes, more teachers and more classrooms are required in the primary school system. In addition to new buildings, remodeled and improved equipment are also necessary. The secondary school system must be expanded to accommodate more than double the present number of pupils, and living subsidies must be provided for many of these. Then universities, now vastly overcrowded, must be enlarged to meet the increased enrollment arising out of the government's student-assistance scheme, an increase greatly needed to train experts for the growing secondary industries and professional and cultural services. A broadening of the present rather narrow academic limits to include a wider range of purely cultural subjects and studies in the social sciences is also essential.

- 7 -

Employment Policy

THE new scale of social services and the method of financing them is plainly geared to conditions of prosperity. It presupposes that the country can maintain a high level of employment. In the face of past experience this may seem to some like willfully blind optimism. But it is not. It is rooted in the conviction that the fundamental cause of general economic depressions is now understood, and that it can be averted by government action. This conviction rests upon the acceptance of what economists commonly call the Keynes-Hansen analysis of the business cycle, or otherwise, the "surplus savings" theory of the cause of general depressions.

This new economic outlook is one of the most striking and significant changes in the Australian thinking in recent years. In 1934 and 1935 there was little more than a hesitant willingness to give serious consideration to the "surplus savings" theory which had at that time received only a partial exposition by J. M. Keynes and J. A. Hobson in Britain. But in 1936 when the former published his epoch-making volume, *The General Theory of Employment, Interest and Money,* Australian economists were quick to recognize its significance. They saw that the features of their own Premiers' Plan which had been extremely valuable in the depression of 1929–35 were not the orthodox measures of government economy and reduction of wages, but the boldly unorthodox measures of reduction of interest rates, lowering of the exchange value of the currency, and government spending financed by treasury bills issued by the Commonwealth Bank. With these object lessons before them, and with the weight of Keynes's authoritative and expert argument in its favor, the "surplus savings" theory triumphed. It has been accepted by all schools of economic thought in Australia and made the basis of statements of policy concerning control of unemployment coming from both sides of the political arena.

In America the Keynes-Hansen thesis is not so widely accepted. There is still conservative opposition to some of its less welcome implications. Further, among laymen in economics both in Australia and America it is not well understood. An understanding of the problem must begin by recognizing that everybody's income is somebody's expenditure. The income of the shopkeeper, the doctor, and many others comes directly from the expenditure of the consumer who buys their goods and services. That of the employee in a private business comes from the expenditure on wages or salaries by the employer, who recoups himself from the expenditure of those who buy the goods or services his employees produce. That of the government employee comes from expenditure of government money derived from taxes or loans. The employer, whether a private individual or company or the government, expends money in wages and salaries for one of two purposes, that is, for consumers' goods and services (such as food, clothing, education, private cars, and houses) or for capital goods (goods used to produce other goods and services, such as factory buildings and machines, business cars and ships, houses, and roads). This gives us the main classifications of the kinds of expenditure that provide our incomes: (1) private consumption; (2) private investment (expenditure on capital goods); (3) government consumption (e.g., defense, pensions, and education); (4) government investment (e.g., roads, forests, and flood control).

If employment is to be kept at a steady level, then the total expenditure from these four sources combined must not fluctuate. That means that any variation in one must be counterbalanced by one of the others. But the trouble is that, if left to themselves without any over-all planning, they tend to move together, instead of counterbalancing each other. Thus, if private investment becomes very active, the money spent encourages private consumption; and the additional taxes that come in and the general feeling of confidence and prosperity encourage government spending. In this way a boom is started. On the other hand, if one is decreased the others tend to follow suit, thus creating a depression.

Of these four sources of expenditure (and of income), private investment is most subject to fluctuations. Depressions and booms usually start in the industries that produce capital goods because there is a fall or rise in the amount of private investment. Private consumption is fairly stable, except that it tends to expand or fall with the total income provided; it does not tend to initiate changes of itself. Government expenditure in peacetime is also fairly stable and so long as it spends only money derived from taxes it has a counterbalancing effect in reducing private expenditures. A reduction of taxation, however, may not be counterbalanced by increased private expenditure; the money not required for taxes may be saved and not invested. Government loans can become inflationary, for the money borrowed and spent by the government goes back into the people's pockets as income and can be spent by them again. This is what happens in wartime, but in time of peace government-loan expenditure is not often extended to the point of an inflationary boom. Moreover, except in wartime, government expenditure is easier than the other types to control.

The problem child of the economic family, therefore, is private investment. It is the most variable and the most difficult to control. So far there is nothing new in the economic analysis. The classical economists could all agree. But what Keynes and his co-workers have brought out so clearly and freshly is the fact that there is, in our twentieth-century world economy, a chronic tendency of private investment to fall short of what is needed from that source to keep up a stable rate of total expenditure and total income.

To understand the reasons for this tendency we may begin by considering a single business, for example, a shoe factory managed by its owner. In setting the price of his finished product the owner takes account of all his costs— wages, salaries of management (including his own), raw materials, services, rent, interest, waste and losses, depreciation on the plant. He then adds a margin of profit as compensation for his risks. This profit may not be great, but it is over and above all his costs. Capital is turned over several times a year and there is normally a profit each time. The persons who receive this profit (over and above rent, interest, depreciation, and salaries of management) usually do not want to spend it on consumers' goods. They want to add most of it to their capital. So long as the business is profitable, therefore, most of the profit accumulates and must find investment. At first it may be invested in the expansion of the shoe factory. But if all or even most shoe manufacturers are also making profits and doing the same, the shoe industry soon reaches a point where no more capital can profitably be invested in it. The shoe manufacturers then invest their profits (either directly or by putting the money in financial institutions which do it for them) in some other industries where there is still room for expansion. And the same is done, on a smaller scale of course, by some of their employees who save some of their wages or salaries.

If there is general prosperity, however, then in due course every industry becomes expanded to the limit. Existing industries must look for new industries in which to invest their profits. But if every industry in the country is generally profitable there can never be enough new ones to absorb the savings available for investment. So investment falls off. Some of the surplus savings are allowed to lie idle in the banks and the rate of investment expenditure falls. The capital goods industries, such as steel and building, must reduce hands. Unemployment appears. Consumption drops and consumers' goods industries must reduce their output. Taxes fall off and the government decides it is necessary to economize, and more people are without work.

General prosperity thus kills itself because it cannot continue to find new investments for all its profits. Its surplus savings choke the economic machine. The downward spiral caused by surplus savings goes on until the loss of profits and the cost of keeping men in idleness eliminate the surplus of savings. Then stability is found at a low level of employment, and the economy of the country must remain on that low level, if it does not fall still lower, until something happens to create new opportunities for investment. One factor that always tends to bring at least a temporary upsurge after a few years is the accelerated depreciation of depression years and the fact that plant and buildings become obsolete even if not used.   In addition, the steady growth of population at length stimulates some new building and other enlargement of output, though this factor is now much less effective than in the past.   A third factor is the development of new industries; but these are not very helpful if they merely replace one kind of consumption with another, and they are far from sufficient to absorb the savings of general prosperity in all established industry.

During the nineteenth century surplus savings were a recurrent but not chronic cause of unemployment.   Industry was expanding all over the world.   When Britain became fully industrialized she invested her surplus savings in the United States, South America, her colonies, and other countries.   General depressions occurred but were temporary, for the prodigious growth of population, the development of new countries, the increasing use of industrial power and machinery soon caught up with the reduced savings and gave scope for new investment.   Indeed, much of the time the demand for new capital outran savings and caused inflationary expansion of credit.   But as more and more countries became fully industrialized and sought to export their surplus savings for investment in other countries the competition for new openings for investment became desperately keen.   It led to war in 1914.

Just at that juncture the United States turned the corner from being an importer of capital (and an outlet for other nations' surplus savings) to being an exporter of capital—a country with surplus savings of her own to invest elsewhere. From 1914 to 1918 the war absorbed the savings of all the world.   For a few years after its conclusion the program of reconstruction provided an outlet for countries with capital to export.   Australia, Canada, and the South American countries were also still expanding, opening up new land and absorbing new population.   But by 1929 the products of these new lands were glutting the markets of the world, and the process of making loans to Germany and other European countries also ceased. The surplus savings of the world had overtaken the opportunities for investment. Finding no genuine new investment, people gambled for a while on the stock exchange, sending shares to fantastic prices. Then the crash came.

From that depression the world did not fully recover until war again created a tremendous new demand financed by the borrowing of the belligerent governments. The great depression of 1929 and the years following was different from all other depressions because, for the first time, the world as a whole had attained a chronic surplus of savings. There was no more opening up of new lands, no great new growth of population to provide openings for investment of its accumulated profits. Prior to 1914 the United States, in most years, helped to absorb the surplus capital of other countries. Now she added to the world's surplus. All that was possible was a partial recovery which overtook the excessive depreciation and inertia of the worst depression years. In Australia a greater recovery was made than in most countries because the measures taken to check the balance of trade created a demand for investment in secondary industries. Yet even Australia had ten per cent unemployment at the beginning of 1939; and in the more fully industrialized democracies the position was worse.

Methods of promoting employment.— These, then, are the causes of the general depressions which have appeared periodically since the era of capitalistic production began. They show that in the present day a high, and on the whole an increasing, level of unemployment threatens to become chronic—the cause being the tendency of savings to outrun investment. How then can unemployment be prevented? There are two possible lines of attack, and they are not mutually exclusive. One is to do something to stimulate higher private investment. The other is to compensate for a drop in private investment by an increase in one or more of the other three sources of expenditure and income, that is, in private consumption, government consumption, and government investment.

It should, perhaps, first be pointed out that an increase in private consumption cannot be obtained simply by increasing wages and salaries. Wages and salaries constitute far the largest part of the cost of production; and the other costs —rent, interest, and profit—tend to vary with them. Thus, to increase wages and salaries all around adds so much to the price of goods that the purchasing power of those wages and salaries is only slightly increased. At the same time the purchasing power of accumulated savings (including insurance) is decreased, and therefore the total purchasing power of the consumer is no greater than before. An unfair distortion of values has been introduced into the economic system and nothing gained.

One of the remedies for financial slumps suggested by Lord Keynes is the stimulation of private investment by the lowering of interest rates. This, he says, should be deliberately undertaken by the central bank as a matter of government policy when unemployment threatens. Lower interest encourages people to borrow money and invest it. It also encourages the purchase of durable goods and houses on time payment. It encourages the erection of bigger and better houses and public buildings and other government investment in works of advantage to the community. And it encourages the owner of money to invest it himself instead of leaving it at interest in a bank or in bonds. There is, however, a limit to the reduction of interest rates. The owner of money must be compensated for the cost and risk of lending and for refraining from the dissipation of his money on projects of personal interest. It is impossible, therefore, to reduce interest rates, in present economic conditions, much lower than they have been in recent years. For that reason such a method of stimulating investment is not likely to be sufficient to overcome the chronic tendency to surplus saving, that is, to underinvestment.

The second and more important method of meeting the problem is that of additional government spending on investment goods (for example, on roads, public buildings, flood control) to make up for the drop in private investment. This has the advantage of giving employment to the very industries which have been allowed to grow slack by the fall in private investment. The government, according to this plan, simply borrows a considerable part of the surplus savings for which no profitable private investment can be found and spends the money to the general advantage of the public. This action, of course, adds to the public debt and to the national interest bill, for it is not possible to find enough public works (such as power dams and toll bridges) which will pay interest on their cost.

In adopting this method of overcoming a depression, however, it is not necessary for the additional government investment to be as great as the total fall in private investment and consumption, since government spending increases private consumption and creates openings for private investment which otherwise would not exist. Yet government spending has to do more than merely prime the pump. Because of the chronic tendency of industry to accumulate surplus (uninvestable) savings in times of general prosperity, the government has to keep up its practice of borrowing and spending enough of that surplus to stimulate consumption and provide fields for investment of the remainder. And if a country has been allowed to sink deep into depression, then it will require great volumes of government spending to lift it out. The pump-priming of the American New Deal was right in its way, but it was inadequate. America was never really lifted out of the depression until economic recovery was promoted by the vast government expenditures in wartime. If it had been possible to stop most of that spending at the point where full employment had been reached, tailing it off to a minimum when that point grew near, then prosperity could have been maintained. But it would not have been possible to cease this additional government spending altogether. General prosperity will always produce a surplus of savings. If the problem is to be met by government borrowing and spending, then there will be a continuous increase in the national debt.

This threat of a continuously increasing national debt has made businessmen and statesmen hesitate to adopt such a plan for overcoming depression. Economists, however, point out that it is not really as dangerous as it seems. In the first place, it is an internal debt. The interest does not go outside the country. It goes into the pockets of the people, and in particular, into those of the income-tax-paying class, and is taken out again in taxes to pay the next year's interest. Every dollar added to the national interest bill on internal debt is a dollar added to the national income out of which the interest has to be paid. The only economically important disadvantage is the psychological one that people find that, in spite of increases in their income, a larger and larger proportion of that income goes in taxes, so that when they add to their incomes they are little better off. This, in the long run, must destroy incentive. It has to be recognized, therefore, that it would be possible for the continuous increase of the national debt to reach a point where the interest bill so increased taxation that the profit motive would break down; the incentive to invest could be so reduced that investment would be retarded and unemployment created by the very measures designed to stimulate investment and prevent unemployment.

Advocates of this plan, however, do not believe that the growth of the public debt would ever be great enough to bring about this impasse. They point out that the national income is steadily rising, because of improving technology, growing population, and other factors, and that there is certainly no danger as long as the interest bill does not grow faster than the national income. If it should do so, then adoption of special measures for its reduction might become necessary. The simplest plan would probably be to add to the death duties and gift taxes a sum sufficient to prevent too great an increase of the national debt. These taxes simply prevent the whole of an accumulated fortune from being passed on to the next generation and do not affect business incentive to anything like the same degree as taxes on annual income. Indeed, they even constitute a stimulus to efforts to increase a fortune so that, after paying heavy death duties, there may still be a considerable inheritance to hand on.

There seems to be no reason, therefore, why the chronic tendency to surplus saving inherent in the system of private enterprise cannot be continuously offset by government expenditure of loan money. The loan money may be either borrowed at interest from those who possess the surplus savings or obtained in the form of credits from a government-owned central bank, such as the Commonwealth Bank in Australia. In the latter case it would be interest-free.

The idea of interest-free credits for the government, instead of loans, has appealed to many people, including some Australian politicians, as a very simple way of financing the needed additional government expenditure. If done too extensively, however, it would be dangerously inflationary. It would leave the surplus savings of private enterprise without even an investment in government bonds. This would drive interest rates very low and, up to a point, would be quite wholesome.   But to have large sums of liquid money lying idle in banks at a time of high employment would constitute an ever present danger of a speculative boom which would be extremely difficult to control.   The inviting prospect of an abundance of free money for the government through credits from a government central bank is, therefore, one that must be approached with great caution.   For the most part, the additional government expenditure must be financed by adding to the national debt; and any undue growth must be controlled by such special taxation as that on death duties and gifts or by a general capital levy.

Some economists who would accept the analysis as thus far presented express doubts, however, as to whether, in a country with fully developed industries, it is possible to find enough useful public works to absorb the amount of government spending necessary to offset the deficiency in private investment.   If this should ever prove to be the case, the problem can be met by reducing the taxes that fall on the lower-income groups, thus giving people who normally spend almost the whole of their incomes more money to spend. The revenue lost in this way would have to be made up by loan and the additional spending on consumers' goods would make up for the deficiency in spending on private investment.

This plan offers the simplest and speediest method of adjustment to prevent both depression and inflationary boom. The government can plan whatever public works and social services are thought desirable and arrange its budget to allow for a small deficit to be financed by internal borrowing. This deficit should be a little under what is estimated as sufficient to offset the tendency to surplus saving, but the administration should be given power to remit a portion of certain taxes that fall on lower incomes and raise an equivalent sum in loans or central bank credits immediately it has reason to suspect that national expenditure (and national income) is declining.

With our modern pay-as-you-go method of collecting income taxes the government has a good yardstick for measuring variations in national expenditure and income every month. As soon as a decline appears it could be offset by remitting a certain amount of the monthly tax, for example, a flat rate of so much deducted from everybody's tax for a month. And this could be repeated and varied as much as seems necessary. The additional income thus received by individuals would almost immediately go into additional spending on consumers' goods. The community could be taught that it was a patriotic duty to spend it and the response would be almost universal. When the national income recovered, as revealed by the monthly returns, the tax could be immediately reimposed. Thus the power to vary taxation from month to month, financing the deficits by borrowing, would give the administration an adequate instrument to control those tendencies to depression and boom which otherwise threaten the system of private enterprise with recurring chaos and eventual disruption.

The same result, of course, can be accomplished, though with less speed and accuracy, by the government's power to vary taxation from year to year. It is only necessary to get rid of the traditional conception of orthodox political economy that sound finance requires that national budgets must be balanced, as nearly as possible every year, and that deficits should not be allowed to accumulate. The new analysis of the economic system, which we owe primarily to Lord Keynes, shows that these apparently obvious propositions are fundamentally unsound. Because of the psychological propensity of the people to save more than they can invest, leaving private budgets unbalanced on the credit side, the government must spend a little more than it receives, adjusting its deficits to balance the surplus saving of the people. And if, in the course of time, the accumulated deficits grow unmanageably large, then they must be reduced not by a further charge on income, but by a charge on accumulated capital. This could be done by a capital levy. But the simplest and most painless way of doing it is to take from each person a portion of his or her estate at the time when it is passed on to someone else, either by bequest or by gift.

Australian government policy.—   In May, 1945, the Labor government issued a white paper to define its policy on the problem of unemployment. This document shows a complete acceptance of the Keynes-Hansen thesis. It lays down the fundamental premise that "full employment can be maintained only as long as total expenditure provides a market for all the goods and services turned out by Australian men and women." [1] It then proceeds with the following analysis of the problem and proposals for its solution.

Expenditure may be broadly divided into: (a) private consumption expenditure; (b) public expenditure on current services such as defense, transportation, police, and social services; (c) private capital expenditure; (d) public capital expenditure; (e) expenditure from overseas. Major changes in the amount of employment are due to fluctuations in the third and fourth parts, for private capital expenditure depends upon the variable factor of personal judgments of business prospects, and in the past, public capital expenditure has varied with it because governments have believed that they should expand their activities in good times and economize in bad times. In reality, however, the reverse policy should have been pursued. Expenditure from overseas is also variable in Australia and difficult to control because of a large export trade in primary products, the variations between

---

[1] *Full Employment in Australia* (Government Printer, Canberra, 1945). All the quotations in this section are from this document.

good and bad seasons, and changes in the prices of primary products overseas.

The government therefore proposes that public capital expenditure should be varied to offset the unstable factors in demand for labor. "The essential condition of full employment is that public expenditure should be high enough to stimulate private spending to the point where the two together will provide a demand for the total production of which the economy is capable." It should create a tendency toward "a shortage of men instead of a shortage of jobs," and those temporarily out of work due to sickness, seasonal employment, and such minor causes should receive unemployment pay and retraining for new types of work if necessary.

It is recognized that this policy will need careful administration. Care must be taken that total expenditure does not go too high, causing inflation. An important factor here will be the government's control of credit through the Commonwealth Bank, which can be used to stop a boom or to stimulate private investment. In general, interest rates will be kept low. "In particular it will be the responsibility of the Commonwealth Bank to ensure that the banking system does not initiate a general contraction of credit or contribute in any way to the growth of unemployment through a decline of expenditure."

The government envisages no difficulty in finding worthwhile projects for public capital expenditure sufficient to maintain its full employment policy. Rather, it is feared that, given the assurance of prosperity, private capital expenditure may go so high as to make it difficult to find men and materials for needed public works. "Provision for the maintenance and development of public capital assets . . . will require a level of public capital expenditure substantially higher than before the war . . . housing and slum clearance,

8182 *Employment Policy*

community centres, hospitals and libraries, roads, railways, bridges, harbours, aerodromes, electrical and other power-undertakings, administrative buildings, land development through irrigation, afforestation, water conservation, prevention of soil erosion, flood control, reclamation. . . . If private spending seems likely at any time to expand to a level where it may prevent the completion of urgently needed public capital projects, the Commonwealth and State Governments should seek means by which they can determine which capital projects, public or private, are the more important to the community, and accord priority to those projects."

In regard to fluctuations in net expenditure from overseas the government's policy is to be based on the following principles: (1) to seek agreements with other countries to maintain a policy of high employment and thus keep up the demand for each other's goods; (2) international collaboration to expand world trade and mitigate fluctuations in prices of raw materials; (3) diversification of Australian exports; (4) measures to stabilize the incomes of Australian export producers to offset short-term fluctuations in demand for their products; (5) to compensate for fluctuations in expenditure from overseas by expansion in public capital expenditure and other appropriate means.

Having thus broadly stated government policy, the document goes on to discuss the special problems of full employment. It recognizes the danger of inflation and says about the only thing that can be said in advance: "Avoidance of this threat depends on the skill with which governments can control their expenditure policies. Experience will progressively improve the technique of this planning." It discusses the need for an efficient employment service to reduce transitional unemployment and to facilitate the transfer of employees from declining to growing industries by retraining programs, vocational guidance, and removal from place to place. It refers to the danger that, with the assurance of full employment, businessmen will be content to continue existing types and methods of production rather than seek new products and new methods; the remedy proposed is government assistance in research and encouragement to competition and enterprise. Similarly, the danger of workers being unwilling to change their occupations and of their seeking to restrict admission to their crafts is met by an appeal to trade unions to recognize that, with an assurance of full employment, there is no longer any need for restrictive measures. There is no mention, however, of any danger of the inefficiency of workers due to a removal of the disciplinary fear of unemployment. Such fears are probably exaggerated, however. The inefficient worker can still be discharged and forced to take the least desirable jobs and to lose time in drifting from one job to another.

How to finance a program of full employment is not adequately discussed in this document. It mentions as "the chief possible sources" taxation and borrowing either from the public or the central bank. The chief source of revenue, it is recognized, should be taxation. This is probably inserted as a repudiation of "social credit" theorists (some of whom are found among Labor Party supporters) who argue that the expenses of government can and should be financed by central bank credits. This section of the document then goes on to say that taxation cannot meet the whole problem. It may be made to yield sufficient resources, when the economy is fully employed, to cover "at least all public expenditure on current items, including the maintenance of existing assets" and also "some contribution toward public capital expenditure." But "there are limits on the extent to which taxation can be used." This evidently envisages a policy of "deficit financing," which entails a continuous growth of the public debt. There is no discussion in the white paper, however, of whether this debt may become dangerously large or how such a problem should eventually be met. All we have to guide us here as to the government's intentions are the following cautious statements which indicate a policy which is a compromise between taxation to absorb and spend surplus savings, adding to the interest-bearing public debt, and utilization of free central bank credits.

"Taxes will be designed to have the least possible restrictive effect, both on the readiness to undertake private capital expenditure, and on the efficiency with which production is undertaken. Levels of taxation and existing methods of levying direct taxation are being closely examined, and consideration will be given to such changes as may seem necessary. Borrowing from the public is on a voluntary basis and avoids some of the disadvantages of taxation, but leaves a debt on which interest must be paid. Financing by the Commonwealth Bank can be used to advantage up to the limit of available men and resources, but if carried beyond this point it would gravely threaten the real incomes of workers and low income groups and would result in conditions so unstable that full employment could not be maintained."

This seems to suggest a policy which would use interest-free Commonwealth Bank credits or treasury bills, the interest on which accrues to the profit of the government's own bank, to finance public works up to the point of full employment of manpower and materials. For public works needed beyond this point, or to absorb an accumulation of private money seeking investment and threatening inflation, government bonds would be issued—and with a flush money market the interest would be low. Taxation would be kept high on high incomes in order to absorb a considerable portion of surplus savings, yet low enough to provide incentive for investment. Finally, death duties and gift taxes (which fall on accumulated capital rather than on current income) would be utilized to prevent the interest bill on the national debt from growing faster than can well be sustained by increase of the national income. This last point is not explicitly mentioned, but it is not likely to escape the government's financial experts as they seek for taxes "designed to have the least possible restrictive effect" on capitalist enterprise and efficiency.

The feature of the employment problem which gives Australian statesmen and economists most concern is not how to find enough useful public works to keep the people employed or how to finance such undertakings, but the variability in what the white paper lists as the fifth component of national income, expenditure from overseas. Australia may pursue a policy of full employment, but if other countries do not do so, then there may occur a serious fall in the demand for, and price of, Australian exports such as initiated the great depression in 1929. If Australia counteracted this fall in national income by expanding government spending, this would keep up the level of her imports while that of exports (and the payment for them) fell off, and no country can continue to endure for any length of time an adverse balance of payments, least of all a country with a large overseas debt. Therefore, the problem of avoiding a depression imported from overseas is one that seriously exercises the minds of Australian statesmen.

For this reason, H. V. Evatt, Minister for External Affairs, has frequently emphasized, at San Francisco and at other international conferences, the need for international agreements to pursue policies of high employment. This is also the reason for Australia's long hesitation over acceptance of the Bretton Woods proposals. It is frankly feared that the American Congress may refuse to take the measures necessary to prevent another depression. And a depression in America would depress prices and markets, especially for raw materials, everywhere. It might then be necessary for Australia, in order to save her policy of high employment, to take drastic measures to safeguard her balance of payments. Australian statesmen therefore wish to be sure that there are no commitments in the Bretton Woods or any other international agreement which would prevent them from doing what they believe might be necessary to safeguard themselves against the effect of other countries' neglect to adopt an adequate employment policy.

The protective measures envisaged in the white paper on full employment are the seeking of an international agreement to maintain high employment and the negotiation of trade treaties for expanding commercial relations. If these are not effective then it is expressly stated that any temporary decline will be met by resorting to a quantitative restriction of imports; and if the decline proves to be permanent then it must be met by a reduction of the exchange value of the currency in relation to that of other countries. Australia has no faith whatever in the laissez faire theory that universal prosperity is guaranteed by the removal of restrictions on international trade. She is convinced that, unless all countries maintain an internal policy of high employment, then removing the restrictions on trade (or, in particular, surrendering the power to impose restrictions) merely means the exposure of those countries that have the wisdom to maintain a policy of high employment to the consequences of the folly of those that do not.

What the brains trust is thinking.— The group of economists who framed the policy of the Premiers' Plan in the great depression have often been called "Australia's Brains Trust." They have continued to be influential. There are few countries, if any, where the economists in the universities and in places of importance in the civil service are listened to with so much respect by the ministers responsible for shaping public policy. And this remains true from whichever side of the political arena the ministers are drawn. It is therefore of no small importance to learn what these gentlemen are thinking.

Probably the leading figure in the brains trust of 1931 was D. B. Copland. During the war he did a remarkably successful piece of work as Commonwealth Prices Commissioner, heading the Australian counterpart of the American Office of Price Administration. In January, 1945, he gave the Godkin Lectures at Harvard University, which have been printed as a book entitled *The Road to High Employment*.[2]

At the outset of these lectures Professor Copland announced his concern to maintain the system of private enterprise, but declared that if it is to survive it must remedy the defects revealed by the great depression. The complete domination of the system by the capitalistic entrepreneur must give way to a large measure of public control. The possibility of successful nationalization of industry has been proved by the success of the statutory corporation and, although the democratic countries show, he believes, little inclination to carry the process of nationalization very far (this was said, it must be remembered, in 1945), nationalization is the alternative in so far as private enterprise fails.

Apart from nationalization the elements and instruments of public control in a democratic system have been greatly developed, he points out, in recent years. By progressive taxation and by extension of social services greater equality of income and a higher level of consumption have been achieved. In particular, it has been found possible to supply the community with "collective goods and services" such as education, health services, housing, roads, parks, and li-

[2] D. B. Copland, *The Road to High Employment* (Harvard University Press, Cambridge, Massachusetts, 1945).

braries; and this must be an increasing function of government. Again, the war has shown that a democratic economy is capable of tremendous expansion and successful direction of its productive effort. It proved that government expenditure can step up demand in all fields of endeavor, increase the national income, and raise standards of living even apart from any direct benefits from such an expenditure. It disposed of the myth of insufficient finance and the inevitability of fluctuations of employment, and taught nations to base their calculations of what they can do on a "man-power budget" instead of on a "finance budget." In retrospect it shows that the heroic measures taken by Australia to cure the depression of the thirties would have been more successful if government expenditure had not been so severely reduced.

Specific reasons are given for the view that private enterprise cannot, of itself, provide long-term full employment. Chief of these is the fact that the higher standard of living of modern communities has shifted the emphasis from basic needs to luxury and semiluxury goods, and that this does not provide sufficient scope for investment. It does not suffice to absorb the even greater amount of savings that accumulate with the continuous rise of income. Thus the world of today lacks the "capacity to consume." And the more unequal the incomes of the community, the greater is the tendency to build up surplus savings. "The rate of investment in these circumstances must be increased; this has not been done by private enterprise and must be undertaken by the state for the benefit of the whole community." [3]

Although insisting that the state must undertake to keep public expenditure sufficiently high to maintain "a stable level of employment with work for all" [4] Professor Copland objects

[3] *Ibid.*, 36.
[4] *Ibid.*, 46.

to the term "full employment" and to the slogan of "more jobs than workers to fill them." He is opposed to the policy stated in the Australian white paper and in agreement with an American government report which suggests a level of from five to eight per cent unemployment. [5] He criticizes the Beveridge plan for England as being unrealistically "perfectionist" in its advocacy of "full" rather than merely "high" employment and says that the former could not be maintained without undue regimentation and danger of inflation. "We cannot weaken the incentive of competition for work without supplanting it with some form of discipline." [6] For in a short market for labor some employers will offer higher pay and start a vicious spiral of wages and prices. Thus it is argued that a certain minimum pool of unemployment is the only alternative to labor regimentation, price control, and the fixing of maximum as well as minimum wages.

On this point there is evidently some difference of opinion between Professor Copland and the Labor government. The Liberal and Country Parties, now the official opposition, would agree with the professor's more cautious position. Both parties, however, would agree that there will always be some unemployment, due to seasonal factors, fluctuations in particular industries, and changing of jobs, and that there must be unemployment pay for those temporarily out of work. In practice there would probably be little actual difference between the two sides, for the opposition has, in its semi-official propaganda literature, also endorsed the program of high employment maintained by government expenditure.

A pamphlet distributed by the Liberal Party expressly states that "in a free economy, which is an economy which depends upon private investment as its mainspring, there is

[5] *Report of the Technical Committee of the National Resources Planning Board on Security, Work, and Relief Policies in the United States* (Government Printer, Washington, March, 1943).
[6] Copland, *The Road to High Employment,* 49.

an almost chronic tendency for savings to exceed investment. . . . The result is a tendency toward a permanent deficiency in total expenditure and chronic unemployment." The remedies suggested are "to make money for financing construction available at low interest and, in a period of threatened depression, to vary the rates of interest and amortization payments," and "to dovetail public construction with private construction. Such a contracyclical policy can be a major stabilizing influence." [7]

In budget policy it is urged that governments should "strike a balance over a series of years rather than annually" so that "public expenditure, especially public investment expenditure, could be increased in periods of business recession, thus incurring deficits. The corollary would be to wipe out deficits and build up surpluses when business was buoyant, especially when boom conditions were developing." This would seem to deny the necessity for almost continuous deficit financing. But a later statement shows that even a long-term balancing of budgets is more a hope than a conviction. "We are not as optimistic as some writers on the practicability of implementing a policy of long-term budget balancing. We can see both statistical and political difficulties. . . . On the other hand, it seems to us important that public financing should have a contracyclical pattern as one of its main characteristics."

In discussing loan policy this pamphlet refers to "the vexed question whether money is to come from borrowing from the public or through the expansion of bank credit." Idle savings, it is maintained, should be tapped as far as possible, but "failing that, and in a situation where substantial productive resources are idle, the expansion of bank credit will be sound." At the same time the warning is uttered

[7] *Stability and Progress* (Institute of Public Affairs, Sydney, 1945), 13, 24.

that care must be taken "to avoid expansionist policies likely to lead to inflation . . . and to avoid building up a public debt which the expected future productivity of the community cannot conveniently support." [8]

It will be seen, therefore, that in the matter of employment policy essentially the same principles are recognized by both the opposing political parties. The brains trust has done its work well. Lord Keynes has convinced the economists at the Australian universities, and their experience during the depression and the war has justified his theories, which have now become the basis for political action on both sides. The only differences are in details. Should Commonwealth Bank credits be a first resort or a last resort in financing the needed deficit spending? Should the policy be one of full employment, of more jobs than workers, or of high employment, keeping the unemployment pool down to a level of five to eight per cent? It is such minor questions as these that divide the opposing parties on employment policy.

This confidence of all parties that the solution to the problem of unemployment has been found is well grounded in facts and figures. Its application to Australian conditions has been carefully studied. Dr. H. C. Coombs, Director General in the Ministry for Post-War Reconstruction, has published figures showing how the application of the policy would have worked out had it been adopted in 1938–39 (table on page 192).[9] In the first column of this table is shown the actual position in 1938–39 when, because of ten per cent unemployment, £63,000,000 of the national resources were left unused. In the second column is shown a careful calculation of what would have happened if the government had spent another £10,000,000 of loan money

[8] *Ibid.,* 16, 17, 18.
[9] H. C. Coombs, *Problems of a High Employment Economy* (The Hassell Press, Adelaide, 1944). Dr. Coombs undoubtedly had much to do with the framing of the government white paper on full employment.

on public works.   It is estimated that this would have been
sufficient to start a cycle of additional expenditure sufficient
to create full employment, increasing the national income
from £877,000,000 to £940,000,000.

NATIONAL EXPENDITURE AND PRODUCTION, 1938–1939,
IN MILLIONS OF POUNDS

	ACTUAL	THEORETICAL
Private expenditure on consumers' goods and service	638	665
Private expenditure on investment goods	97	115
Net expenditure in Australia from overseas (i.e., export of goods and services minus imports, but excluding government imports)	20	2
Public expenditure on goods and services: From revenue	88	114
From loans	34	44
Unemployed resources	63	—
Maximum production	940	940

The assumption underlying these figures is the perfectly
reasonable one that private consumption and investment
would increase proportionately to the incomes of consumers
and investors if unemployment were reduced to an unavoid-
able minimum, and that there would be roughly proportional
increases in taxation and in expenditure on imports.   The
result issues in one very hopeful conclusion and, on the other
hand, points sharply to what is likely to be Australia's most

serious problem in pursuing a full (or high) employment policy.

The hopeful conclusion is drawn from the fact that so small an increase in government loan expenditure can produce so large an increase in total national income. In this connection Copland shows that Australia has no real reason to fear that the maintenance of a high employment policy will unduly increase the national debt.[10] He estimates national income after the war at about £1,500,000,000, and says that technological advance, capital improvements, and a growing population should increase this easily enough at the rate of two per cent a year. That means a £30,000,000 increase in national income each year. If seven and a half per cent of this increase were allotted to pay interest on the national debt, that would provide £2,250,000. At three per cent interest that sum would pay for new loan expenditure at the rate of £75,000,000 a year. If, as Dr. Coombs estimates, a high employment policy would require new loan money to the amount of £44,000,000 when the national income was £940,000,000, then £75,000,000 would be quite sufficient to cover the increase when the national income was £1,500,000,000. Thus the ghost of the interest burden of the national debt would be successfully laid, and seven and a half per cent of the annual addition to the national income would be sufficient to take care of it.

The more serious problem pointed out by Dr. Coombs's analysis is the effect of a high employment policy on Australia's balance of payments. In 1938–39 there was an adverse balance of payments of £27,000,000; and Dr. Coombs's figures show that with a high employment policy this would have been increased by a further £18,000,000. Australia is hoping that the growth of her secondary industries during

10 Copland, *The Road to High Employment,* 83.

the war will, in the future, greatly ease her problem of over-seas payments by reducing her imports and increasing her exports. But it is easily seen that a country so largely dependent on overseas trade can be seriously embarrassed if the price or quantity of her exports suddenly falls. In the past this has been met to a great extent by allowing a resultant reduction of employment and general prosperity to decrease imports. In the future Australia is determined that this will not be allowed. For this reason Professor Copland, like most other Australian economists, points out that the country must be prepared, if necessary, to adopt exchange controls, restrict the importation of goods that she can best dispense with for the time, and, if need be, lower the exchange value of her currency.

In a paper presented to the Economic Society of Australia and New Zealand in 1945, L. F. Giblin, a member of the group that formulated the Premiers' Plan in 1931, endorsed the now generally recognized principle that the government must take measures to ensure that the demand for labor is maintained at the maximum level.[11] The most interesting feature of this paper, however, is the explicit recognition of one method of achieving this goal which we have not found considered in the other documents discussed. In these documents the problem has been presented as one of increasing government expenditure. Professor Giblin points out that the goal of increased employment can also be attained by maintaining government expenditure at its present level, reducing taxation, and financing the deficit by loan. If the taxation were taken off the lower incomes and goods in common use this would release money which would rapidly be spent on consumers' goods. This method, he points out, is one that can be pursued along with the others. If taxation

[11] L. F. Giblin, "Financing Full Employment" in *Economic Papers, No. 5* (Economic Society of Australia and New Zealand, Sydney, 1945).

on low incomes were already high it would certainly be desirable that it be adopted.

It will thus be seen that the makers of Australian policy share major convictions concerning the means necessary to avoid the recurrence of a condition of general unemployment. It is this condition which has been the chronic malady of the system of free enterprise for the past quarter of a century. It did not seriously affect Australia and the United States until 1929, though it had fastened its grip upon Britain as early as 1921. But under the guidance of Lord Keynes's new economic analysis both the British and the Australians are convinced that they can avert general unemployment in the future. And all parties in both countries are determined to adopt the necessary practical measures. Differences of opinion arise concerning only the minor questions of means of finance and the possibility of full, or merely high, employment. The former are not very important. The latter will be decided by practical experiment, for all parties want as high a degree of employment as is practicable and none want inflation.

The Commonwealth Employment Service.— General unemployment resulting from the tendency to surplus saving in a modern free economy is not, however, the whole of the employment problem. There are fluctuations in particular industries which constantly throw men out of work. Some of these are inevitably seasonal, especially in the primary industries which constitute so large a part of Australian production. In other industries, such as automobile manufacture, there is also a strong tendency to concentrate production in certain months and slacken off at other times. Technological changes also mean that men are put out of work in one place, or in one industry, even though they may create as much or more employment elsewhere. For such reasons as these there will always be a certain amount of unemployment and it is important to reduce it to a minimum. Much study has been given to this problem in Australia. The states have had offices to facilitate exchange of labor for many years. Then in 1945 the Commonwealth Employment Service was established after a study of the experience of the British and American employment services as well as those of the Australian states. This organization is designed to take over the function of manpower control exercised by the government during the war, but without any powers of compulsion.

This service has been placed under a Commonwealth Director of Employment, with a deputy director in each capital city, a network of district employment offices throughout the country, and a series of special offices for particular classes of workers, for example, professional and scientific personnel, engineering and building tradesmen, and disabled persons. Its function is not to direct labor into specific channels, but to coordinate information concerning the labor supply and demand, and to act as a preselection agency for the employer and a counseling service for the employee. In this connection facilities are being established for special retraining of workers to facilitate their transfer from industries where there is an oversupply of labor to those where labor is needed, for vocational guidance, and for moving workers to new districts.

To ensure the immediate notification of vacancies and of the filling of jobs, teletype machines are being installed in the principal district offices and the central clearing house. Employers are asked to give notice of their labor needs in advance and to do the same as jobs approach completion and men are to be laid off. In this way the transfer of men from one job to another can be made with as little loss of time as possible, and men can be offered jobs as near as possible to their homes. No one, of course, can be compelled to take a job, nor can the employer be compelled to take on any man recommended to him. But the preselection and counseling of the Employment Service can, nevertheless, save a considerable percentage of the time lost between jobs.

Probably the largest field for such saving of lost working days is that of the seasonal occupations employing migratory workers. Wartime experience has shown the value of central coordination of the available labor supply for this type of work. Fruit picking, canning, wheat harvesting, shearing, sugar-cane cutting, and other rural industries require large numbers of workers for short periods in particular places. Where there is a large pool of unemployment these can be drawn from the pool. But when that pool is reduced to a minimum by a high employment policy, then the available labor supply must be coordinated and directed or crops as well as working days will frequently be lost. This has been done during the war under compulsory powers. It has been the function of the new Commonwealth Employment Service to do it by voluntary cooperation of employers and employees, trade unions, and employers' organizations, since wartime compulsions were abandoned at the end of 1946. Its problem thus far has been to find workers for jobs rather than jobs for workers. It reported at the end of November, 1948, only 1,000 persons receiving unemployment benefits and 113,000 vacancies waiting to be filled.

- 8 -

To Socialize or Not

THE structure of the social service state is nearing completion in Australia and is already completed in New Zealand. Providing that full, or at least high employment can be maintained, that structure should remain secure. Undoubtedly there will be minor additions and improvements and modifications of the methods of financing it, but its general features can be regarded as having come to stay.

What then is the next stage? Is the attainment of the social service state to be but a prelude to complete socialism, or is it to constitute a framework of social security within which an economy of private enterprise can function successfully? It could equally well be the one or the other. The major political battles of the future in both countries are likely to be fought over this question. Meantime, the existence of the social service state and high employment (providing the latter is maintained) will give stability to the social order, enabling the question of further socialization to be approached experimentally and debated on its merits.

In the practice of public ownership of industry both countries already have a great deal of experience. They have carried this kind of "piecemeal socialism" or "state capitalism" further than any other noncommunist country with the exception, perhaps, of Britain, and they have been practicing it much longer than Britain has. Further, their ventures of this sort have not all been inaugurated by Socialists. Indeed, most of them have been the work of non-Labor governments, both before and after the rise of the Labor Party.

The most notable of all government industries in Australia is the railway system, which has been publicly owned almost from its inception. It was not an inclination to socialism, however, that brought this about, but rather the fact that private enterprise had attempted to meet the need and failed. In 1849 the Colonial Secretary in London, Earl Grey, advised the governor of New South Wales that it would be wise for the colonial government to retain in its own hands the power to construct railways. This, however, did not meet with agreement in the Legislative Council, which passed a resolution that the introduction of railways could best be effected by the energy and enterprise of private individuals.

In accord with this policy a company was incorporated to construct a line from Sydney to Paramatta, the government guaranteeing interest at four per cent on its stock. But the company exhausted its capital before the line was finished and the government had to come to its assistance. Another railway, in the coal mining area of Newcastle, met with similar difficulties and appealed for aid. A commission, appointed to consider the question of railways in the whole country, came to the conclusion that "private companies could not succeed in constructing railways without Government aid on a scale which ought not to be conceded, and, therefore, these works should be taken up by the Government itself."

In Victoria private enterprise was a little more successful, several short lines around Melbourne being constructed and run at a profit. But the task of building and maintaining lines to serve points at a distance from the capital proved to be beyond the capacity of private enterprise. The government was forced to step in and take over these ventures and, having done so, it pushed railway construction where it was required to serve the needs of the community. Not having to pay dividends to stockholders, it charged rates not at a figure which would show a profit, but at prices considered fair for the service rendered. These were definitely lower than those of the private companies, and the public thereafter showed no disposition to allow private capital again to enter the field. To coordinate the traffic of the state, the private companies were, before long, incorporated into the state system.

Australia was thus launched upon its program of developmental works undertaken by the states not for profit, but as public services. The telegraph and telephone systems, together with the post office, were public services from their inception, as were ports and harbors. Water supply became a function of either state or municipal government. Thus it became an accepted principle that the state should undertake works that were needed for development, even at the risk of some initial or permanent losses, instead of waiting until the demand for such services became great enough to attract private capital to supply them. Losses taken on some ventures could be largely recouped by profits made on others. And if there was a net loss over all, it was accounted a small price for the community as a whole to pay for the resulting improvement in land values and the capacity of the country to sustain an increased population.

All this, however, was state capitalism, not socialism. The aim was not to curtail private enterprise but to increase its opportunities and profits. The state provided facilities for further investment of capital in land, mines, industry, and commerce by undertaking the industrial projects needed for developing the country, which private enterprise was unable or unwilling to afford, or which it could not be trusted to provide at reasonable cost.

These examples of useful state activity in the economic sphere were not lost, however, upon those individuals who were inclined to believe in the socialist principle of replacing private enterprise with a system of state or communal activity. It is not surprising, therefore, that the labor movement, from very early days, looked forward hopefully to the extension of state functions into a complete system of socialism.

The man who did most to convert Australian labor to socialism was William Lane, editor of the *Queensland Worker* in the stormy nineties, a position for which he had sacrificed a well-paid journalistic career. Lane was not a Communist but a Socialist of the type of Robert Owen. As a lecturer and writer he did more than any other man to shape the thought of the trade unions and to inspire them with loyalty and idealism. After the disastrous defeats of the great strikes, however, he despaired of any further success in introducing socialism into Australia and led a band of enthusiastic disciples to found a socialist colony called New Australia in Paraguay. When this failed, as all such colonies have failed, Lane became disillusioned and abandoned socialism. But in spite of this setback and the loss of its most dynamic leader, the socialist ideology continued to make converts and, in 1921, was adopted in principle as the ultimate objective of the Labor Party.

This objective is stated as "the socialization of industry, production, distribution and exchange," to be achieved by "constitutional" means. It replaced a milder statement, formulated in 1905: "The securing of the full results of their industry to all producers by the collective ownership of monopolies, and the extension of the industrial and economic functions of the State and municipality." This had satisfied the Fabians and would probably have satisfied William Lane in his socialist days, but it did not satisfy the small but energetic group who had framed their ideas under the influence of Karl Marx. There was at the time no Communist Party in Australia, but the demand for the new objective came from the radical group influenced by communism. It was immediately christened "the Red objective" by Labor's opponents and served as an excellent weapon in their hands.

The socialist objective, however, is regarded by the Party rather as a statement of its ultimate goal than as its immediate program. It does not fight elections on a socialist platform, but puts forth a "fighting platform" defining the measures which it plans to put into operation in the parliamentary term for which it seeks election. And there has been little tendency to seek support for installments of socialism. In part this has been due to constitutional difficulties. The Commonwealth government does not have the power to socialize industry without first securing an amendment to the constitution. And the hands of state labor governments are largely tied by their Legislative Councils. But it is nevertheless true that they could have moved faster in the direction of socialism than they have.

The reason for this hesitation is, in the first place, that plans for socializing industries do not find much favor with the electors. Moreover, social security and the improvement of the conditions of labor have been prior goals. But with the completion of the structure of the social service state new objectives must come to the fore.   It is inevitable that the issue of socialization will be more and more strongly debated, but it does not follow that Labor will find it easy to make progress toward a socialistic goal.   In spite of the fact that Australia has had considerable experience in public owner-ship of industry, popular ideas on the question are very con-fused.   It is important, therefore, that we should examine the record.

State developmental agencies.— On the question of the government developmental agencies (such as railways and electric supply) there are, broadly, three distinct schools of thought.   There is a right wing minority which believes that they have, on the whole, been failures, that it would have been better to wait for private enterprise to do these things, and that it would be wiser, even now, to dispose of most of them to private companies.   On the other hand, there is a left wing minority which claims that they have proved the ability of public business undertakings to supply economic needs more efficiently and fairly than private enter-prises run for profit; and that therefore they justify a social-istic expansion of government undertakings.   Between these two views is the opinion, held by a large majority, that the general principle of public ownership of utilities has been vindicated; that most of the government's ventures in devel-opmental agencies have justified themselves and should be retained, though some have been ill-conceived and failed; but that private enterprise shows more initiative, efficiency, and consideration for the customer, and that it should be al-lowed to operate wherever competition provides protection against exploitation and where it does not stand in the way of larger developmental plans that can be carried out only by the government.

Opinion on questions of this kind is, of course, influ-enced by political ideology and subtle factors of personal interest.   It therefore does not follow that the majority is right.   That it is not well informed must be admitted.   The press, being capitalistically controlled, tends to exaggerate the faults and failures of public industrial undertakings and creates a misinformed bias against them.   The man in the street forms a rather hazy judgment based on his experience with the service he receives and what he reads in the newspapers.   It is well to recognize, therefore, that the truth about government enterprise in Australia cannot be determined by a Gallup poll or a show of hands.   We must look at the facts presented by those who have carefully examined the record.

Victoria's early experience with state-controlled railways, says F. W. Eggleston,[1] resulted in "chaos, maladministration and patronage," and it was seen that "if the system of State railways was to be continued the railways must be taken out of politics and entrusted to independent commissions."   This led to the development of the statutory corporation as the instrument of state action.   A statutory corporation is an incorporated body with defined powers and functions, the management and finance of which can be entirely freed from all possibilities of political interference. Concerning the record of such corporations in the state of Victoria, Eggleston says that "where complete autonomy has been given, the result has nearly always been good; but Parliament has been jealous of parting with control, some power

[1] F. W. Eggleston, *State Socialism in Victoria* (P. S. King, London, 1932).   This is the most informative study of the question yet published. Eggleston, undoubtedly one of the ablest men in Australian politics, served as Attorney General and Minister of Railways and of Water Supply in the Victorian government between 1924 and 1927.   Though a conservative, he entered upon these tasks as a believer in government activity in developmental projects and public utilities as an aid to private business. His experience as an administrator of these projects, however, caused him to modify his opinions and advocate a considerable limitation of such state activity.

over policy has in most cases been retained, and unsoundness is the result." [2]

The faults and failures of state enterprises lie, he emphatically declares, with the general public, who use their influence over their political representatives to interfere with the policy and management of these concerns in order to gratify various sectional interests. He completely repudiates the common contention that the management, left to itself to perform a public service without the stimulus of a profit motive, will lack interest, vigor, efficiency, or honesty. "The defects usually ascribed to State action—incompetence, patronage, and corruption in internal management—hardly apply to Victoria at all. . . . The great Victorian public services that we have described embody much honest political thought from sincere statesmen, and attract disinterested devotion from capable managers and staffs." [3] This is the result of the adoption of the statutory corporation as the instrument of state action and of the selection by the state of competent men to place at the head of its industrial undertakings. Trouble has come only through those powers which the state has reserved for its own jurisdiction, either through a reluctance of parliament to abandon control over policy or because the dependence of the statutory corporation on government finance has made it essential for the state to reserve some such control.

This endorsement of the efficient management of government agencies under statutory corporations in Australia is generally supported by competent students of the problem. Newspaper criticism of these concerns is constant and frequently grossly unfair. It has created a common impression that public servants tend to be idle, entangled in red tape,

[2] *Ibid.*, 42, 47.
[3] *Ibid.*, 283, 284.

and lacking in initiative. But this opinion is not endorsed by able men with adequate knowledge of the working of government departments and statutory corporations. Thus, no less an authority than D. B. Copland says: "Examples [of the statutory corporation] such as the British Broadcasting Commission, the London Passenger Transport Board, the Tennessee Valley Authority, the State Electricity Commission of Victoria indicate the possibility of reconciling independence of management, efficiency and financial success with political expediency. . . . The statutory corporation has practically all the advantages of the joint stock company in the public utility field plus the added advantage that its very structure, and the source from which it derives its authority, guarantee that it is working in the public interest." [4]

Eggleston reviews the working of Victorian government enterprises and concludes that their success has been directly proportional to the degree of their independence of political interference. And the failures due to political interference he attributes not to the corruption or incompetence of politicians, but to their weakness in the face of determined pressure groups urging that government enterprises be made to serve special interests, or to the fact that a laudable desire to develop the country and add to its population has led to the undertaking of ventures which could not possibly be financially successful.

The worst of the failures discussed by Eggleston is that of the Closer Settlement Board, designed to assist small farmers to establish themselves on the land. After the first World War this board entered on elaborate schemes for the settlement of returned soldiers, immigrants, and others. Its function was to purchase large estates or Crown lands, divide

---

[4] D. B. Copland, *The Road to High Employment* (Harvard University Press, Cambridge, Massachusetts, 1945), 5.

them into suitable farms, provide the necessary amenities, and finance settlers in building homes, purchasing stock and machinery, and in living until their crops matured. Private finance companies had previously done this same thing but on a smaller scale and with carefully selected farmers. The Closer Settlement Board set out to act on a grand scale for people with very small means and often without much farming experience. As a result the majority of the settlers soon found themselves in financial difficulties. They used their political influence (and that of the returned soldiers was especially great) to secure further help. The board, not being a profit-making institution, received its funds from the government, which therefore exercised some control over its policy, and concessions were made to the settlers which could not be economically justified.

The chief trouble, however, was that the scheme was attempting the impossible. Land values in Victoria were inflated; hence settlers were placed on blocks that were too small, because to give them farms of really economic size would have saddled them with an impossible debt. The conditions were such that only thoroughly experienced men of exceptional ability as farmers could succeed. Many of them did succeed and became possessed of independent farms, free of mortgage. But the failures were numerous. Finally came the disastrous fall in prices which was a prelude to the great depression; and by 1931 nearly half the settlers had been forced off their land by accumulated debt, and about one third of the capital invested by the government was lost.

The second most serious financial loss was that incurred in irrigation projects undertaken by the State Rivers and Water Supply Commission. The need of irrigation in a dry country like Australia is obvious. Private capital has undertaken it on a small scale, but not with financial success to the entrepreneurs. Only the government could do it on the scale needed. Eggleston recognizes that this is the case and gives credit to the commission for carrying out its tasks with great ability and imagination. Further, the government engineers who were asked to report on the proposals advised against expenditure on irrigation because, they said, it could not be made to pay in the conditions prevailing in Victoria, there being no great rivers easily dammed and no great local market for the products of irrigated farms.

Enthusiasm for developing the country and making the most of Australia's scanty water supply, however, over-rode financial caution. The commission was financed and instructed to carry out a large scale plan. It has done this with skill and economy; but the cost has been far too great for the interest bill and working expenses to be paid by charges on the water supplied to farms.

The Victorian railways, says Eggleston, are soundly and efficiently run. This includes the construction work-shops, the coal mines, refreshment concessions, and other services run as subsidiary to them. The commissioners are not independent, however. Parliament decides, on the recom-mendation of its own committees of inquiry, what new lines shall be built. The commissioners are bound to obey any order in writing from the Cabinet, but the Treasury under-takes to repay them any cost thus incurred. The commis-sioners must also receive the consent of the Cabinet for any changes in fares and freights or in salaries over five hundred pounds a year. Thus there is room for a good deal of political interference. This has manifested itself chiefly in decisions to build railways for developmental purposes which do not pay interest and working expenses. But poli-tics sometimes makes its way into smaller matters as well; and Eggleston gives a typical example of one of these.

The commissioners wished to purchase and use a num-ber of large freight cars, these being much more economical than small ones, but not so convenient to shippers of goods in small quantities. Opposition members suggested that it was intended to make the large cars the universal standard equipment and roused sufficient protest to defeat the proposal. On another occasion a decision to make a general increase in fares and freights to meet an all around rise in costs of operation resulted in the defeat of the government at an election.

All the state railways in Australia have occasionally suffered financially from this sort of political interference. But it is also true that both the people and politicians are learning the need of avoiding such interference. However, the railways are not regarded as a business the chief function of which is to earn profits, but as a government agency designed to render a public service at the least possible cost. There is not the slightest possibility of the adoption by any considerable body of public opinion in Australia of the policy advocated by Eggleston that the railways be sold or leased to a private company. No private company would provide the service that the state railways do on lines that serve the needs of thinly populated parts of the country. Yet the nation would be the loser if much of this service were withdrawn. From the standpoint of the nation small freight cars which save the farmers' time and produce may be more economical than large ones which save expenses for a railway company.

In general, the Australian railway systems pay working expenses and part of the interest on their capital cost. The New South Wales railways, for example, in the period 1935 to 1940, earned an average of 3.6 per cent on their capital investment in spite of nonpaying lines and concessions and rebates to various primary and secondary industries assisted for national reasons. In the years since 1940 profits have been still greater. In the years from 1938 to 1943 the Victorian railways showed a net profit after paying all expenses, including interest and a sinking fund. These, of course, were years of high employment. In depression years all the states have had to accept heavy losses, the paying lines being unable to balance the deficits incurred on those laid down for developmental or political purposes.

One misfortune of the Australian railway system is the lack of a uniform gauge. Owing to vacillating counsels, the railways of New South Wales were started on the standard gauge, those of Victoria and South Australia on a broader gauge. Later, Queensland and Western Australia, having vast areas with a scattered population, adopted a narrow gauge for reasons of economy. Nearly all interstate commerce (even between Victoria and South Australia, where there is no difference in the gauge) goes by sea, since the large cities are all on the coast. The small saving to be made by the adoption of a uniform gauge would therefore not pay the interest on the cost. Queensland and Western Australia seem to be determined to retain their narrow gauge railways indefinitely. The three central states, however, are now planning, with the help of the Commonwealth government, to introduce uniformity in the size of the gauge at a cost of fifty million pounds. To secure internal rail communication between the principal industrial areas for purposes of military strategy is one important reason for this plan. But the project will put the railway system as a whole still further in the red, and the interest bill will have to be met almost entirely by taxation.

As interest rates fall the problem of debts on the railways, however, will become less serious. All the state railway systems will be enabled to approach nearer to competely paying their own way. Apart from the burden of the non-paying lines serving the needs of thinly populated pastoral and agricultural areas, they could completely pay their own way. But most of these lines are amply justified on national grounds as making possible the utilization of land that would otherwise be idle, which adds much more to the national income than is lost in interest and working expenses. Further, even though, through their own folly, the people find their railways somewhat more costly than they need be because they have demanded more service than it was wise to ask, they at least have the satisfaction of knowing that they are receiving that service at cost. They would be well advised, however, to give the railway commissioners complete freedom in control of operations and determination of freights and fares, allowing them special subsidies, such as are often paid to private companies, for nonpaying services.

Concerning the other government enterprises in Victoria, Eggleston has much less criticism. To some of them, notably the Savings Bank, the Harbour Trust, and the Melbourne and Metropolitan Board of Works (which includes the city water supply), he gives unstinted praise, pointing out that they are independent of political influence. He recognizes that the Tramways Trust is efficiently run, but objects to the provision which enables the government to fix the fares.

The main conclusion to be drawn from his analysis as a whole is perfectly clear and well sustained by his argument. A state enterprise run by a statutory corporation which is free from political interference can carry out industrial and commercial projects of all kinds with efficiency and initiative. Governments can (and those studied generally do) select for their management able administrators. But the *sine qua non* of financial success in such enterprises is their freedom from political interference. The pressure groups operative in a democratic system are so strong that they divert the organization to uneconomic service of special interests if they are allowed to influence its operation; but well-selected public servants, left to themselves, take pride in directing a public agency for the common good.

Electric power.— The most remarkable and the largest of all government enterprises in Australia is the State Electricity Commission of Victoria. Prior to its establishment there were in the state (as in the rest of Australia) a large number of independent power plants, most of them municipally owned. These depended almost entirely on the supply of black coal from New South Wales—a supply constantly interrupted by industrial troubles. The state was known, however, to possess huge deposits of brown coal (lignite) which had scarcely been touched. This was investigated and analyzed and found to be suitable for the generation of electricity if special methods such as were used for similar fuel in Germany were adopted. To do this, however, required considerable command of capital and technical knowledge. No private company was willing to undertake the task, for success seemed speculative. Further, there was a general feeling that the possibilities were such that their advantages should be retained for the community by state operation.

The state's need of some new source of electric power was so great that there was no serious opposition to the idea. Therefore legislation was passed in 1918 by a non-Labor government to set up a statutory corporation to undertake the generation and distribution of electric power throughout the state, and especially for the purpose of utilizing the supplies of brown coal. After the project was well under way, however, it was found that a serious mistake had been made in the analysis of the coal upon which operations were based. Most of the coal for the analysis had been taken from a smaller deposit which had been worked for some time by a private company. This coal, it was discovered, had a much lower moisture content that that of the larger deposit where the commission's works were established. Some expense and much research work were required to design new furnaces to burn coal with a higher moisture content. The difficulties were overcome, but the result was that the cost of power per unit was not as low as the original estimates had indicated.

Eggleston praises the tenacity, the will, and the unrelaxed research work by which the commission overcame all difficulties, pioneering in a new field of technology and planning an industrial undertaking on a larger scale than anything else in the country. It has utilized water power as well as coal, and by means of a series of strategically located generating plants, the commission is able to supply electricity to almost the entire state. Largely as a result of this assured and cheaper supply of power, the manufacturing industry has grown enormously in Victoria. At the time Eggleston wrote (1932) the commission was still laboring under the burden of debts accumulated during its developmental and experimental years and its profits were small. He recommended that it be leased to some private company for operation, though no private company, he thought, would be willing to take it over with its accumulated indebtedness. It had commenced to supply power in 1924 and showed its first profit in 1928. In the depression years, 1930–31, however, it again showed a loss, which may be the reason for his pessimistic judgment. In the next year, however, it again showed a profit and by 1943 it had wiped out its past losses and accumulated reserves of ten million pounds. Its capitalization was then twenty-eight million pounds and its profits for the year £844,206. Meantime it has kept the cost of electric current down to a minimum.

The success of this undertaking is of special significance because it was pioneering in a new field. The only people who had had any experience in the use of lignite at that time were Germans, and in those years just after the first World War public opinion would not permit the importation of German experts for any purposes whatever. The commission therefore had to rely on Australian engineers and scientists to solve its problems by their own investigations. The whole venture was highly speculative. If the brown coal could be efficiently used it would prove a great national asset. But the cost of solving the problems concerned with its use was greater than any private company at the time was willing to risk. Defenders of private enterprise, in Australia as elsewhere, usually lay stress on its value as providing an initiative, a willingness to take risks with its capital in order to win profitable prizes. But the State Electricity Commission of Victoria has shown that this virtue is not peculiar to private enterprise. It has proved that a statutory corporation can be just as energetic and venturesome in tackling new and difficult problems, and just as efficient in routine operations, as any organization of private capital.

At the end of 1945 there were in Australia only two electrical companies of any importance still in the hands of private enterprise. And early in 1946 one of these, the Adelaide Electric Supply Company, was taken over by the government. This was done by a non-Labor government whose declared policy is the maintenance of private enterprise. Its action is therefore significant of the convincing experience throughout the country of the value and success of public ownership of such utilities. The Adelaide Electric Supply Company had a good record of efficient service, its rates were recognized as reasonable, and its profits were limited to seven per cent on ordinary shares; but a question as to the method by which it should be allowed to raise new capital for expansion of its services led to the appointment of a Royal Commission to inquire into its operation.

For some time now in Australia all such commissions have recommended public ownership; and this was no exception. Even the company's own representative on the commission gave his vote in favor of a recommendation to the government to take over. The commission found that the privately owned company, though quite efficient, was no more efficient than publicly owned corporations elsewhere in Australia and that government ownership, if the company were acquired at the existing market price of its shares, would save the community two million pounds a year in interest and dividends, the government being able to borrow at much lower rates than even the safest of public utilities. A further reason for the recommendation was that no private company could be expected to develop its services except in accord with its own interests, but that the state required a coordinated supply of power which would utilize the profits on densely populated areas in a program of decentralization.

In the face of this recommendation the government felt it necessary to comply. There was opposition from the conservative members of its own party which nearly succeeded in blocking the measure in the Legislative Council— the upper house, still elected on a householder and property franchise. But the act for acquisition went through, the government carefully explaining that its action in socializing the electric supply of the state was not to be taken as indicating any renunciation of its faith in the validity of private enterprise in all ordinary, competitive business and industrial concerns.

State competitive enterprise.— It may be taken as an established policy that Australia is committed, as a whole, to the principle of public ownership of utilities. And the process of taking over these concerns from private enterprise is nearly complete. But this is merely a measure of state capitalism, not socialism. Though supported by Socialists, the deciding motive is not the creation of an installment of socialism but the securing of an improved basis for a general economy of private enterprise. Public opinion does not at present, and never has, supported socialism on general principle. This was shown, for example, by a Gallup poll in 1946 which returned a definite negative to a question concerning proposals to nationalize the air lines.

Nevertheless, Labor governments have, in the past, made a number of ventures into fields of competition with private enterprise with the double purpose of forcing prices down by creating a yardstick by which to measure the efficiency and cost of private business and of establishing an educational example of socialism in operation. The record of these ventures is somewhat mixed. Many of them were very successful. Others were disastrous failures. Even the successful ones, however, were not allowed to continue for long after the Labor governments which established them passed from office. They were sold out by the political supporters of private enterprise on grounds of general policy, that is, that the government should not enter into business competition with private persons. The two most important series of undertakings of this character, however, were established under public authorities comparatively free from political influence. One is that of the early Labor governments of New South Wales before the split over conscription. [5] The other is due to the governments of Fisher and Hughes during the first World War.

One of the undertakings in New South Wales was a state brickworks, which had a remarkably profitable career from 1910 to 1936. It was established to break the price control of a very close combine in the industry. A Royal Commission in 1919 reported that its loan capital of £87,000 had been reduced by £20,000 from profits and that it had accumulated a further £20,000 in reserve. In 1924, its

[5] For an account of these undertakings see H. V. Evatt, *Australian Labour Leader* (Angus and Robertson, Sydney, 1942), chapters 42 and 68.

record year, the auditor-general reported a profit of £27,511, and pointed out that it had achieved this while selling bricks at 53 shillings a thousand while the combine charged 73 shillings. Its prices had, in fourteen years, saved the government £135,000 and the general public another £100,000. A stone quarry established a little later than the brickworks had a similar success. Started with a capital investment of £160,000, in 1924 it showed accumulated profits of £72,000 and a similar amount in reserves against depreciation. A third undertaking was the acquiring of the Monier Pipe and Reinforced Concrete Works in 1914. The auditor-general's report in 1924 showed that this concern, on a capital of £17,000 furnished by the Treasury, had in ten years paid all trading liabilities and interest and set aside profits and reserves totaling £103,000.

During the depression years these industries suffered along with those of private enterprise, particularly as they were concerned with the hardest hit of all industries—building and construction. The anti-Labor government which defeated William Lang announced its intention in 1933 of selling all three concerns. The leading Sydney newspaper pointed out that in their history to date they had together earned profits of £932,000 in addition to supplying materials below the costs of private enterprises. Of these profits £227,000 had been shared with the workmen and £178,000 had gone into reserves, leaving £300,000 net, partly invested in the works. The sale was postponed for a time because of such powerful opposition even from conservative quarters. But it was eventually carried through, the three works being sold for £370,989. In the words of a Royal Commission which later investigated the sale, the reason was simply that "as a matter of policy the government was determined to 'get out of business' and not to continue to compete with private enterprise."

Some of the state undertakings of this period, however, were not so successful. A state sawmill established in 1919 made a profit of nine thousand pounds in its first two years, but thereafter showed losses, the main reason being the cancellation of a large contract by the Commonwealth government which left the mill with huge stocks of timber to dispose of on a falling market. A little later five thousand pounds was needed to extend the railway by which timber was hauled and the non-Labor government refused to grant this additional capital and sold the mill. The auditor-general subsequently reported that had the railway extension been made no loss would have occurred. Evidently a government interested in the success of the undertaking could have made it profitable, but it was already becoming the policy of anti-Labor parties to liquidate Labor's socialistic experiments as unjustifiable entrenchments on the proper sphere of private enterprise.

Another unsuccessful enterprise was that of the New South Wales state trawlers. Australia had never developed deep-sea fisheries and their possibility had never been thoroughly explored. A Royal Commission in 1912 recommended, on the basis of some experimental evidence collected, that commercial trawling be initiated either by the government itself or by a private company. Sydney's fish supply was, and is, poor and expensive; so the government accepted the responsibility. The enterprise, however, was placed under the management of a scientist who was more interested (perhaps wisely) in using the trawlers for further, more thorough exploratory work than in an immediate supply of cheap fish and a balanced budget. Further, much higher prices could have been charged and still have given Sydney a reasonably priced fish supply. After four years of such experience a non-Labor government extended the enterprise by adding considerably to the trawling fleet at a time (1919)

when the cost of shipbuilding was at its peak.   The business,
however, never paid for itself and a few years later, when
shipping was at a low ebb, the trawlers were sold at a great
loss.   Assets costing £200,000 were disposed of for £50,000.

Probably the most spectacular failure in the history of
Australian state enterprise, however, is that of the Queensland butcher shops and cattle stations.   They succeeded in
reducing the cost of meat to the Brisbane customer to little
more than half its previous price, serving at their peak twenty-
five thousand families.   For the first eleven months they
showed a profit.   The enterprise was killed, however, by
cattle rustling on the ranches and inefficiency in the management of the shops.   The cattle stations lost £1,375,000 in
eight years.   During the same period six other Queensland
government enterprises showed a surplus of £75,000. [6]   All
were sold by a non-Labor government which came into
office in 1929.

The proportion of financial success and failure in the
government enterprises of New South Wales and Queensland is probably very similar to that of private enterprise.
But it must always be remembered that the purpose of these
industries was not merely to make profits but to render a
public service, and this they certainly did.   The fault was not
in their organization.   Their managers were reasonably free
from political interference.   Professor Bland, one of Australia's more conservative economists, has expressed the
opinion that the provisions of the New South Wales Special
Deposits (Industrial Undertakings) Act under which they
were constituted are "adequate."   And the Queensland act
was similar.   He agreed with the report of the Royal Commission of 1918 that "the success or failure of each enterprise depended primarily upon the management and then

[6] B. G. Fitzpatrick, *The Australian People* (Melbourne University
Press, 1947).

upon the nature of the operations undertaken." Concerning those still in operation in 1929, he said that they "have gone on from strength to strength, and even the doctrinaire individualist would be perplexed to find adequate reasons for their abandonment." [7] The only conclusion that the evidence seems to support, therefore, is that the state can run business undertakings with neither more nor less efficiency and initiative, on the whole, than private capital. The question as to which is the better system must therefore be decided on other grounds, such as those concerning security, equity, and freedom within the social order.

Commonwealth enterprises.— The Commonwealth, too, has had its ventures in state trading. The first of these were the Commonwealth Woollen Mills and Clothing Factory established in 1912 by the Fisher Labor Government to supply cloth and uniforms for the Australian Militia, postal employees, and others. The clothing factory gave better conditions to its employees than did private enterprise, turned out work of high quality at less than prices contracted for privately, and showed a profit. Nevertheless, the Liberal-Conservative Fusion Government, which held office for fifteen months after June, 1913, took government work from the factory and gave it to private contractors. The return of the Fisher Government and the outbreak of war restored the fortunes of the factory. Work on construction of the mills was also held up for six months by the Fusion Government so that they were not ready for operations when the war started. They commenced work, however, in 1915.

Both the mills and the factory operated very profitably and with great savings to the government during the war years. After the war, when returned soldiers wanted civilian clothing and found themselves being charged exorbitant prices, they appealed to the government to allow the Common-

---

[7] F. A. Bland, "The Administration of Government Enterprises" in the *Economic Record*, Melbourne, May, 1929.

wealth mills to supply them, through their own organization, with suit lengths. This was done and, according to figures later quoted in parliament, soldiers were able to obtain for £1/11/6 suit lengths for which the retail price was £7/7. At the same time the mills showed a handsome profit. On a government investment of £295,000 they made a profit in five years, after allowing for interest, depreciation, and sinking fund, of £142,691.[8]

The government, however, now in the hands of a non-Labor administration of which, in December, 1921, S. M. Bruce, a former dry goods merchant, became treasurer would not allow the mills to compete with private enterprise by selling to the public.[9] They had a capacity, developed through the war, of 600,000 yards a year, but the government needed only 150,000. It was therefore decided to sell them. In 1922 when Bruce became prime minister, the mills, on which an independent appraiser had placed a valuation of £ 267,159 for plant, building, and lands, were sold for £155,000. [10]

A much larger venture into competitive enterprise was that of the Commonwealth shipping fleet. This had its origin in a fleet of fifteen cargo ships purchased in 1916 by Labor Prime Minister W. M. Hughes. To these were added twenty-one vessels taken from Germany during the war. This fleet was, of course, extremely profitable during the war years in spite of the lower freights charged and some losses through enemy action. After the war, between 1919 and 1922, twenty-one other vessels were added, including five fast passenger ships of 13,851 tons called the Bay liners.

Under Australian Arbitration Court awards all these ships gave their seamen much better conditions than those prevailing on British, European, and Japanese ships. This

---

[8] Hansard, 100 : 2287, 2301.

[9] A later decision of the High Court shows that had they done so, it would have been declared contrary to the constitution.

[10] D. J. Amos, *The Story of the Commonwealth Woollen Mills* (E. J. McAllister and Company, Adelaide, 1934).

constituted a financial handicap similar to that which has always made it impossible for America to develop her own merchant marine for overseas trade without subsidies from the government. Further, from 1921 onwards, British shipping companies began to face the difficulties of the post-war slump and large numbers of ships were laid up. Also the great British shipping combine, or Conference, under Lord Inchcape, made a strong attempt to drive the Australian ships out of business. It established a "deferred rebate" system under which shippers received rebates on freights if they did not ship goods on vessels not controlled by the Conference. The Australian Seaman's Union also displayed a disastrous lack of foresight in creating a good deal of industrial trouble for the line in spite of the fact that their conditions were so much better than on competing overseas vessels. Under these circumstances it is not surprising that the Commonwealth Line found difficulty in competing at a profit.

In 1921 Lord Inchcape offered either to purchase the Commonwealth Line or sell the ships of the Conference in the Australian trade to the government. The Commonwealth Line was keeping down freights and saving large sums for primary producers, but there were too many ships in competition for the available trade and both it and the Conference were in difficulties. Lord Inchcape's offer was refused. But when Bruce replaced Hughes as prime minister at the end of 1921, the line lost its only staunch supporter in the government.

In 1923 Prime Minister Bruce presented a statement to parliament showing that, if the value of the ships were written down to what he judged them to be worth in the existing depressed conditions of world shipping, the line showed a loss of £2,645,761. The line was then reconstituted under a very capable board of three gentlemen with very high salaries, increasing the managerial expenses threefold. It was charged with five per cent interest on the new low valuation of the ships. It was also compelled to pay taxes, although the Australian government was at the time paying subsidies to its competitors. On these terms the line was required to pay expenses or meet them by sale of its ships. In these circumstances the vessels gradually had to be sold for what they would bring at a time when unused shipping was laid up in anchorages all over the world. By 1927 nothing was left but the five Bay liners and two others. It was not deemed politic to sell these without a preliminary investigation, so a committee from both sides of parliament was called on for a report. It stated that the line had brought about reductions of freights and prevented increases and recommended that it be retained. A second report, after hearing further evidence in camera, changed this recommendation and the fleet was sold. The buyer was Lord Kylsant, a member of the Conference; but after paying the first installment of £580,000 he went bankrupt, leaving Australia to whistle for the remainder of the bargain price of £1,900,000. Private shipping in those days was experiencing similar difficulties to that of the government. Too many ships were competing for the available trade of the world.

The losses of the Commonwealth fleet and other losses in government enterprise have received great publicity in the Australian press. Little is said of those that have been profitable. This kind of propaganda has succeeded in creating a very general impression that the government loses money on almost everything it touches. Few people are aware of the extent to which the losses have been due to unsympathetic policies of politicians not in favor of the government's entering into competition with private enterprise. The result is that proposals for nationalization of anything other than utilities of the kind which are already almost everywhere government-owned are not popular.   In the coming battle over the question of further socialization both sides are likely to draw a great deal of ammunition from the history of past experience.[11]   But in the utilization of that experience for purposes of propaganda the proponents of private enterprise are now a long way ahead.

In a somewhat different category from other government enterprises is the Commonwealth Bank.   When first established it was given all the functions of other banks and Labor supporters intended that it should enter into competition with other banks and bring about their gradual extinction. The manager, however, moved cautiously.   He established a savings bank (using the facilities of the post office) which has continued to function successfully.   He accepted, but did not pursue, ordinary business, keeping interest on fixed deposits at one-half per cent below other banks.   The bank's chief customers were the government and the trade unions. During World War I it saved the government £3,261,000 on the costs of floating loans in London.   At the end of the war it had accumulated about £1,847,000 in profits.   After the war the popularity of the bank greatly increased and it began to expand its general business.

In 1924 the Bruce and Page Government, in pursuance of the policy of not allowing government concerns to interfere with private enterprise, changed the constitution of the bank, placing it under a Board of Governors consisting of the secretary of the Treasury and six other persons who, it was specifically required, "are or have been actually engaged in agriculture, commerce and industry."   This removed the bank from government control and placed it in the hands of

[11] In February, 1949, legislation was introduced to aid shipbuilding and to enable the government to operate a fleet of steamers in overseas and interstate trade.   The line is expected to comprise about forty vessels and is designed to relieve the existing shortage of shipping.

people who would confine its functions to those of a central bank, not allowing it to compete for ordinary banking business. Indeed, as was found during the depression, in time of crisis it placed the government in the hands of the bank rather than the bank's being in the hands of the government.

Bearing this experience in mind, the Chifley Labor Government, in 1945, introduced new legislation having three main purposes: 1) to ensure that the financial policy of the bank should be in harmony with the main decisions of government policy; 2) to strengthen the central banking functions of the bank; 3) to expand the bank's general banking business by active competition with the trading banks. This last function, however, is placed in a special department (under the general management of the governor of the bank), the accounts of which are kept separate from those of the central bank. This trading department continues the savings bank, rural credits, and mortgage bank activities previously established and adds to them the provision of financial assistance for the development of small industries and housing loans on *crédit foncier* terms.

The management of the bank is now placed in the hands of a governor assisted by an advisory council which is acknowledged as being representative of some of the best financial brains in the country. To ensure that the government shall have ultimate control of policy, however, there is a special provision that the governor shall inform the treasurer from time to time of the monetary and banking policy and, in the event of any difference of opinion which it is found impossible to overcome by discussion, the treasurer may inform the bank that the government is prepared to accept responsibility in the matter and the bank is then required to follow the government's policy. This does not mean that the bank is now likely to be subject to political interference in minor matters, but it does mean that, in major problems of financial policy such as those faced during the depression, the view of the government will prevail.

Past experience had shown that the trading powers of the bank do not tend, as some of its early proponents hoped, to the gradual extinction of private banking, for private business, on principle, favors private institutions. But it is specifically provided in the new act that the general banking division "shall not refuse to conduct banking business for any person, by reason only of the fact that to conduct that business would have the effect of taking business from another bank." The principal effect of the provision, which soon began to manifest itself, was to give support to small industrial undertakings which found themselves strangled by the rather conservative and cautious policy of the ordinary trading banks. This is likely to prove of importance in the period of rapid development of secondary industry upon which Australia is now entering. The cautious policy of the private banks might well weight the scales in this development altogether too much in favor of large established companies.

The most important implications of the bank act of 1945, however, lie elsewhere. In the first place it gives the government the financial power to pursue a policy of full employment if it so desires, even though the governor and advisory council of the bank should wish to limit its financial resources to such as would suffice for a policy of high (or not so high) employment. In the second place, if ever the Commonwealth is given power to nationalize industries and engage in manufacturing and commerce, then its power over the bank will greatly simplify the problem of financing such enterprises.

The powers of the Commonwealth in these matters have, however, been strictly confined by decisions of the High

Court. Not only is it restricted to trade and commerce with other countries and between the states, but a decision of 1926 asserts that the Commonwealth's power to regulate interstate trade does not extend to the establishment of manufacturing or engineering businesses for general commercial purposes. And when the Commonwealth, in 1945, wished to nationalize interstate airways the Court decided that to create such a monopoly was prohibited by the section of the constitution providing that trade and commerce between the states shall be "absolutely free." The Commonwealth government, has, despite this ruling, established air lines of its own under a statutory corporation, but these have to be run in competition with private lines as long as the latter are determined to remain in operation.

In 1947 came a test case for the present prospects of further socialism in Australia. The Chifley Government, having been re-elected for the second time in September, 1946, and thus establishing a record for a national Labor government, decided to press the policy of socialization in the one sphere that still seemed constitutionally open. A bill was introduced to nationalize the whole of the banking system of Australia. The opposition challenged the government to test public opinion on the issue by submitting it to a referendum, but this was refused. Anti-Labor forces in control of the upper house in the state of Victoria therefore decided on extraordinary action to force a test vote. They rejected a supply bill of the state Labor government, thereby forcing a state election. The election was in reality a test vote on the question of nationalization of banking, and Labor was soundly defeated, losing half its seats. It was therefore made evident that the federal Labor government was pressing its program of socialization beyond the will of the people. The legislation was, nevertheless, pushed through by the strong Labor majority in the federal parliament.

The constitutionality of this act of nationalization was immediately challenged in the courts, and enforcement of the act was held in abeyance pending judgment. The chief constitutional question at issue was whether the power to legislate for control of an industry (which the federal government undoubtedly has in the case of banking) includes the power to prohibit or take over private enterprise in that field. The High Court of Australia delivered judgment in August, 1948, declaring the legislation invalid, and this decision was upheld in an appeal to the Privy Council in London, provision for which is made in the Australian Constitution. More important than the legal issue, however, is the fact made clear by the Victorian elections that in this case Labor is pressing its program of socialization beyond the point favored by public opinion in general. Australians are certainly convinced that some measure of socialism is good but there is no majority yet ready to support socialism simply for socialism's sake.

Orderly marketing.— Much less spectacular, but more far-reaching as essays in planned economy, have been the provisions for "orderly marketing" of primary products. These have been developed among the most individualistic section of the whole community, the farmers. They are typical examples of the Australian tendency to turn to the state to provide a framework within which private enterprise can function more effectively. In every case state action has arisen from the difficulties encountered by primary producers in marketing their products overseas.

The first organization of this character was in the dried fruits industry. The large-scale irrigation work which was completed just toward the end of the first World War resulted in a great expansion of vineyards and orchards for production of currants, raisins, and other dried fruits. Prices at the time were good and a great many returned soldiers took up irrigated blocks with high hopes. But shortly after their vines and trees began to bear fruit, world prices dropped severely. Australia, with a high standard of living and the costly irrigation from her scanty rivers, could not compete with Mediterranean countries so much nearer the British market. Export prices were well below the cost of production. The Australian market was protected by the tariff but was easily swamped by the great quantities produced. The only solution seemed to be to keep the Australian price as high as the tariff would permit, sell the balance overseas for whatever price it would bring, and pass legislation that would ensure a fair share of the protected home market for everyone.

Growers therefore appealed to the Commonwealth government, and the necessary legislation was passed. It provided that the scheme must receive the approval of a majority at a poll of growers before it could come into operation. This was done and the organization was established. It provided for a statutory board, of which some members were elected by the growers and some appointed by the government. This board was given power to control the export and sale of dried fruits, setting standards, fixing prices, and conducting publicity. All growers were required to sell their whole crop through the board. If forty per cent of the total year's crop was sold overseas and sixty per cent on the home market, then each grower was paid accordingly. He received the Australian price for sixty per cent of his crop and the overseas price for the rest. The home consumer was charged what has been called "a fair Australian price," but he paid more for his dried fruits and raisins than the Londoner did for the same Australian-grown article.

The same solution was applied a few years later to the problem of surplus dairy products which were glutting the Australian market and could be exported only at a price below the cost of production. There was already in existence a Dairy Produce Control Board, similar in organization to the

Dried Fruits Board, to control standards and assist in the overseas marketing of dairy produce. When surplus butter became a serious problem, a voluntary pooling scheme, known as the "Paterson Plan," was established to sell through a pool and share the advantage of the higher price obtained by price-fixing in the home market. But some creameries refused to join the pool and sought to sell the whole of their produce on the home market. In 1934, therefore, legislation was passed making the pool compulsory, as in the case of dried fruits. Similar schemes have also been put in operation for the sugar industry, although this is under the control of the Queensland government. And in 1936 an act was passed to apply the same solution to the problem created by the low export price for wheat.

In this way a situation has developed whereby the Australian consumer has been called on to pay extraordinarily high prices for products that should be cheap, in order to support the expansion of primary industries. The process is plainly uneconomic. Its only justification is that it is the complement of protection to the manufacturer. The farmer is compelled to pay high prices for manufactured goods because of the tariff; and this raises his costs so that he cannot export at a profit. Therefore he is permitted to recoup himself by charging the Australian consumer a high price under protection of a tariff and a monopoly organization.

In 1936 a blow was struck at this whole scheme of things by the High Court. It declared that the practice of fixing a home consumption price for primary products on an interstate market was a breach of the constitutional provision that interstate trade should be absolutely free. The wheat scheme was therefore dropped. The sugar pool was unaffected, that having been established as a Queensland state monopoly by agreement with the only other sugar-producing state, New South Wales. The dried fruits and dairy products pools have continued on a voluntary basis. During the war they were maintained by wartime regulations under the special defense power of the Commonwealth. How long voluntary pools with a fixed home price can survive the passing of those regulations remains to be seen. An attempt to amend the constitution so that legislation for compulsory pools could again be introduced was defeated in the referendum of September, 1946. This means that, in the future, marketing pools must be purely voluntary or must depend on obtaining agreement for uniform legislation by the states or by the Commonwealth and states combined. To secure the stabilization of the wheat industry, a bill seeking to bring this about was passed by the federal parliament in July, 1946. It created a statutory authority to guarantee the farmer a fixed price for his wheat, with powers to limit the output if world prices should again fall below Australian costs of production. Opposition of several states has, however, thus far prevented it from coming into operation.

If the pools fail, the taxpayer will have to find some other way of subsidizing some of Australia's agricultural industries. At the same time it must be admitted that the pools have overstimulated production of some crops to an uneconomic extent. If the "home price" practice is continued, or if subsidies are given, they will need to be accompanied, as is contemplated in the wheat legislation, by provisions for quantitative control of crops that receive such benefits. In the export market orderly marketing in some form will certainly continue. It has been extended to many other products besides those that have received the benefit of a special home price. The various boards for primary industries perform important duties in standardizing, improving, and assisting in the marketing of primary products. They do not replace private enterprise but they control its operation in the interest of the producer. In the future they can be expected to develop their functions still further in the direction of providing for the "ever normal granary" and of maintaining guaranteed prices for the farmers' products.

Housing.— The most extensive government enterprise in the near future is likely to be found in the field of housing. The reason here, as elsewhere, and as in the case of most other Australian government undertakings, is the failure of private enterprise to meet the needs of the public. A survey conducted in 1944 revealed that a quarter of a million city people (one in every fifteen) were living in substandard dwellings. The building industry in Australia had never erected more than forty thousand houses in one year. The arrears were so great at the time that, allowing for normal expansion, it would require seventy thousand houses to be built each year for ten years to catch up. Even this does not allow for any considerable immigration, and plans in that field will require a still greater expansion of homebuilding and its maintenance over an indefinite period. The extent of the need was therefore shown to be such that only a combined program carried out by the Commonwealth and all the states could hope to meet it.

Such a program has now been worked out and is in operation. The combined Commonwealth and state authorities have organized the allocation of materials, carried out research, trained new workers in the building trades, imported trained construction workers from Britain to build houses for British immigrants who are to follow, financed private home-building schemes on lines similar to those of the Federal Housing Administration (FHA) in America, and built large groups of houses with a varied but limited number of designs by mass production methods. By June, 1948, the building industry had surpassed its prewar record in annual production of homes. The houses are for sale or for rent. Most of them are rented, however, and the states are therefore destined to become, to an ever increasing extent, the landlords of the people.

This is not a one-party program. It is supported by the leaders on both sides of the political fence. Prior to the Commonwealth's entrance on the scene, active housing programs had been set in operation by both Labor and non-Labor governments in the states. These projects were usually started with the idea of slum clearance; but they have gone on to that of the creation of garden suburbs for working-class and middle-class homes, equipped with community centers, parks, and every modern amenity. This program is only in its infancy; but the general feeling is that it will be successful. Enthusiastic and idealistic citizens are working together with hardheaded businessmen on the state housing agencies, the function of which is to execute the details of the plan. The response of former slum dwellers to the new environment created for them has been most gratifying. Gardens are the passion and pride of the Australian suburbanite; and the people from the congested areas have set out to rival their neighbors, and the neighboring suburbs, when given a house with a plot of land in which fruit, flowers, and vegetables can be grown.

Financially, too, the response has been excellent. The 1946 report of the South Australian Housing Trust, for example, states that, in seven and a half years of operation, with £293,893 rents receivable during the period, it has had to write off £1/1/6 as irrecoverable. And the rents charged during this period have all been economic rents, that is, sufficient to pay interest on the cost of land and house, together with depreciation, upkeep, and other expenses. The trust balances its accounts without profit and pays interest to the state government at the rate at which the money is borrowed.

This does not mean, of course, that the task of slum clearance can be carried out without expense. That task has, as yet, hardly been begun, for the arrears of housing are still too great.   The new Housing Agreement between the Commonwealth and the states makes provision that losses incurred in slum clearance and the provision of housing shall be shared, three-fifths being borne by the Commonwealth and two-fifths by the state.

Another interesting and important provision of this agreement is that for rental rebates.   Under this scheme low-income families needing a larger house than they can afford are to receive a rebate on the economic rent of the house provided for them such that they will not pay more than one-fifth of their income in rent.

Most of the actual building has been done by private contractors, but nevertheless the state agency plays a large part.   It becomes, in effect, a great employer of contract labor for which it provides the materials and gives over-all direction, while allowing subcontractors to make a profit by organizing and directing certain parts of the work.   It takes out of that part of the building industry which it controls (and that is likely to be the major part of home construction for many years) all the more speculative elements, the larger profits, and the gains from jerry-building.   In addition, part of the construction work has been done directly by state agencies.

The new housing program, therefore, involves a large intrusion of the state into the sphere of private enterprise. This being the case, it is not surprising that the plan is being subjected to a constant fire of criticism.   While materials were scarce they were controlled and directed, so long as wartime powers lasted, toward the building program of the states for low-cost housing.   There were protests, therefore, from builders who wanted materials for more expensive homes.   The powers given to the state agencies to acquire land by compulsion in order to build large groups of houses together have also aroused protests. The land salesmen, in past years, have subdivided most of the land around the cities and sold it often at ridiculously high prices. Some of this land has been taken over by a state authority at a price adjudged fair, but considerably below its cost to the unfortunate victim of the land salesman. This, too, creates protests. And the press, which always defends private enterprise, makes the most of these difficulties. It is possible, therefore, that the advance of the new housing program may be hampered by political interference. But the need is so great that any such setback is not likely to be more than temporary. The large-scale operation of the government in the field of housing seems to have come to stay.

Monopolies.— The weak point in the defenses of private enterprise in Australia is the extent to which industry is in the control of monopolies. At present the great majority of the people are convinced that industry in general is best left in the hands of private enterprise. They are suspicious and critical of every new movement in the direction of state socialism or state capitalism. They accept or call for such ventures only where private enterprise has clearly failed to meet a need or in the accepted field of operation of public utilities. Further, the constitution favors private enterprise. The powers of the federal government are very severely limited, and in the states the Legislative Councils stand as a solid barrier against socialistic ventures. The powers of the states are also limited by the fact that they do not control their own currency, could not prevent a flight of capital, are limited by the Loan Council in their capacity to borrow, and cannot (since the recent Financial Agreement) decide the rate of their own income tax. Private enterprise is therefore well protected by both public opinion and the constitution. So long as the federal government is not given powers to nationalize industry, there is no prospect of any considerable move in the direction of socialism.

As far as can be seen at present, the only factor that might bring about a change in this situation is the further growth of monopolies, especially if it is accompanied by unsocial practices. Australia has such a small population, and modern industry tends so much to large-scale organization, that the tendency to monopoly is almost inevitable. During the last twenty-five years the organization of Australian industry in the control of a few great companies has increased enormously. The holding company, almost unknown a quarter of a century ago, has come into extensive operation. And interlocking directorates among these organizations are exceedingly common.

The Broken Hill Proprietary Company is the greatest of these concerns. It began as a silver-lead mining company at Broken Hill, accumulated large profits, and invested these, in 1915, in steel mills. In 1935 it absorbed its only serious competitor, the Australian Iron and Steel Company. It is a very close corporation, having never issued a single share for public subscription, though it has extended its list of shareholders in the absorption of subsidiary industries. [12] It now dominates the steel industry of Australia completely and runs its own coal mines and ships. It has been extremely well managed and is one of the most up-to-date and efficient steel works in the world. During the second World War it was a source of great strength, producing steel of practically every type needed for munitions and armament. It declared dividends of fifty per cent in 1915 and 1916. In 1919 it capitalized one and a half million pounds of reserves and distributed them to shareholders. Several times it has sold new shares to its shareholders for less than their market

[12] B. C. Fitzpatrick, *The Rich Get Richer* (Rawson's Book Shop, Melbourne, 1944).

value. , Thus its great assets have been chiefly built up by its profits. On its capital as now expanded it makes from four to six per cent profit, but it would be very difficult to say how much of this capital is water.

By many the B.H.P., as this company is familiarly called, is regarded as a public benefactor. It is certainly an industry of enormous importance and value to the country. But that very size and importance makes many look upon it with fear. As secondary industries develop, the whole economy of the country is beginning to rest upon this one company as its base. Its directors, therefore, bear an enormous responsibility and wield extraordinary power. The company could easily become an octopus to strangle the independent industrial life of the country. If it tends to do this it can hardly avoid creating a political movement that will overthrow it and start Australia on the high road to complete socialism. The same result might be brought about by the continuance of what is at present a somewhat intransigent attitude towards its employees. This has resulted in communist domination of the Ironworkers' Union. A prolonged period of industrial unrest in such a basic industry as steel could only issue in some form of government control if not complete nationalization. This situation has already been reached in coal and, if greater contentment cannot be created among the workers, it can also happen in steel.

In the coal mines the trouble is not due to monopoly, but rather to the lack of it. Free competition has resulted in a haphazard distribution of pits, often operated by companies with insufficient capital. The result has been great waste of coal through inefficient development of underground operations, slowness in development of mechanization, and lack of the facilities necessary to create content among the workers. The owners have met discontent by fighting against concessions. During the depression unemployment was terrible. The owners found that they could defeat strikes as long as large surplus stocks of coal were kept on hand. But a prolonged strike early in the recent war exhausted stocks. Since then the country has lived from hand to mouth. Union organizers deliberately keep production down so that no stock pile can be accumulated. They have demanded and are beginning to get radical reconstruction of the industry.

The demands of the miners include proper ventilation of all pits, properly policed safety precautions, automatic sprayers to keep down dust, modernized bath houses, tramways to save miles of walking underground, regular weekly wages instead of piece rates, and security against lockouts and unemployment. Only government control could give them these things. And measures to initiate such control and reorganization of the industry have recently been worked out by the Commonwealth government and that of New South Wales in combination.

In 1946 these two governments evolved a plan which gives a government agency power to reorganize the industry without destroying private ownership except in special cases and as a last resort. Such a step required uniform legislation in both Commonwealth and state parliaments and had, therefore, to secure the consent of both the Labor Party and the opposition which was in control of the upper house in New South Wales. This legislation established a Joint Coal Board as a statutory corporation drawing its powers from both the state and federal governments. This board was given power over such matters as the opening and closing of coal mines; methods of working; mechanization; the use and distribution of coal; prices and profits; the health and safety of workers and their welfare both in the mines and in their communities; employment and training; statistics and research. If cooperation is not forthcoming from the owners and managers the board is empowered to assume control of, or to acquire and operate, any mine. And it may suspend or exclude from the industry any superintendent, manager, or other employee who acts in a manner which is prejudicial to the industry. The financing of all these measures is the responsibility of the Commonwealth government.

This is a new experiment in control of industry falling just short of complete socialization and also in state and federal cooperation. It may provide a model for much wider application. The new Joint Coal Board commenced operations early in 1947. Its program is necessarily one of long range reform and it will take many years to exercise its full effects. Its first years give promise of success. The coal output for 1948 has equaled the all-time record set in 1942 when the country was faced by Japanese invasion. Industry, however, has been expanding so fast that coal is still in short supply.

It would become tedious to enter upon the ramifications of monopoly and near-monopoly organization in Australia, for there is very little real competition left among the major basic industries. Fortunately, the outstanding leaders in these organizations seem to possess a considerable sense of public responsibility, a quality which may save the monopolies from abusing their power. It would be impossible to try to break them up by use of legislation like the Sherman Anti-trust Act. If a small country like Australia is to be equipped adequately with efficient, large-scale, secondary industries, then a great deal of monopoly is inevitable. It would be too wasteful for the country to attempt to enforce competition. The alternatives therefore are that private enterprise, under large-scale organization and with monopolies in wide-spread control, shall conduct itself with consideration toward the consumer, the small businessman and the employee, or a prolonged struggle, a growing discontent, and an eventual revolt will introduce nationalization of all big industry by act of parliament.

- 9 -

Nationalism

AUSTRALIAN loyalties are gathered into four concentric circles—the State, the Nation, the British Commonwealth, the United Nations. Of these, national loyalty is undoubtedly the strongest. But this was not always so. State and imperial loyalties have in the past competed with the national sentiment. The nation, it must be remembered, was born only in 1901. Prior to that there had existed a number of politically separate British colonies which thought of themselves merely as so many provinces within the British Empire. The main loyalty at that time was to the old country, which was commonly spoken of as home even by the Australian-born.

The immigrants of the nineteenth century, on the whole, did not like Australia. It was a hard, dry, land of "sin, sun, sand and sorrow." The bush and the plains were never as green as the woods and fields of England. The squatters grew rich quickly—and that was a compensation. But the small farmers battled with droughts and pests—including the English rabbit, brought out to provide food for the foxes which, in turn, were brought out to provide English gentlemen with something to hunt. Even the squatter had his troubles in times of drought, as expressed in the bitter irony of "Banjo" Paterson's [1] lines,

> Oh! its grand to be a squatter
> And sit upon a post
> And watch your little ewes and lambs
> A givin' up the ghost.

But the Australian-born grew up to love Australia. They saw beauty in the careless freedom with which the eucalypts stretch their arms to the sun. They reveled in pastoral occupations, in horses, cattle, and sheep. They learned to love the wonderful blue of the mountains in the clear, dry air. They roved freely from sea, to hills, to hinterland, and rejoiced in the great open spaces. They discovered that Australia was all one land, one undivided continent for an undivided people. They discovered, too, that it had its own individuality, and that individuality stamped itself upon them. They were British and proud of it. But they were British with a difference. They were a new nation.

It was the first World War that really brought the national spirit to birth. They believed in the things they were fighting for—the rights of small nations, the sacredness of a "scrap of paper" that contained a man's pledged word, the democracy for which the whole world must be made safe. Their whole way of life and the social order they had made were rooted in that sort of faith and made them ready to fight for it. The prophetic eye of their favorite poet had foreseen it.

[1] Andrew Barton Paterson, Australian poet, 1864–1941.

There are boys out there by the western creeks
   who hurry away from school
To climb the sides of the breezy peaks
   or dive in the shaded pool,
Who'll stick to their guns when the mountains quake
   to the mighty tread of war,
And fight for the Right or a Great Mistake
   as men never fought before.

There are boys today in the city slum
   and the home of wealth and pride,
Who'll have one home when the storm is come
   and fight for it side by side. [2]

Australia came out of the first World War with a sense of national unity and individuality, with pride in her achievements and a determination to play her part in the world of nations. She insisted on being given control of the strategically placed islands to the north of her which had been taken from the enemy. She took her place in the League of Nations and used her vote with independence. She supported the system of collective security, hoping to see it grow strong enough to keep the peace. But she kept firm her connection with the British Commonwealth for reasons both of sentiment and security.

There was a certain brashness about some of the early manifestations of this new sense of independent nationhood. It was overboastful concerning the achievements of Australian armies. It was oversensitive to criticism. It was parochial in the attitude adopted toward newcomers to the country. But these marks of national adolescence are disappearing, and in their place signs of a certain maturity of outlook are manifesting themselves in recent Australian

[2] Henry Lawson, "The Star of Australasia" in *Winnowed Verses* (The Pocket Library, Angus and Robertson, Sydney, 1944).

literature and in discussions of national problems and international affairs. Statesmen are facing the new world situation with sober realism. Plans are being laid with a frank recognition of the mistakes of the past. Writers and artists are beginning to cherish and depict the Australian scene with faithfulness and affection, as the newer school in the United States does with the American scene.

The Australian people are developing a mature patriotism that can look without shame on what is unlovely in the past, yet cherish the best and face the future with courage. This sentiment is expressed in a poem, the title of which, as a symbol of their country, must still be a shock to many Australians, and which would hardly have been possible two decades ago. Yet today it is selected for an anthology published by a group of writers who are dedicated to the cultivation of a literature that is distinctly Australian.

BALLADE OF THE CONVICT'S DAUGHTER

My love has sailed across the water
And all for the sake of the convict's daughter!
He gave me a ring; he gave me a pledge;
Yet he said goodbye by the flowering hedge—
He said goodbye and my heart grew colder
For he wore her name upon his shoulder
He wore her name for the world to see . . . .
And little he thought or cared of me!

But the convict's daughter comforts me
As I sit in the dusk by the flowering tree.

I wept and I pleaded that he might stay
But I lost all hope when he turned away
For she was lusty and young and fair
And the Southern Cross she wore in her hair
And her eyes were the blue of the Southern Seas
And her hair was the gold of the wattle trees

And her laughter the ripple her creeks had
    taught her . . . .
Oh my love would have died for the convict's
    daughter!

Yet the convict's daughter comforts me
As I sit in the dusk by the flowering tree.

Now he has gone and his sudden laughter
Lost in the hush that has followed after . . . .
For he sleeps at Crete, beneath the sea
With his fingers curled as a child's might be
But I hear his voice, and I understand
How deep was his love for his golden land
"The convict's daughter" hear him call
"Is the grandest lady of them all!"

And the convict's daughter comforts me
As I sit in the dusk by the flowering tree. [3]

31 Immigration.— Australians, in their pride in their
country, have always envisioned its growth through immigration. Comparisons of the size and population of the continent with that of the United States have led to exceedingly
optimistic estimates of the possibilities of future development.
More exact scientific knowledge of the conditions of agriculture, of rainfall, wind and water erosion, soil and evapora-
ation have scaled down these hopes. Particularly have the
expectations concerning the potentialities of the tropics had
to be greatly reduced. The rainfall of the North is heavy
for a few brief months, the rest of the year being hot and
dry. The result is a terrible problem of erosion—wind erosion in the dry months and the washing away of the soil,

[3] Sheila Sibley, "Ballade of the Convict's Daughter" in the *Jindy-
worobak Anthology, 1945* (Georgian House, Melbourne, 1945). By
kind permission of *Salt,* Melbourne.

powdered to dust in the dry season, in the torrential rains of the wet.

Nevertheless, it is agreed that the country as a whole could support several times its present population. Some experts have placed the optimum for general prosperity at fifteen millions. On the other hand, there is good agricultural authority for the opinion that eventually the land may be made to produce food for fifty millions. This, however, presupposes enormous capital expenditure for irrigation and other projects. Further, Australia probably should remain an exporter of considerable foodstuffs to industrial populations in Britain and Europe. Reasonable estimates, therefore, place the possibilities, with known methods of production, at twenty to thirty millions.

More important than the question of the ultimate possibilities, however, is that of the rate at which immigrants can be absorbed into the country. Here Australia's record is much better than is generally supposed. Indeed, through most of her history, she has shared with New Zealand the distinction of having the fastest-growing population in the world. In the decade of 1911 to 1921, when immigrants were pouring into America from Europe so fast that they could not be satisfactorily assimilated, the United States had an annual increase of population (including natural increase) of 14 per 1,000. In the same decade the increase in Australia, New Zealand, and Canada was 20 per 1,000; that of Japan, 9; Sweden, 7; and of England and Wales, 4. In the forty years between 1881 and 1921 the New Zealand rate of increase was 23; Australia was second with 22, followed by America with 19 and Canada with 18. In the years from 1921 to 1939, however, the declining birth rate lowered the total increase in spite of a very vigorous immigration policy (prior to the depression), which cost her considerable financial losses in the state schemes for irrigation and settling migrants on the land.

Pointing to these figures, the Commonwealth statistician, [4] in 1928, showed that if the existing rate of two per cent increase a year (which was close to the maximum of any country in modern times) could be maintained, then the population would double itself every thirty-five years. The depression which set in the next year, however, stopped this rate of growth. Immigration for a time ceased and has never recovered its former rate. The postwar policy of the Ministry of Immigration aims at restoring at least an annual increase of two per cent. Allowing for natural increase this would require seventy thousand immigrants a year. If this and no more can be done, then Australia's seven and one-half millions in the census of 1947 will have reached fifteen millions by 1981.

A statement of government policy, issued in August, 1945, emphasized the need of avoiding past mistakes in any immigration policy. Australia, said the Minister, wants immigrants; but she will not mislead any immigrant into coming to the country until there is a reasonable assurance of his economic future. The country's first duty, he pointed out, is the rehabilitation of men of the armed forces; the second, the provision of housing for the existing population. A third obstacle to an immediate immigration program is the lack of shipping.

The first of these hurdles has already been overcome; the change-over from war to peace has been achieved without the appearance of any unemployment; there has, rather, been a manpower (and still more, a womanpower) shortage. The

[4] C. H. Wickens, "Australian Population: Its Nature and Growth" in *The Peopling of Australia,* edited by P. D. Phillips and G. L. Wood (Macmillan, Melbourne, 1928).

second difficulty, housing, will remain a major problem for many years. Immigration cannot wait until it is entirely overcome. Yet no very great numbers can be admitted until the housing shortage is considerably relieved. The third difficulty, shipping, is being overcome with greater rapidity. Space was found for thirty thousand people in 1947 and for seventy thousand in 1948. Early in 1949 shipping was secured and plans made for another two hundred thousand immigrants by the middle of 1950, half of them to be displaced persons from Europe. This is an achievement of considerable merit, for the five or six weeks' journey by sea from Britain is no small obstacle, since a ship can make only four round trips a year, and the poorer-class immigrants cannot afford the passage money. Thus government assistance must again be forthcoming, so that financial problems once more stand in the way of any long-continued large-scale movement of population.

Finally, there is the question of jobs for the new arrivals. In the past Australians have always thought of immigration in terms of land settlement. But the immigrant finds Australian farming conditions so different from those he has known at home that all too often he does not succeed. If there is a further rapid growth of industrial towns, there will be opportunities for small farmers from Europe on truck farms in good rainfall areas in conditions to which they can fairly readily adapt themselves. But the typical Australian large-scale farming in the dry areas and cattle and sheep raising have to be done by men with a thorough understanding of conditions. Further, this sort of development has already been pushed so far that, except in the tropical North, it must in the future grow slowly.

The question of jobs for new arrivals therefore turns upon the growth of industry in the towns. It is here that

Australia is on the eve of a great expansive movement. With its basis laid in a magnificently equipped and efficient steel industry, the opportunity exists for manufacturing of all sorts. The raw materials are, for the most part, to be found in the country. With its wide range of climate almost anything can be grown. In its vast spaces nearly all minerals are to be found. Almost every kind of secondary industry has already made a start, and only labor and materials are needed for the process of expansion. With these opportunities, and with full employment deliberately maintained by the government financial policy, the question of jobs for immigrants is only one of how quickly factories can be built and equipped for them to work in. Already Australia produces more meat, dairy produce, breadstuffs, fruit, and sugar than she can consume. Increasing other food crops is a simple matter. The question of the rate of absorption of immigrants, therefore, is only one of the rate at which the houses and factories can be built to supply their needs.

It is an economic fact, not always clearly understood, that in a country with a modern, industrial economy, supplying most of its own needs, immigration does not increase the available labor supply. It actually diminishes it. So long as there is capital looking for investment and no great surplus of housing and industrial plants, the immigrant makes more work than he performs. In his first year he needs a house and furniture, with all the municipal amenities. He needs a place in a factory, a machine or tools, and materials with which to work. If the population is growing fast enough and if the land, materials, capital, and managerial and technical skill are available, there will be no unemployment. The whole community, including the newcomers, will be kept busy with the program of expansion needed to accommodate the increasing population. Immigration can cause unemployment only if immigrants arrive too fast for factories to be built to supply them with jobs and with their other needs. And the erection of houses, of course, competes with that of factories.

It might be suggested that there may also arise a problem of balance of payments between exports and imports, for an increasing population will mean more local consumption, more imports, and fewer exports. But this problem will largely be solved by the immigrants bringing a little capital with them, by investments from abroad in Australian industries, and by an increasing tendency for the products of these industries to replace exports from abroad. The balance should easily be met by a gradually expanding export trade.

In these circumstances it would not be surprising if the earlier aim of the Ministry of Immigration—to restore the rate of increase to two per cent a year—is for many years far exceeded. Two per cent was a figure maintained with eight per cent of the workers unemployed. With a full employment policy, and with the constantly increasing powers of production of modern industry, it should be possible to raise the standard of living and at the same time increase the rate of expansion of factories, houses, and farms faster than before. The new effort at expansion must be made without the help of external government borrowing such as was practiced in connection with the developmental programs of the past; but the enormous increase in the national income achieved during the war shows that capital and material resources should be available for a great program of expansion in time of peace without resort to the money markets overseas.

The material conditions exist, therefore, as soon as the immediate housing and shipping shortages are overcome, for a great immigration program which will double the population in much less than thirty-five years. But where are the immigrants to come from if the problem of the declining birth rates of the Western world is not overcome? If the figure 1 is taken to represent the birth rate that is needed to maintain the present population, then that for the white population of the United States in 1940 was .95, of negroes 1.07, of Australia 1.04. Just before the war it was in England .78, Scotland .96, Germany .98, France .9, Switzerland .80, Sweden .78, Russia 1.7. All those countries with less than unity are faced with a declining population if they continue at only that birth rate. Perhaps the trial of war, with its terrible revelation of the need of manpower, will stimulate a deliberate effort to increase it. But many thoughtful persons, looking at the figures for the birth rates of western Europe, have doubted whether Australia can find the immigrants she needs unless she is able and willing to take them from southern and eastern Europe or from Asia.

It must be recognized that there is not now, and will not be for a considerable number of years, any enthusiasm for the admission of Germans or Italians. That is the psychological effect of the war; and in considering the possible success of immigrants in a new land it is a fact to be reckoned with. It may be difficult to obtain immigrants from countries in the Russian sphere of influence. There is already in Australia a nucleus of Greeks and Yugoslavs successfully established, and more would be welcomed. Moreover, in spite of the declining birth rates in western Europe, investigations have revealed in several of those countries a surprising interest in Australia and a desire to emigrate there.

Toward the end of 1945 the Australian delegates to the International Labour Organization at Geneva were constituted a committee to enquire into immigration. Their investigation revealed that in Britain, Switzerland, Holland, and Norway there are many thousands of people eager to emigrate to Australia. There is also some interest in Denmark, Sweden, and Finland, though none in France and

Belgium. In Norway they found a very active Australia Migrants' Club carrying on active propaganda to develop migration to Australia. Australia is their choice because of what they know of the country and their contacts with Australians during the war. If it were possible to accept European immigrants now, in 1949, a stream could be started which would probably continue for some time. The difficulty is that these people may have settled down at home or gone elsewhere before the housing and shipping problems are sufficiently overcome. Yet efforts will, no doubt, be made to secure a beginning of migration from these countries while the opportunity is so bright; and the stream, once started, should grow, providing the present employment and social policies are maintained.

In Britain today, migration is not looked upon as a matter of finding an outlet for surplus population, but as one of securing a better distribution of British people within the Commonwealth. British industries are establishing branches in Australia and planning to move some of their people with the industry. Britons are eager to go in considerable numbers. At the end of 1947 Australia House in London had a list of half a million registered prospective emigrants. Such a movement will not necessarily mean a decline of population in Britain, for, as the industrial center of a considerable section of Europe, British industry can, if necessary, draw supplies of labor from European countries. As the New Englanders moved out to occupy the West and their places were taken by Europeans who, in course of time, became good Americans, so the old Englanders can move out to the Dominions and their places will be taken by Europeans who will become good Britishers.

In the light of these facts and probabilities it would appear, therefore, that for the next twenty years Australia will have no real difficulty in finding all the immigrants she can absorb, and she can do this without drawing on populations which, by reason of their different ideologies, might prove difficult to assimilate in large numbers.   It would be a magnificent achievement if Australia could, in that time, build houses and factories and develop farms to supply five million people in addition to her own natural increase.   That would practically double the population in two decades, providing a reasonable natural increase is maintained.   It would require shipping and housing for a quarter of a million immigrants a year, which would be a great but perhaps not impossible task.   But if Australia can provide the opportunity, there is little doubt that, among the British, Scandinavians, Dutch, Swiss, and Greeks, with a sprinkling of others, there will be a quarter of a million people a year ready to seize it. The immigration program therefore is not likely to fail for lack of suitable immigrants.

Australia's primary concern with immigration is not the desire for an increased population for defense purposes. Her security rests with the United Nations, the British Commonwealth, and her good friend, the United States.   Moreover, a few million more inhabitants could not make an appreciable difference in the scales of world war.   However, because she is dependent upon other countries for her protection, it is necessary that she be able to justify herself morally before them.   To do that she must show convincingly that she is not selfishly excluding from her shores people who want to come and who would make good use of her resources. She must show that she is accepting into her national life a stream of newcomers as great as her economy can bear, as fast as homes and livelihood can be provided for them. If she is really doing that, then there can be no complaint if she selects from among those who desire to come the type of people who, by reason of their ideological background, are most easily assimilated into her way of life, people who will strengthen rather than weaken her democratic social order because they already understand it and appreciate it.

Probably, the greatest question mark attached to the problem of Australia's future, however, is not that of the quantity and quality of the immigrants she will receive, but that of the birth rate which Australians and the new immigrant population can sustain; for most of the countries from which Australia might hope to receive immigrants in the near future have a birth rate as low as, or lower than, Australia herself. From 1932 to 1938 the net reproduction rate was just below the figure necessary to maintain a stationary population. During the war there was, as in America, a very great increase. The hope that some of this increase can be sustained rests upon the fact that the war has awakened both government and people to the seriousness of the situation. Child endowment, social security benefits, educational aid, and housing subsidies for large families are the beginning of a program for the restoration of the normal, healthy family of three or four children. Other aid will follow to lighten the economic burden of parents. More nursery schools, organized and subsidized domestic help, an expansion of the present services for child care and advice to mothers, and, above all, adequate housing with modern conveniences are planned and needed. It is hoped that, with such aids, a reasonable rate of natural increase can be maintained. If not, then European immigration will not solve the problem, and it will be only a question of time until the present Australian type will be overwhelmed by an influx from Asia.

White Australia.— It is probably true that a greater rate of increase could have been maintained in the past if Australia had been willing to accept immigrants from Asia.

But this is true only on the assumption that the Asiatics would have been content to accept a lower standard of living. The advocates of Asiatic immigration have, for the most part, been divided into two classes. One has desired cheap labor for factories and farms, in particular for tropical and subtropical agriculture. The other, on humanitarian grounds, has seen in Australia's "great open spaces" a means of relieving the overcrowded areas of India, China, and Japan.

It is on the first ground that serious attempts have been made to introduce non-European immigrants. When convict labor became scarce in New South Wales after the cessation of transportation in 1840, some pastoralists and other employers began to recruit labor from China. But when gold was discovered the Chinese laborers left their employers to seek their fortunes on the gold fields. And news of their success brought several thousands of their fellow countrymen following them. When the surface gold played out they, like the white miners, turned their hands to farming and manufacturing, especially to market gardening and cabinetmaking. Most of them had no intention of staying in the country longer than was necessary to accumulate enough money to represent a small fortune in China. They did not bring their women with them. They lived on low economic standards, undercutting the white worker and gardener who was trying to make a home for himself and his family. Many of them might have brought out their wives and settled permanently had there not been a great deal of ignorant prejudice against them. This, combined with genuine economic objections, resulted in the restriction of Asiatic immigration, carried out first by the states and later by the Commonwealth.

The second important attempt to introduce cheap labor was the importation of Melanesians (Kanakas) from the

South Sea Islands for the sugar plantations of Queensland. These people were brought in as indentured laborers for a term of years, on the understanding that they would then be returned to their islands. The sugar planters throve on the profits made from what was little better than a system of slavery; but Queensland paid dearly for this greed in the introduction of tropical diseases. This and the methods of recruiting the Kanakas, as well as their treatment on the plantations and the resentment of displaced white labor, aroused a strong public reaction. In 1904 further importation was prohibited and the Islanders were, in the next few years, returned, as far as possible, to their homes.

These were both attempts to introduce non-European labor for the benefit of the Europeans. Had such policies been allowed to continue they would have created in Australia a biracial society in which the whites maintained a precarious position as a ruling caste, denying full economic and political privileges to an exploited coolie class and crushing a "poor white" population between the upper and nether millstones. From this danger the White Australia policy was designed to save the country. And it has succeeded.

The humanitarian criticism of this policy, however, envisages a very different situation. It would have Asiatics admitted with their families and given the full status of citizenship. It would have them employed at trade union wages and given the opportunity to acquire farms and houses equal to those of the rest of the community.

This idealistic view, however, fails to grasp the real difficulties of such a program. No working class in any country sustains high standards of wages except by its technical skill and political cohesion. The first generation of Asiatic laborers would inevitably be exploited. They could not help but undermine the political and social order which democratic processes have painfully developed and maintained only at the usual price of liberty—eternal vigilance. Further, the unpleasant fact of race prejudice cannot be set aside. Australians are no more immune to it than other people. Any considerable non-European immigration would create a race problem which would add to the world's difficulties rather than relieve them.

To the Asiatic peoples themselves the gain from a change in Australia's policy would be slight. They could not be absorbed into the economy of the country at present working-class standards of living any faster than Europeans. If Australia should open her doors to fifty or one hundred thousand Asiatics a year, or even a quarter of a million, it would not create a ripple in the human tide of Asia, where the annual natural increase of India alone is five millions. The problem of the overpopulated countries of Asia is one that no program of emigration anywhere in the world can solve. Its only solution is the application of scientific methods to control the birth rate as well as the death rate. Until the people of Asia have learned to do both, their lot will continue to be unhappy; and to export any considerable number of them to other lands would merely be to spread the area of unhappiness.

One further objection to a policy of purely European immigration, however, should be considered. It is the doubt as to whether the resources of northern Australia, such as they are, can be satisfactorily developed by Europeans. If they cannot, then there would be a case for urging that Asiatics be admitted to at least the tropical part of the country. The primary objection to this plan is that, once admitted to the North, it would be an extremely invidious distinction to insist that they must be kept out of the rest of the country. With democratic citizenship an Asiatic northern Australia would create distinct Asiatic states within the Commonwealth. The class, caste, and racial distinctions of Asia would inevitably make themselves felt. Political differences with the South over labor conditions and many other questions would appear. It would be most unlikely that an Asiatic North and a European South could remain united in one Commonwealth. The question of secession and the danger of armed strife would inevitably arise. Instead of purchasing peace with her Asiatic neighbors by such a concession, Australia would create one more of those minority problems which are among the most fertile sources of war.

Experience with the settlement that has so far taken place in tropical Australia, however, sets aside doubts as to the ability of people of European extraction to develop its resources. Those resources, it must be remembered, are not great. The principal industry of the far North will probably always be the raising of cattle. The area that has a high enough rainfall to compensate for tropical evaporation and make agriculture possible is not large, and ages of erosion in the long dry season have denuded the soil. Nevertheless, a quarter of a million white people are already living north of the Tropic of Capricorn, chiefly engaged in raising and milling cane sugar. And there is certainly room and a good livelihood, in cattle raising and agriculture, for several millions more.

The people of tropical Queensland are healthy. Tropical diseases that began to manifest themselves in the days of Kanaka cheap labor have been overcome to such an extent that Queensland has passed from the condition of having the worst health record in the Commonwealth to that of the best. The infant-mortality rate is lower than the average for the Commonwealth; the birth rate, higher. Further, the people born in Queensland have better health records than those born outside the state. Not all of Queensland is tropical, but it is all at least subtropical and the health of those in the definitely tropical areas is as good as those in the South. Also there is no difference in health between the inhabitants of the moist, humid, coastal areas and those of the dry interior.

These results are attributed by a competent authority to three factors: "1) The successful institution of adequate measures of preventive medicine; 2) the exclusion of races with lower standards of life and higher rates of disease and reproduction; and 3) the continual increase in locally born inhabitants." [5] To those who live in the country, he says, the third factor is obvious. There is a process of complete physical adaptation of the organism as a response to the continued influence upon it of the distinctive physical stimuli of low latitudes.

On grounds of health, then, there is no real obstacle to the development of northern Australia by white settlers. What, then, has delayed settlement in this part of the country? The answer is fourfold. In the first place, most of it is the poorest part of the country (apart from the arid interior) in natural resources of soil and usable rainfall; it is isolated, subject to hurricanes and to great variations in rainfall. Then too, white settlers have been ignorant of the uses to which it can be put, of how to deal with its peculiar problems, and of how to live healthily in a tropical climate. Moreover, the crops it will grow are those that come into competition with the cheap colored labor available elsewhere,

[5] R. W. Cilento, "White Settlement in the Tropics" in *The Peopling of Australia,* edited by P. D. Phillips and G. I. Wood (Macmillan, Melbourne, 1928). Dr. Cilento was for many years Director of the Division of Tropical Hygiene of the Commonwealth Department of Health.

and the known methods of cultivating these crops have been dependent on a supply of such cheap labor. And finally, the climate is one that people accustomed to temperate zones find uncomfortably hot for a large part of the year. Only the prospect of large economic rewards could persuade many people to endure the heat when there was land and opportunity available in the delightful climate of the South.

The last is the most serious barrier to settlement. Yet it is not insuperable. Those who have become accustomed to the climate of northern Australia generally grow to like it and become its most enthusiastic advocates. But pioneering in the tropics certainly requires considerable powers of endurance. It is especially trying for women to have to maintain domestic life in primitive housing conditions in a hot climate. But in increasing numbers they are doing it. Even primitive housing can be kept open to the breeze and great heat can be endured if one has a breeze and shade. Further, housing conditions and the general amenities of life are being rapidly improved. People are learning to adapt their architecture and clothing to life in the tropics and to save labor by use of machines. Modern air conditioning has only just begun to come into use. It may, before long, transform the whole situation. It is the cattle-raising industry that will open up the North. Men can ride the ranges and the boundaries in tropic suns and find life good. If their women can live in air-conditioned homes, if they can sleep and do office and professional work in air-conditioned rooms, if the few necessary shops, warehouses, factories, and meat plants can be air-conditioned, then the problem of the white man's life in the tropics will be solved. For the greater part of the year no air conditioning would be necessary, but it would provide the needed relief when the heat becomes intense. It will probably be found that life can be made comfortable in the tropics by means of air conditioning in the summer just as cheaply as it can be made comfortable in cold regions in the winter by means of central heating.

There would seem, therefore, to be no good reason why Australia should not continue to build up its population solely from European sources without risking the race problem that any departure from that policy would almost certainly introduce. Nevertheless, that policy should, and could, be framed and administered on lines that would be much less objectionable to Asiatic peoples. A beginning has been made in this direction in a provision for reasonable freedom of temporary residence for students, businessmen, and tourists from non-European countries. And the Labor Party, in reaffirming the White Australia Policy in 1945, was careful to state that it was maintained not on racial, but on purely economic grounds. This repudiated former statements maintaining the policy on grounds of racial purity as well as the objection to cheap labor.

It is time now to go further. Australian citizenship should be offered to the few non-Europeans resident in the country. The policy of rigid exclusion should give way to one that would allow the entry, for purposes of residence, of a small number of selected non-Europeans who, by reason of their standard of culture, would not offend popular prejudices or enter into competition with manual workers. No other means of exclusion is necessary than the need of obtaining a passport visa; and it would suffice as a statement of general policy that passports for entry of proposed residents will receive the Australian visa only in cases where consular officials see no barrier to the economic success and social happiness of the individual as an Australian citizen. In all but a small number of cases the fact of being of non-European origin would constitute such a barrier and the visa would be refused.

The transparent device of a dictation test in some European language (one being chosen that the non-European does not know), which is the present instrument of exclusion, is clumsy and a little disingenuous. It dates from the era before British passports and is now quite unnecessary. It and the absolute rigidity of the exclusion policy should be abolished in the interest of harmonious relations with Asiatic countries.

Imperial relations and foreign policy.— Australia, in fact and in thought, is less dependent upon Great Britain, and yet more firmly attached to the British Commonwealth of Nations, than ever before in her history. In the past the predominant body of opinion has taken the British association and British leadership for granted. It was perfectly content to leave the direction of major policy for the whole Empire and Commonwealth to the British Government. As one shrewd observer stated the position in 1938: "Where Britain is concerned the Australian mood is not one of impartiality or detachment. For that reason any lengthy discussion of Australia's right to remain neutral in a war in which Britain was engaged would be academic and unrealistic." [6] The Statute of Westminster, which gives to the Dominions the right of secession and of neutrality, though it meant a great deal to South Africa and Ireland and cemented the friendship of the former with Britain, was received without enthusiasm in Australia and New Zealand. The parliament at Canberra has never officially ratified it as a whole.

This situation, as pointed out by former Attorney General J. G. Latham, [7] is due to the fact that the vast majority

[6] H. L. Harris, *Australia's National Interests and National Policy* (Melbourne University Press, 1938).

[7] J. G. Latham, *Australia and the British Commonwealth* (Macmillan, London, 1929).

of Australians have never doubted that they could have all the liberty they wanted in their relations with Britain and never wanted to sever their own fate from that of their kindred on the other side of the globe. This attitude was reflected in the position taken by the non-Labor prime minister, R. G. Menzies, at the outbreak of hostilities in 1939 in announcing that when Great Britain is at war Australia is automatically at war also.

A new attitude was reflected in the action of the Curtin Labor Government when Japan struck at Pearl Harbor. Australia declared war on her own responsibility twenty minutes before it was done in Great Britain. And this step was taken deliberately "in order to emphasize that Australia's right to go to war or make peace was inherent in the Australian people themselves and was not to be decided for them by a parliament at Westminster or anywhere else." [8] Yet this show of independence was not designed to suggest any tendency of Australia to dissociate herself from full relationship with the British Commonwealth, but rather her determination to take a more active part in the direction of its affairs. The same minister who, in the words just quoted, pointed out the significance of the government's independent action in declaring war on Japan, emphatically declared in the same speech, "Any person who suggests that we should break away from the British Commonwealth is either mad, or bad; he is a fit subject for a lunatic asylum. We know that we cannot possibly hold 3,000,000 square miles of the British Commonwealth of Nations if, as a people of 7,000,-000 we regard ourselves as a completely independent nation. We must help the British Commonwealth of Nations to de-

[8] From a speech by A. A. Calwell, Minister of Information and Immigration in the federal parliament, March 26, 1946. *Commonwealth Parliamentary Debates, 17th Parliament, 3rd Session No. 4*, 604–610.

velop its strength. The stronger the British Commonwealth of Nations becomes the stronger, too, each of its units becomes."

These are the words of an Irish-Australian Labor politician whose sentimental attachment to England is something less than zero. They represent, therefore, a purely realistic appraisement of Australia's interest in the maintenance of the British Commonwealth. But those Australians (and they form probably a majority of Labor supporters, though not of the opposing parties) who, like the speaker just quoted, value the British association rather for its strategic advantages than because of any cultural nostalgia or sense of kinship, are determined that Australia must have a larger say in the direction of the policy of the British Commonwealth (so far as it has a common policy) in peace and war.

The distinctive attitudes of the two parties in this matter of imperial relations are most vividly portrayed by their respective positions on the question of the recall of Australian divisions from the Near East in 1942. In this connection the Labor minister continued, "I cite also the opposition of honorable members on the other side to the recall of the 6th and 7th Divisions of the Australian Imperial Force to Australia. The Labor Government wanted to bring them back, but honorable members opposite wanted them to stay in Egypt, and later, wanted to divert the 7th Division to Burma. Indeed, Mr. Churchill, without reference to the Australian Government, did divert the 7th Division to Burma, but the Commonwealth Government ordered its return to Australia and told Mr. Churchill that it held him responsible for the safety of every member of the convoy. It was said at that time that if the 7th Division were not in Burma that country would be lost and the gateway to India would be opened to the enemy. The Churchillian policy was to save India even at the expense of abandoning Australia. . . . We on this side claim that Australia has the right to determine its own policy, but honorable members opposite prefer to accept, almost without question, the policy of the British Government from time to time. . . . As a member of the Australian Labor Party and as a Minister in an Australian Labor Government, I proudly proclaim my Australian nationalism. I am a nationalist before I am an internationalist." [9]

This speech does not represent the majority opinion in Australia, but it does represent the majority opinion among the working class. This change of attitude has been wrought by the hammer blows of historic events. First there was the discovery that the British fleet could no longer shield them at times of world conflict. Then came the surrender at Singapore of a British army 100,000 strong, including an Australian division, to one third that number of Japanese, trained in jungle warfare, for which neither the British, nor the Australians under British leadership, had been trained. Finally came the revelation of the material strength and efficiency of the American fighting machine. These successive events have shaken the complacent acceptance of British leadership in the minds of all that section of the community whose education has not so imbued them with a sense of the cultural predominance of England as to create habitual acquiescence in whatever emanates from there.

The result of this impact of events has not been a tendency to break loose from the British Commonwealth. Nor has it been a tendency to change from a leaning on England to a leaning on America. It has, instead, issued in a conviction that Australia and New Zealand, together, must make their voices heard in the British Commonwealth and in the United Nations. In the former Australia is of sufficient im-

[9] *Ibid.*

portance to be heard with respect if she raises her voice. In the latter she has found, through the leadership of her Minister for External Affairs, Dr. Evatt, that by rallying the small nations of the world to join her in insisting on their rights her voice can also be heard.

To the non-Labor parties the policy thus pursued appears a mistaken departure from Australia's proper and traditional support of British policy. This was made clear by R. G. Menzies in 1946. "The basic defect of the Australian Government's policy or, at any rate, the policy of the present Minister for External Affairs, is—in practice and probably also in theory—that it aims at utter independence of Australian thought and action (which for seven million people in a remote island continent, is more pretentious than sensible) as if no special British relation existed at all. . . . The United Nations is experimental. It must be tried, but not beyond its strength and its true nature must not be mistaken. If some of us continue to emphasize that the British Empire is not experimental, but tried and proved, it is merely because we know that every nucleus of peace and non-aggression and goodwill within the international structure is a mighty source of strength for the United Nations organization." [10]

Between these two positions the difference is not really sharp. Both recognize that Australia's security rests upon the maintenance of the United Nations and the British Commonwealth. Both are directed to maintaining the strength and integrity of the two organizations. But one is moved by a sentimental and cultural attachment and the memory of an historic association to place the emphasis on the British

[10] From a speech by R. G. Menzies, Leader of the Opposition, in the federal parliament, March 20, 1946. *Commonwealth Parliamentary Debates, 17th Parliament, 3rd Session, No. 3*, 437–444.

connection and leave the leadership to the senior partner. The other, adopting a more critical attitude toward the historic policy of Britain, especially as to its imperialism, seeks to play an active part in implementing a program of security and freedom for small nations through both instrumentalities.

- 10 -

Underlying Concepts and Attitudes

ONE of the best moving pictures produced by the infant Australian cinema industry is "Forty-Thousand Horsemen," a mingling of history and fiction based on the activities of the Australian Light Horse in the Palestine campaign in the first World War. In one scene a group of soldiers around a camp fire discuss the question of what they are fighting for. Finally, one man sums up his conception of the war's objectives in terms that are intelligible and acceptable to all: it is being fought for "the right to tell the boss what to do with his job if you don't want it." The rough phrase states vividly the essential condition of that freedom for which the youth of Australia have volunteered to fight in two world conflicts. There can be no real freedom without economic freedom. The essence of slavery is not that a man must obey his employer's orders, but that he cannot leave that employer if he wants to. Freedom means that if a man is dissatisfied with the conditions under which he earns his livelihood he has the opportunity to seek better conditions elsewhere.

A more sophisticated soldier of the second World War might have expressed the same conviction by saying that the conflict was part of the struggle for the four freedoms, and that the other three freedoms could never be real without the fourth—freedom from want. It was thus expressed by one of the most conservative of Australia's former prime ministers. "All our aspirations are summarized in President Roosevelt's Four Freedoms. The desire of the ordinary man and woman is to live in a world from which the fear of war has been banished, and in which there is the opportunity to earn a decent livelihood, freed from the nightmare of destitution in times of unemployment, sickness and misfortune."[1]

There are those today who tell us that we cannot have both freedom and security, that we must either surrender our freedom in an economy planned and regimented along communist or fascist lines, or we must accept the insecurity of a laissez faire economy in which private enterprise and free competition bring some victoriously to the top while others are crushed in the struggle. If there is any meaning to be read in Australian political history it is the refutation of this thesis. If there is any underlying conviction on which we may be sure the Australian public will act, it is the thesis that freedom and economic security are both possible and inseparable. Every threat to freedom is treated as a threat to economic security, every threat to economic security as a threat to freedom.

No man is really free to leave a job he does not like unless he has a considerable assurance that he can find another.

[1] S. M. Bruce's farewell address to the Australian people on March 24, 1946, before his retirement to England. Text supplied by the Australian Broadcasting Company.

But the Australian's pride is stung to the quick if he is forced to show servility to his employer in order to keep his job. He despises a yes-man. He hates class distinctions. He is ready to make economic sacrifices to maintain his sense of social equality and independence. But there is a limit to the economic sacrifices any man can make. He must have access to the means of production or perish. If he has no productive property of his own, then he must find someone to employ him. If he knows that to give up the job he has is to find himself without means of support, then he knows he is a prisoner—a wage slave. If the employer demands that he be servile, then he must be servile or starve. No man is free unless he is able to defend his self-respect, if necessary, by throwing up his job with the assurance that he can find another.

There is therefore no real freedom for any man without economic security—without the assurance that there will be access somewhere to the means of production, or a market somewhere for the services he has to offer. This bitter lesson people learned everywhere in the days of the great depression.

In some countries the people, finding they had lost both security and freedom, were ready to accept a promise of the former without the latter. They bartered liberty for bread. In other countries the loss of both was endured for years in the hope that it would not be permanent. Australia, more vigorously than any other country in the world (except, perhaps, New Zealand), set to work to restore security and freedom together by means of democratic social planning.

Planned economy began in Australia when the state undertook to give the people the railway service which private enterprise could not provide. It was extended when the country abandoned the prime tenet of laissez faire by adoption of a protective tariff. This step led, in turn, to the activity of the state in the "orderly marketing" of primary products. And the mistakes and extremes of a tariff shaped by the influence of pressure groups led to the formation and growing influence of the Tariff Board, shaping a scientific tariff, so that the politician feels himself called upon to decide only questions of general policy. Similarly, the statutory commissions, which now control so large an area of the country's economic life, combine the control of the expert planner in matters of detail with the democratic decision of matters of broad policy through the people's ministers and parliaments. Above all, in the relation of employer and employee the old shibboleths of freedom of contract and collective bargaining have given way to the new province for law and order.

In brief, the Australians have, typically, sought to enlarge their freedom by the extension of the reign of law; they have used the activity of the state to open safe channels for the activity of the individual. They have insisted on democratic control of the state; and in their reluctance to extend federal power they have sought to keep the state close to the people. But in the problems faced by a handful of people struggling to make good use of a vast and difficult country they have discovered that the democratic state can be turned into a useful and powerful instrument of cooperative action. The common man manifests the same suspicion of the expert that he does in America. He does not return many scholars and scientists to parliament. He prefers the common touch in his political representatives. But both he and his political representatives are learning to make use of the expert in the execution of policies and as adviser in the shaping of them. In this way the planning which has been forced upon Australia in the struggle for that economic security and opportunity which is essential to real freedom has been developed in a way which provides that security without infringing upon the people's liberty. The only freedom that is being lost in Australia by the development of her planned economy is the freedom of the few to dominate the lives of the many by securing control of the means whereby the many must earn their livelihood.

The political caldron.— This development of a planned economy is the work of all three of the major parties active in Australian politics—the Labor, Liberal, and Country Parties and their variously named political antecedents. This is emphatically true of industrial arbitration, the orderly marketing of primary products, and public ownership of utilities. The only differences on these questions are in matters of detail in the planning. To a considerable extent this is also true even of the broader issue of socialization versus private enterprise. "The apostles of private enterprise realize that there are certain activities such as transport, electrical power and other vital services which should be controlled by the State on behalf of the people as a whole. On the other hand, the apostles of State enterprise recognize that many industries, particularly those producing consumer goods, should be left to private enterprise."[2]

Australia is committed, therefore, to a planned economy as surely as she is committed to the maintenance of democratic freedoms. Concerning the details of planning, of course, the opposing sides can strive mightily. In general, Labor wishes to go further and faster than its opponents. Both sides criticize each other concerning the methods and means chosen to attain similar ends. Each accuses the other of aiming eventually at extremes which it knows the country will not tolerate. The political pendulum swings to and fro. Every government makes political mistakes and its opponents can always be wise after the event and convince the constituents, in due course, that the time has come for a change.

[2] *Ibid.*

No really conservative party can long hold office in Australia. That does not mean that there are no conservatives in Australian politics. They are there, and they are active and influential. But no party could win an election under that name. Conservatives therefore find their place in the parties opposed to Labor along with those of a liberal but nonsocialistic turn of mind. The popular strength of the non-Labor parties has come from their absorption into their leadership of men like Hughes and Lyons who have broken with Labor over the handling of such crises as conscription and the great depression. And the conservatives in these parties are constantly finding themselves forced to give support to liberal measures in order to win votes for their party and maintain its solidity—as, for example, in the Liberal Party's adoption of the proposal to extend child endowment to the first child.

On the other hand, no really radical proposal ever appeals to the Australian electors. There is a large block of electors, chiefly of the lower-salaried class and small farmers, whose vote is turned first to one side and then to another. This floating vote sways the elections. In general it is anticonservative, but it is never radical. It requires time to get used to a new idea, and those who would move too far or too fast get out of touch with it. It is impatient with industrial unrest and if there are too many strikes it will vote against Labor. It is not doctrinaire but ready to judge every proposal on its merits, whether socialistic or not. The terms "private enterprise" and "free economy" are catchwords that have lost their power. Socialism has ceased to be a bugbear, but it has not become a moving slogan. The people expect much from the government—they expect it to step in and do for them whatever private enterprise fails to do. But they dislike government regimentation and they have only fretfully submitted to restrictions necessarily imposed by the war.

They are, on the whole, convinced that those things within the power of private enterprise and within the sphere of real competition are likely to be done more graciously and efficiently in that way than by the government.

Probably the greatest weakness in the Australian political situation is the scarcity of really able leaders. There are a few outstanding men on both sides, some of whom would make their mark in any gathering of the world's statesmen. But there are not enough who have both the ability to handle the problems of ministerial office and the capacity to think for themselves and resist the pressures of interested groups to which they are subjected. Such pressures can be resisted only by men of special ability, prestige, and force of character.

The Liberal and Country Parties, representing the classes that are economically better off, are more easily able to find men with education and professional and business experience. But the rewards of political life are not sufficient to attract many really able professional men; and business men and farmers rarely go into politics early enough to learn thoroughly the broader business of statesmanship. The trade-union movement selects as its leaders men of considerable native ability, the best of whom tend to attain the prize of parliamentary election. But most of these men have to overcome the initial handicap of poor education; and the rank and file of the working class tends to be suspicious of intellectuals. Both parties suffer from the fact that promising men are often lost by the swing of the political pendulum. And both have found it difficult to obtain a sufficient number of men of ministerial caliber and experience in a party consisting of a little more than half of a House of seventy-five members and a Senate numbering thirty-six.

In order to lessen this difficulty the 1948 parliament passed a measure to increase the membership of both houses

—the House of Representatives to one hundred and twenty-two members and the Senate to sixty. But even this still does not solve the problem of that insecurity of tenure which makes it so difficult to persuade able men to run for political office and to retain them in parliamentary bodies long enough to gain experience and knowledge sufficient for cabinet responsibility. Here a new departure seems to be called for, a departure which Australia and every other democracy—especially those with small legislatures—should seriously consider.

The problem of insecurity of tenure in parliament could be largely overcome by electing two members in each constituency, the one at the top of the poll to have both a voice and a vote and the second highest in the ballot to have a voice only. The result of an election could then change the voting strength of the parties in the legislature with little or no change in the personnel. Providing a member could win the preselection ballot (or primary) of his party he would, in a two-party system, retain his seat—with or without a vote. The insecurity of political office would be reduced to a minimum. Abler men and women would be attracted to seek election. And members would retain their seats long enough to gain political experience and knowledge of the affairs of government. Australia in particular, with her large-scale government activity in economic affairs, would be well advised to adopt such a method of improving the efficiency of her parliament and cabinet.

The Cooperative Commonwealth and class war.— The Australian philosophy of the state is neither that of individualism nor of socialism. It might be called that of the Cooperative Commonwealth. Still an unwritten philosophy, the cooperative idea is tacitly assumed by all three major parties in their appeal to the electors because they know the electors believe that the state is the chief instrument of cooperative action whereby the people undertake to do all those things that can be better done collectively than individually. The function of the government as policeman—as an authority regulating and confining the activity of the individual—has become overshadowed by that of the government as an instrument of economic and cultural activity.

There are other cooperative instruments, including producers' and consumers' cooperatives, trade unions, and joint stock companies, but these are sectional and partial organizations. The all-inclusive piece of social machinery is the state; and to the Australian it has an all-inclusive purpose. He is not afraid of it, for he feels himself in control of it; and he is learning constantly how to use it to meet his needs. If there is anything wrong that cannot be readily remedied by the individual himself, then he insists that the government do something about it. What is demanded is not state paternalism, but the interest and cooperation of the state in solving the problems of the individual. If the solution requires some regulation of individual activity the citizens are ready to submit and cooperate so long as the results are worthwhile, but they demand a change if they find that the new law or institution tends to limit their power and freedom more than it enlarges them.

There is nothing revolutionary about this conception of the state. It is definitely evolutionary. The Australian politician does not promise a "new deal," but he constantly speaks of a "fair deal." A "fair deal" means equality of opportunity and the adjustment of burdens according to the ability to bear them. And it means constant adjustment. There is nothing rigid about this typically Australian conception of the function of the state. It is purely experimental. The state is a piece of machinery to be used for any purpose for which it can be made to work successfully; if one method does not succeed another must be tried. Voters have shown reluctance to extend the power of the federal machine, but that is not through any sense of the sacredness of the constitution. It is rather that the voter feels that he exercises more personal influence in the local state machine and prefers to keep as many functions as possible for the machine where he feels his own weight is more effective.

The structure of social security, which the citizen believes he has a right to expect of the state, is now almost complete. All parties are committed to its maintenance and completion. The same may be said of the policy of high employment. No government is likely to live long which does not maintain that policy with vigor. Over the socialization issue political battles will be fought, but socialization will advance just so far as the people become convinced that it justifies itself in practice—and no further.

The issues within the Cooperative Commonwealth therefore, though important, are not vital. All the three major parties can function within this concept and have a useful part to play in the constant readjustment and perfecting of the structure of the state which embodies it. Outside of this area of thought, however, lies the force that is really opposed to it—doctrinaire communism. Whether this force constitutes a real threat to the structure of the Cooperative Commonwealth only the future can reveal.

Thus far the Communists have elected only one member to a state parliament (Queensland) and none to the federal. But they have obtained positions of leadership in many of the more important trade unions. Their aim is to capture the trade-union movement and through it the Labor Party, making the Communist Party (even if called "Labor") the official opposition. From that position they would hope that the opportunity would eventually arise whereby they could, constitutionally or otherwise, lay hold of the reigns of government. Thereafter there would be no more free elections.

The economic, political, and military successes of the Russians greatly enhanced their prestige during the war years in Australia as in America. Australian Communists followed the party line, first opposing the war as "imperialist" and then, after the attack on Russia, urging all-out cooperation. During this latter stage they won popularity with the workers, for they proved themselves very active and successful in keeping men on the job, increasing output, and securing improvements in pay and conditions of work. By the time the conflict was over they had placed themselves in a strong position in the trade-union movement.

The peacetime policy now being adopted by the Communists is definitely intended to see that the Cooperative Commonwealth shall not be allowed to function successfully. A contented working class is of no use to a revolutionary movement. The first objective of their attack is the Arbitration Court system. Strikes have been fomented against the rulings of the Courts; however, this policy has not had the effect desired. It has weakened the grip of the Communists on the unions. But it has also weakened the popularity of the Labor Party in the country. If the Communists should succeed in continuing to stir up industrial strife it must end in the defeat of the Labor government and would probably bring about an attempt by a non-Labor government to crush the Communist-controlled unions with punitive legislation. Such an attack would strengthen Communist sentiment in the whole working-class movement. Those who had suffered for the cause might well be admitted into the Labor Party. Labor would be further weakened at the polls, but Communist influence within the Party might become dominant. In this way the conservatives within the non-Labor parties might defeat the political Labor movement, but in doing so, help to put communism into the place it covets—the official opposition.

If the propagation of the class war should thus succeed in stultifying or breaking down the Cooperative Commonwealth, it would not necessarily mean an ultimate victory for communism. In Australia as in other highly civilized countries of today, the so-called masses on whom the Communists rely for their strength are now a decided minority of the whole population. If the middle class, which is now by far the largest class, becomes sufficiently annoyed by the industrial turmoil of militant unions it will support repressive measures. The government in power has only to allow unemployment to develop and the tactics of militant unionism can be defeated. All Australian industrial history shows that direct action is successful only in times of prosperity and of full employment. And civilization has now reached the stage where full employment can be maintained only by deliberate government activity. It is thus within the power of any government to defeat direct action and break militant unionism by allowing unemployment to develop. Normally, the middle-class vote would not be likely, in the future, to tolerate a government that allows unemployment. But unemployment following on industrial strife will not be blamed on the government, but on the makers of industrial strife.

It therefore would appear that the Communist program is likely to be self-defeating. If the unions are persuaded to surrender the arbitration system for direct action they will defeat the political Labor movement and strengthen conservative and reactionary influence in the non-Labor parties. They will bring about unemployment which will defeat direct action in the industrial field; and they will put power into the hands of those of their political enemies who will use the forces of law to suppress them.

On the other hand the use of strong measures to repress trade-union militancy led by Communists would probably not succeed in such repression without a prolonged battle which, in its earlier stages, would strengthen the grip of the radical element upon the trade-union movement and the political Labor movement. And victory in that battle could be won by the employers only after the development and during the maintenance of a considerable measure of unemployment. So long as the spirit of militancy remained in the union movement the restoration of prosperity would only create the opportunity for that militancy to manifest itself again in action. No one who knows the Australian working man can reasonably believe that repressive measures directed at his chosen leaders can ever lessen trade-union militancy. Repressive measures can therefore only prolong the status of class war and unemployment, every temporary revival of prosperity merely reviving militancy on the one hand, strengthening political reaction on the other, and flinging the country back into depression.

It is improbable, however, that these gloomy possibilities will be realized. They are pointed out here simply to indicate the consequences that would be likely to follow the policies advocated by the extreme Left and extreme Right in Australian politics. The policies of both extremes are self-defeating, and therefore it is doubtful that they will find much support among a people as politically competent as the Australians. The Cooperative Commonwealth therefore appears to be very securely founded in spite of the rumblings of class war.

Most of the stress in the present political and industrial life of the country is due to the aftermath of the depression. The paradox of povery in the midst of plenty was particularly striking in a young, underdeveloped country like Australia. The worker is convinced that it was unnecessary. But he fears that it may be brought upon him again. He is determined to make all the political and industrial gains he can while the present postwar prosperity lasts. For that reason he is impatient with the slow-moving Arbitration Court awards based on the statisticians' figures of living costs (which do not adequately reflect all increases) and the cautious estimates of judges concerning the ability of industry to stand wage increases and reduction of hours. There has, therefore, been a tendency to listen to Communist advice concerning direct action; and strikes have been frequent.

There are already signs, however, that this phase is passing. Communists have lost some important positions in the trade-union world as a result of the postwar strikes. Labor relations will certainly improve as it can be brought home to the consciousness of the worker that there is to be no more large-scale unemployment. It would greatly help if there could be some emphatic pronouncement by the leaders of industry, banking, and all three political parties to the effect that the causes of general depressions are now understood and that all are determined to support future action by whatever government is in power, so that full employment will be maintained.

Two things seem to be necessary if any improvement is to be obtained in the attitude of the Australian worker toward his work. One is the assurance that when a job is finished there is always another waiting to be done, that improved methods and high production will not mean that there is less work to be distributed among those seeking employment, now or in the future. The other is that the Arbitration Court practice of reducing wages when the cost of living falls must cease. The worker must be assured that he and all his class will be allowed to share in the benefits when they cooperate to increase output per man and lower the general price level. If the leaders of Australian political and industrial life will give these assurances they will rapidly find a change in the psychological attitudes of the workers.

Class conflict is no new thing in Australian life. It has been manifest, as our historical chapters have revealed, from the beginning. But Australia has, from the beginning, been moving toward the elimination of class struggle. Nowhere in the world is wealth more evenly distributed. Never in the country's history has it been more evenly distributed than it is today. The sister dominions of Australia and New Zealand, with their new schemes of social security, family endowment, and high employment, promise to be among the first countries in the world able to make the proud boast that they have permanently and completely abolished poverty from their shores. They are lands where it will be exceedingly difficult for anyone in the future to grow very rich, but where it will be impossible for anyone to be very poor. There will still be considerable differences of income and larger differences in possessions. But even these will tend to decrease, and if, in the face of the world uncertainties of the twentieth century, these conditions can be maintained for a few decades, the spirit of the class war will die. A genuinely classless society will have been achieved without a dead level of equality—not by means of the class war, but in spite of it. The structure of the Cooperative Commonwealth, the main features of which are already formed, will be stabilized, the details filled out and improved. Future generations will be able to adapt and perfect it free from the internal stresses of a class struggle which they will have outgrown.

- 11 -

Contemporary Party Policies:
The Liberal Party

by A. Grenfell Price
and Colin G. Kerr

THE Liberal Party of Australia is vigorous and progressive, and possesses a remarkable degree of unity considering that it is composed of autonomous state branches. Its members work by the yardstick of experience and common sense. They are alive to the need for remedying abuses and for going ahead in a moderate and cautious spirit, but they regard the New Order in its more extreme forms with a wary and skeptical eye.

There is no Conservative Party as such in Australia. The Liberal Party is conservative in the sense that it resists socialism, but both its platform and personnel are in general highly progressive, as is shown by the fact that Liberals under various names have been responsible for the chief advances in Commonwealth social legislation—for example, industrial arbitration (1904), old-age and invalid pensions (1902–08), and child endowment (1941).

Together with the Country Party, the Liberal Party of Australia represents those people who support democratic liberalism as against communism and state socialism. It is an adult party, reinforced by experienced older men and plentifully infused with younger men who have helped to defend the country in war and are determined that its fine record of achievement shall be maintained in peace.

The Liberal Party's opponents—as distinct from the many thousands who support liberal principles in general but whose conditioning inhibits them from having truck with anything bearing the name Liberal—call it reactionary. The reason for this apparent contradiction in terms may be sought for back in the days when Liberals were regarded by a large section of the people as being anti-Labor, that is, antiworking-class. But a reason more significant of our times is that political terminology has changed its color in Australia, as elsewhere, during and since the war; and terms are now being bandied about which have little or no connection with the parties to which they are applied. If Communists can claim to be democratic, it is no wonder that Liberals can be accused of being reactionary.

The opponents of liberalism are chiefly to be found in the left wing of the Labor Party and in the Communist Party, whose agents are now entrenched throughout the trade-union system, and who work in an uneasy but nevertheless actual alliance with the militant industrial elements of Labor.

In point of fact, no party can govern Australia without the support of the workers; and in times of difficulty like the war of 1914–18 and the depression of the early 1930's, the Liberals were undoubtedly supported by many members of the trade unions.

Today, it is noticeable that the Labor Party, which recruits under the banners of freedom, progress, and planning for economic security, is appearing under a darker aegis— that of a bureaucracy which believes that the way to human happiness is through more and more government action and control.

During the war many Australians regimented their lives in a service pattern for several years in order to fight fascism in the field, while many others on the home front submitted to governmental regimentation on an unprecented scale in order, in the words of the late John Curtin, to "back the attack."

This state of affairs was so nearly inevitable in the circumstances that it is unnecessary to question it in retrospect. The point at issue is whether the mentality of regimentation by government shall be encouraged to persist and develop still further in Australia. The Liberal Party says no, and in doing so it is prompted not by a concern for vested interests, which are already in the melting pot, but by a conviction that the individual in the new social order now emerging must not be frustrated by excessive governmental controls. It believes that only by shifting the emphasis from controls to high production and free enterprise within a government framework can prosperity be achieved.

Liberals recognize the danger of wartime controls being clamped permanently on a nation which is punch-drunk from controls and which may scarcely have the will to resist. The question as to what extent Australians have lost the sense of their rights and responsibilities as individuals is an absorbing one to the Liberal Party and this explains why phrases like individual rights, free enterprise, and incentive to earn and save appear so often in Liberal writing.

Federal Labor, which still claims to have saved Australia during the war, despite the fact that it did little more than pluck the fruits planted and tended by the Liberal and Country Party governments before it, has emerged with waning credit. Punitively high taxation, ruinously wasteful spending, and an inability to govern, as distinct from controlling, are its distinguishing features. In Liberal eyes, federal Labor wears the dingy livery of a bureaucracy composed largely of mediocre men whose passionate zeal for power far exceeds their ability to use that power in the interests of the people.

Under their ineffectual cloak, communism flourishes. Foreign relations deteriorate alarmingly; huge stores of future calamity are laid up in the way of lost trade and lost good will with our nearest neighbors, the Dutch; real power shifts from the seat of government to the union bosses on the waterfront and in the mines and factories, and the country drifts inexorably into a state of chaos. Frustration is the keynote of daily life—and this in the midst of plenty.

Liberals point to a paradoxical state of affairs in which the very people who tolerate inefficiency and condone lawlessness are also the busiest planners, meddlers, and graspers after power that the country has ever seen.

The Communists, who until recently were regarded as rather funny in much the same way as Hitler was regarded by the British world in the early thirties, have demonstrated to a dazed public that they hold Labor spellbound and can make the whole population of Australia dance to their tune. Labor publicly repudiates any alliance with them, yet at the same time Labor Ministers confer with Communist union bosses in frantic attempts to settle the constant lawless strikes which the Communists call whenever the tactical situation suits them, and usually for no other reason at all. The Communists, on their side, urge a united front with Labor against the Liberal "reactionaries."

Liberals believe that if Labor offers a strangling but muddling bureaucracy, the only thing the Australian people can expect from communism is a stark dictatorship. But the Communist Party, like its fellow socialist body, the Labor Party, hides its purpose under the old brave banners of freedom, progress, and economic security. And human nature and intelligence being what they are, the Communist Party is growing in power in Australia, especially among the young, irresponsible, and discontented. Moreover, by a system of staff work which is purely military, the Communists control the key unions of supply and transport, and through them they influence the daily lives of all Australians.

The Liberal Party is the implacable enemy of communism. The only effective resistance to communism in Australia comes from the Liberal and Country Parties and from strong Catholic elements within the Right and Center ranks of Labor. Considerations of political expediency, however, often hamper the Labor enemies of communism, although credit is due to them for the tenacity of their resistance. The Liberal Party, with its strong influence in city communities as well as its widespread rural interests, is the group best fitted to fight the Communists. The Liberal Party, unlike the Country Party, does not wish to see the Communist Party declared illegal. (Communist sabotage of the war effort made this step necessary during the administration of the Menzies Government. And the Communist Party was an illegal organization until the Labor government lifted the ban, on receipt of a Communist undertaking to behave, thus allowing the Red Fifth Column to function freely again.) The Liberal Party does not want to see Communists prosecuted as Communists; but when they become lawbreakers, it will have them brought to account, particularly when, in defiance of court rulings, they foment strikes which paralyze the community and throw thousands out of jobs.

The Liberal Party's hatred of communism, it may be said, goes further than politics and reaches back into morals. In denying the individual his rights of private ownership, and in representing him as a mere unit in an all-important state, the Communist makes the moderate and cautious Liberal see red. And that is what is happening today. That, above all, has made the Liberal Party take the offensive.

The Liberal Party of Australia, under that name, was formed late in 1944. It was the result of a conference convened in Canberra by R. G. Menzies, leader of the United Australia Party and prime minister from 1939 to 1941, in an endeavor to secure unity among the non-Labor political organizations and to form an Australia-wide federal body, working under a common constitution and with common objectives. The party actually came into being at a conference held in Albury in December, 1944.

There is still no amalgamation between the Liberal and Country Parties, except in South Australia, but an ultimate amalgamation is one of the aims of the Liberal Party. To contest the federal election of 1946, a happy arrangement was reached to ensure that when both Liberal and Country Party candidates were standing there would be no real conflict between them, and an exchange of preferences was agreed upon. For the Senate, joint teams, consisting of two Liberals and one Country Party candidate, were selected.

Thus was brought about an Australia-wide Liberal Party, working for a common purpose and with a single constitution, but in which state divisions have complete autonomy in the control of their own affairs, including the selection and endorsement of parliamentary candidates. Its objective, as set out in the constitution, is to create an Australian nation in which an intelligent, free, and liberal democracy shall be maintained by: 1) parliament controlling the Executive and the Law controlling all; 2) freedom of speech, religion, and association; 3) freedom of citizens to choose their own way of living and life, subject to the rights of others; 4) the protection of the people against exploitation; 5) the encouragement of individual initiative and enterprise as the dynamic force of reconstruction and progress.

Stress is laid on Australia's place in the British Commonwealth of Nations, on national defense as "a matter of universal duty," on preference to ex-service men and women in employment, on social benefits on a contributory basis and free from a means test, and on education. The Liberal Party wants to see an Australia "in which family life is recognized as fundamental to the well-being of society, and in which every family is entitled to live in a comfortable home at reasonable cost, and with adequate community amenities." In other words, Liberals desire a free but stabilized society—one in which the people have individual responsibilities and enjoy certain communal benefits—as distinct from the pauper state of the Socialists.

In stating its aims for Australia as a nation, the Liberal platform specifies full Australian participation in the United Nations organization and acceptance of the responsibilities arising under the charter. And as a first practical contribution to the success of the U. N. it demands close collaboration with Great Britain and the other British countries, not only on the political plane, but by active association in the problems of Empire marketing. Great Britain is recognized as the best customer for most of Australia's primary products.

The Liberal emphasis on Australian relations with the Mother Country contrasts strongly with the Anglophobia of the Communists and the churlish indifference to the affairs of the British Commonwealth displayed by the Labor Socialists even after the outbreak of World War II.

The Liberal platform says that Australia must have a clearly defined foreign policy. Australia is a continent of seven million people, with the myriads of an awakening Asia on her doorstep. She has long held to the White Australia policy, for economic rather than racial reasons, because the Australian workman refuses to have his standards lowered by the importation of coolie labor. The Australian workman, however, in the absence of properly supervised union ballots, now takes his orders from the union boss. We thus have the situation of Australian workmen supporting the cause of Asiatics in Indonesia, regardless of the gallant part which the Dutch played in delaying the Japanese attack on the Australian continent.

The new Liberal policy towards population and immigration has not been developed in detail, but in the past the Liberal Party has furthered immigration in contrast to the selfish Labor policy of isolation. Liberals wish to see the country placed on a healthy economic footing by means of reduced taxation and increased production, and they hope that an influx of population will follow. The policy, significantly, begins with the encouragement of home and family life by appropriate economic measures and by financial assistance to the states for the extension of maternity services and infant welfare. Liberals recognize that the Australian baby is the best immigrant, and they have accepted the idea of charity beginning at home as a truism which must not be overlooked.

The Liberals austerely go on to say that they wish to give "encouragement and assistance to those persons of British race who desire to settle in Australia." A campaign for obtaining "suitable migrants to the limit of Australia's absorptive capacity" is advised, together with proper publicity methods and the development of amenities to attract tourists.

It would be wrong to say that in specifying migrants of British race the Liberals are exercising racial discrimination. Like their American cousins, the Australians curtailed colored immigration after unfortunate economic and health experiences with Chinese and South Sea Islanders. They have found that Germans and Italians form racial groups that are difficult to assimilate and that Southern Europeans, imported for the primary industries, drift to the towns. The Liberals have imposed those limits not arbitrarily, but in the conviction that Australia first needs to set her own house in order and that she may then go on to admit migrants who may be expected to play a worthy part in the life of the country.

Closely linked with the question of population is that of defense. Under Liberal leadership the Commonwealth was the first British nation to put compulsory military service on the Statute Book, and the Liberal Party still stands realistically for this unpopular but necessary means of defense. Labor prefers to evade the issue and refers to the adequacy of the existing services. It keeps an eye on the votes of those millions who are unwilling to give even a small part of their time to training for the defense of their country. One of the things that lost the non-Labor parties the 1943 elections was their forthright advocacy of conscription. Labor preferred to use the volunteer forces until they were drained dry in battle. It is true that the Japanese menace forced John Curtin, the Labor prime minister at that time, to persuade both caucus and parliament to permit Australian conscripts to serve in a small area in the north of Australia, but this was poor recompense when drafted American troops were doing so much to help save the Commonwealth.

Liberals believe that pensions and retiring allowances must be provided for all permanent forces. Munitions industries, with research facilities, must be maintained. The military survey of Australia, its territories, and surrounding waters must be completed. In all problems of defense, Australian plans must be coordinated with those of the other British countries.

The Liberal attitude contrasts with that of Labor, which has never shown itself defense-minded, largely because of its isolationist outlook and its desire to expend all available funds on social services. As late as 1938 Curtin, then leader of the opposition, said, "Any increase of defense expenditure after the Munich Pact, as far as Australia is concerned, appears to me to be an utterly unjustifiable and hysterical piece of panic propaganda." And E. J. Holloway, later Minister for Labor and National Service, said, "I do not charge the Government with not spending enough money on defense . . . . I think it is spending too much."

Then war came. Prime Minister Menzies pledged Australia's immediate and full support. He sought the aid of all political parties "because we are all Australians here, and we are all British subjects." The Australian people flocked to the call, particularly after the fall of France when England lay open to invasion; but Labor's reaction was to seek to limit the Australian contribution to continental defense. Curtin spoke out against the dispatch of an expeditionary force—this at a time when Churchill, the realist, was dispatching forces which Britain could ill spare from a beleaguered homeland to meet the enemy on the banks of Suez, Australia's western gateway.

Some of the most striking differences between the Liberal and Labor Parties may be seen in their attitudes toward constitutional matters. The Liberal Party wishes to have an elected national convention to review the working of the Constitution and, where necessary, to make recommendations for its amendment. The aim of such a convention would be to preserve the federal system and to simplify and improve the machinery of government by the rearrangement of powers between the states and the Commonwealth. The Labor attitude is that, if the Party wants to amend the Constitution, referendums should be made directly to the people, with strong directions to them to follow the party line.

In matters of public administration generally, the Liberal Party looks to the states far more than does Labor. Liberals remember that the states are still sovereign states and that they have not abused that sovereignty. Labor tends toward unification and bureaucracy in the myopic belief that a bureaucracy entrusted with tremendous powers will be able to exercise such powers on behalf of the people. The Liberal Party, although strongly conscious of the federal concept, is alive to the danger of a centralized bureaucracy in Canberra, which is distant from all the Australian capitals except Sydney.

Probably neither the Liberal nor Labor Party has fully grasped the American principle of using the states as a proper decentralized agency by which the people's standards can be raised through the distribution of federal powers. Liberals, however, believe in preserving state rights. The six Australian state governments cover an area larger than that of the American Union, and Liberals think that the men on the spot know what is best for their own state. They are sympathetic toward local governing bodies and do not despise them as "curb and gutter authorities."

Liberals believe in an efficient and well paid civil service, but will not tolerate bureaucratic control. They demand the retrenchment of wartime government departments which are no longer necessary and the progressive removal of unwarranted restrictions on industrial and civil activities.

In finance, as might be expected, Labor's policy is directed towards socialism. The Liberal policy leans toward private enterprise, but Liberals believe that private enterprise should function within a government framework and that certain public utilities—for example, railways, telephones, heat, and light—are in some cases best operated as government enterprises. As R. G. Menzies has said, an elector need not be a Socialist to believe that the state should run the railways or the tramways or some big source of electrical power.

In the field of air transportation, the Liberal Party stands for "no nationalization—no monopoly," whereas Labor has already attempted, unsuccessfully, to obtain sole control of

Australian airlines. Regarding land transportation, Liberals recognize that Australia's huge distances may prevent a private concern from trying to operate at a profit, particularly as far as freight is concerned. The Australian railways, for example, generally operate at a loss caused in great measure by freight charges being kept down to a level that primary and other producers can afford. It is thus seen that the Liberal Party, although it does not stand for "rugged individualism" in its completely unfettered sense, is opposed to the classic Labor objectives of the socialization of industry, production, distribution, and exchange.

These objectives have involved Labor in a fantastic expenditure of public money. The Liberal Party wants to cut down on wasteful government spending by eliminating extravagance and inefficiency, and, with that task accomplished, to reduce the income tax by forty per cent from its 1946 level and place social services on a contributory basis. Here the motives are both practical and moral, if the terms may be so used. The Liberals would reduce taxation in order to give the ordinary man some incentive to earn and save with the knowledge that his earnings will be under his own command instead of in a great measure going down the government sink. They want to introduce contributory social insurance, free of a means test, so that the citizen may feel that he has earned the benefits to which he is entitled and not that such benefits are a "charity" in the modern sense—in other words a dole which is as remote from true charity as a stone is from bread.

It is only by a reduction in taxation that any incentive can be given for the worker to earn higher wages and for the employer to extend his enterprises. Only by providing an incentive to work and to expand can Australia hope to produce the goods which she and the rest of the world so badly need to replace the wastage of war. Liberals believe, therefore, that if taxation is cut to such an extent that the current of economic life flows again with unrestricted freedom, the net return to the Treasury will not show a loss.

Another lively problem in Australia today is that of the nationalization of medical services. Liberals oppose it on the ground that it would lower the whole standard of medical practice and that the public health would suffer. The doctor-patient relationship, so important from the psychological as well as the clinical angle, would be broken up; consultations would become like army sick parades; the patient would not be able to choose his or her own doctor; and the doctor himself would tend to adopt the civil service mentality, looking to his departmental head for recognition and approbation rather than to his colleagues or patients.

As far as the writers are aware, no alternative plan to the nationalization of medicine has been put forward by the Liberal Party, but it is altogether possible that the party would endorse a scheme such as that of the British Medical Association in England, whereby doctors vastly increase the scope of their social service work while retaining their identity as individual practitioners.

Australia, like every nontotalitarian country, is wondering how to gain sufficient peace in industry for the production of even the necessary bare minimum of goods. The Liberal Party has no magic wand to wave, but it believes that the industrial situation would be very much better if the following common sense rules were observed. Wages should be the highest and conditions the best that the industry concerned can provide. There must be a constant educational campaign against the employee's notion that the interests of the employer and the employee are opposed and against the employer's view that claims for increased wages and better conditions should be automatically contested. Profit-sharing schemes should be introduced wherever practicable. There must be provision on the fullest scale for prompt conciliation and arbitration. Moreover, the democratic control of unions by a secret ballot is essential. The workers must be given the right to say whether they wish to strike or not, whether they wish to have Communist leaders or not.

Liberals reject the idea that industrial arbitration and direct action can go together. Their platform makes provision for action against those responsible for illegal strikes. They also say that the basic wage should be brought into line with the increased cost of living.

The Liberal Party does not fall into the evident Labor error of thinking of the whole population of Australia in terms of industrial workers and bosses. It believes in helping the small businessman and small farmer and in regulating monopolies harmful to the public interests.

12

Contemporary Party Policies:
The Country Party

by J. P. Abbott

TOWARD the end of the first World War it became evident that a new political philosophy was crystallizing in rural areas. Dissatisfaction with the handling of wartime marketing operations, instability in the price structure, fluctuating production, and a realization of the need for cooperation between primary producers in the disposal of their products strengthened those farm organizations already in existence, brought new ones into being, and inspired sympathetic spokesmen in the Commonwealth and state parliaments.

It became apparent in those years also that the rapid growth of large cities was no passing phase, but represented a movement which would perpetuate dominance of the political field by the representatives of metropolitan areas. More than half the population of Australia was already grouped in a few coastal cities; and the voters in those cities were able to secure the enactment of programs inimical to the welfare of the inhabitants of the vast areas of primary production outside the metropolitan zones.

The realization that this position was being rapidly consolidated induced rural leaders to seek political means for correcting the lack of balance in Australian affairs. Subdivision of the unwieldly states of the federation was actively advocated. A People's Convention was sought to revise the constitution. Electoral reform was demanded.

Though there were active sympathizers of the rural movements in the national parliament, there was no parliamentary Country Party before 1918. In that year a returned soldier named Stanley Melbourne Bruce was nominated as the National Party candidate for the Victorian electorate of Flinders, following the appointment of the previous member (Sir William Irvine) to the High Court. The Labor Party announced that it would contest the seat; and the Victorian Country Party entered the field with a candidate also. The voting system which operated at that time was the "first-past-the-post" system under which the candidate polling the most primary votes would win, even though he may have polled only a little more than a third of the total votes cast. The rural movement had heartily condemned the system, but used the Flinders by-election as a means of achieving its first political victory. The Country Party agreed to vacate the field on the condition that the National Party introduce the preferential system of voting forthwith. The National government, following the election of S. M. Bruce, introduced the necessary legislation, and the Country Party contested and won another by-election later in the same year conducted on preferential principles, defeating the National Party candidate, the Labor Party candidate, and two independents.

In the following year (1919) ten Country Party members were elected to the Commonwealth parliament from various states, and in the ensuing three years they conducted vigorous guerilla warfare against the National government led by W. M. Hughes and against the Labor Party. The original party was led by an old campaigner from Tasmania, W. J. McWilliams, who very soon handed over the leadership to the Party's whip, returned at the 1919 elections, Dr. (now Sir) Earle Page.

The party was immediately under fire from all quarters. Vested political interests resented the entry of a third party into the arena, and while they contended that the traditional two-party system was the mainstay of stable government, neither the National Party nor the Labor Party offered to obliterate themselves to permit the continuance of the two-party standard. The Country Party made no apologies for standing firmly by its determination to maintain its independence. The Labor Party had not yet recovered from the disintegration which followed a major disagreement among its members on the conscription issue when its leader (W. M. Hughes) led a number of his supporters out of the party room to form the National Party in conjunction with the Liberal Party of that day. The National government emerged from the war years in triumph, but like many other triumphant wartime governments, the tree of success spread the seeds of dissolution.

When the 1922 elections were over, the Country Party had increased its numbers to fourteen. What the Hughes Government dreaded had come to pass. The Country Party held the balance of power. The Party had made its attitude clear at the 1922 elections—both in regard to its far-reaching policy and in regard to cooperation with other parties. In the 1922 election manifesto the Country Party leader (Earle Page) declared: "The question has been raised as to how far the C.P. is prepared to work in harmony with other parties in Parliament. In this regard, we can only say that while we are not prepared to enter into any entangling alliances which would in any way destroy the entity of the C.P., we are prepared to co-operate with any other representatives of the people upon the floor of the House, or in the conduct of the country, who hold the same ideals and principles which we advocate. . . . The Party is prepared to accept the full responsibility attendant upon its entry into politics, and should it be called on to take up the reins of government, it will not shirk its duty."

The Country Party made it clear also that it would not enter into any arrangement with the National Party except on clearly defined terms. Replacement of the National Party's leader by a more acceptable person was a primary requirement, and the countrymen sought guarantees that the comprehensive policy enunciated by their leader at the elections would be carried out. Finally S. M. Bruce became leader of the National Party, and a coalition government was formed, with the official title of the Bruce-Page Government. The Country Party accepted five portfolios; its leader was recognized as a joint leader of the government and deputy prime minister; and strong guarantees were given on policy. The Bruce-Page Government gave Australia a stable and fruitful administration for the next seven years.

In the sphere of policy, the Country Party was in a strong position. During the previous years the party had forged upon the political battlefield an integrated national policy of reconstruction and development. Knowing what they wanted, the countrymen were able to attain an incredible number of constructive achievements, as the history of the next ten years was to prove. The policy speech of the Country Party leader at the 1922 elections forecast a comprehensive program of financial adjustment, a policy which suggested the machinery ultimately established and incorporated in the Commonwealth Constitution for the stabilization of the debt position, the National Debt Sinking Fund, and the

Australian Loan Council, now very well known to the Australian people as the salient features of the "Financial Agreement."

The speech outlined the reconstruction of the Commonwealth Bank along the lines of legislation which was enacted during the next few years, placing the bank under the control of an independent Board of Directors, representative of various industries, and withdrawing the note issue from political control.

It drew attention also to the outstanding characteristic of Australian primary production—fluctuations due to periodic dry seasons, which tended to unstabilize the national position, militating against continuity of employment in both city and country. Abundant seasons brought low prices which adversely affected the ability of the farmer to purchase goods and services. Scarcity meant low returns and poor buying capacity. Only in average seasons was there stability. Australia's first policy was to guard against these fluctuations. Apart from the general reconstruction of the Commonwealth Bank already referred to, the Party advocated the establishment of a Rural Credits Branch to finance orderly and cooperative marketing, and this was established by the composite government some three years later.

Finally, the policy speech promised to give every assistance to the establishment of cooperative control of meat, wool, wheat, sugar, fruit, and other primary industries by placing each in the hands of marketing organizations on which the producers' representatives would be in the majority. This clause was the basis of the comprehensive marketing legislation passed during the next few years which has set the pattern of Australia's export marketing structure ever since. Export control boards were established for dairy products, meat, dried fruits, and canned fruits, and grants were made on a pound-for-pound basis to enable primary industries to maintain effective marketing and sales promotion campaigns in suitable markets, a provision which led to the expenditure of over one million pounds on such advertising by the time the second World War closed up the normal avenues of trade.

"In regard to tariff policy," says the Party's manifesto, "the party is prepared to grant reasonable protection to Australian production, but where it is necessary for any industry to receive further assistance, it should be by way of bounty. It will fight for a reduction of duties on the staple necessaries of the producers, and for the admission of implements and tools of trade free of duty when made within the Empire."

This is, by and large, the existing outlook of the Country Party. The tariff is, and always has been, a bone of contention between the Country Party and all other parties, whether labor or conservative. The Country Party is, generally, the advocate of low tariffs; the Labor and other (conservative) parties are advocates of higher protection. After the first World War, primary producers saw the manufacturer protected from outside competition by ever rising duties, while they themselves were obliged to sell their wool, wheat, and dairy products in the open markets of the world at world prices. Their position was worsened by the fact that high duties increased the cost of their implements and plants for the production of goods sold for low world prices. During the depression of the thirties, the Country Party criticized vigorously the tariff policy of the Scullin Labor Government which was marked by unprecedented embargoes, prohibitions, and other tariff devices imposed partly from economic and partly from protective motives. The Country Party was likewise a severe critic of the first Lyons Conservative Government which succeeded the Scullin Government, and declined to participate in its activities, mainly because of the difference in tariff policy.

Being a small party numerically, it became evident to its members within a short time of its formation that opposition to its tariff policy was too strong to permit successful frontal attack. Therefore, from about 1924 onwards, the Party evolved a policy "to permit the producers to break into the vicious circle" themselves. The Home Consumption Price policy of the Party, based on the principle of a domestic price for certain agricultural products, was in the process of evolution. This was regarded as a means of offsetting the effects of the tariff on the goods which producers must buy, and represented for the primary industries the equivalent of tariff protection for the manufacturers and wage fixation for the employees.

In 1926 the deputy leader of the Country Party, T. Paterson, propounded and obtained acceptance of a stabilization plan for the dairying industry. The scheme provided for the payment of a levy on all butter produced in Australia sufficient to pay a bounty on export sales. The local price was raised by the amount of the bounty, while the return to the producer on all butter produced was increased by approximately the difference between the rate of bounty paid and the rate of levy charged. This was a voluntary plan, but it was superseded in 1934, at the request of the industry, by a statutory equalization scheme which, however, was invalidated in 1936 by a decision of the Privy Council as contrary to the interstate free-trade principle of the constitution. The scheme was able to continue, however, by voluntary arrangement between the manufacturers and the Commonwealth Dairy Produce Equalization Committee, Limited. The effect of the arrangement was that local and export prices were distributed equitably among manufacturers by means of quotas. The committee fixed basic quotas and equalized returns to factories through an equalization fund. As the result of a comprehensive survey made by a Royal Commission on the wheat industry, sponsored by the Country Party, the wheatgrowers also received a home consumption price for the first time in history, and the principle is firmly established in the Party's policy.

Early in 1946 the Party crystallized its price policy still further, and the platform of the Australian Country Party now contains the following significant clauses:

> 1) For a period of ten years, payment of incentive-guaranteed minimum prices to producers to ensure continuity of production, to provide the ascertained costs of production plus a fair margin of profit to the producer, and to ensure a reasonable standard of comfort as well as the ability to pay not less than standard wages to employees.
>
> 2) Home consumption prices for all products consumed in Australia, fixed from time to time on the basis of costs of production and parity, plus an allowance for the burden on the export industries caused by Australian national policy in the case of wheat, the margin over production costs originally fixed to be at least maintained.
>
> 3) The cost of production to be ascertained by a representative interstate commission continuously investigating all production costs, including marketing and transport costs.
>
> 4) Guaranteed minimum prices to be determined after a survey of the ascertained production costs and price prospects, and varied upwards or downwards in accordance with the fluctuations therein.
>
> 5) A Stabilization Fund to be set up for each export primary industry so desiring, to which shall be paid (a) fifty per cent of the annual excess export realizations of the produce over the guaranteed minimum price, the other fifty per cent being distributed

among producers, and (b) proceeds of all other sales above the guaranteed price. Such fund to be used to maintain the guaranteed minimum price. The marketing of the product and the management of the stabilization fund to be vested in producer-controlled boards, such as the Australian Wheat Board and the Dairy Produce Board.

6) The difference between the export value of the product consumed in Australia (other than for human consumption) and the price determined by the government for sale to other primary producing industries for production purposes shall be paid out of consolidated revenue to the board controlling the marketing of the industry. This provision is to keep down costs to the consumer and prevent increased costs in other industries without loss to the industry concerned.

Current policy also places heavy emphasis on a national program of developmental undertakings based on regional organization. The Party proposes the establishment of special authorities, vested with Commonwealth and state powers, to undertake the balanced and integrated development of economic zones, involving provision of transport, establishment of suitable industries, water and power development, and organization of services generally. The Commonwealth should accept continuing responsibility for initiating and financing such schemes.

Water conservation programs should be initiated by the Commonwealth with state cooperation "until every stream which flows through areas of inadequate rainfall, and every stream which can be diverted into such areas, is brought so completely under control that no flood waters, which can be profitably used, are allowed to flow to waste." Soil erosion is accepted as a national problem of the first magnitude, and the Country Party proposes Commonwealth action to investigate and remedy its defects in cooperation with the states. Full development of hydroelectric resources and the exploitation of both black and brown coal deposits for the generation of electric power is also part of this comprehensive developmental program.

The Party's present program devotes special attention to the stimulation of rural development and a wider distribution of population by decentralization of industry, more intensive land settlement, and the provision of modern amenities in rural areas. Adequate transport services, extension of health and hospital services, educational, cultural, and recreational facilities for rural people, better rural housing, and the provision of basic services such as water and sewerage, power, and refrigeration are also stressed.

The Country Party advocates that Commonwealth Savings Bank funds should be earmarked for specific developmental projects—to assist local governing authorities to provide housing, to assist home building for persons of limited incomes, to foster approved secondary industries in rural districts, to assist land settlement by loans at lowest possible rates of interest, and to build up the funds available for the Mortgage Bank.

The industrial policy of the rural movement endorses the maintenance of the conciliation and arbitration system, recommends compulsory secret ballots conducted by the Industrial Registrar before strikes are held, and suggests an expert investigation into the existing basic-wage formula.

The Party is pledged to support a "White Australia," and believes in a vigorous immigration program to encourage, first, persons of British stock and, second, newcomers from the United States and other foreign nations.

A comprehensive policy of social security to give freedom from want and ensure the means of securing adequate food, clothing, and housing is part of the platform which also supports a national insurance scheme on a contributory basis to cover health, medical care, and superannuation.

The Country Party stands for the fullest collaboration with Great Britain and the rest of the British Commonwealth in international affairs, in defense plans, economic reconstruction, and the restoration of trade, aviation, and shipping.

Finally, the Country Party believes essentially in free enterprise as opposed to socialization.

13

Contemporary Party Policies:

The Labor Party

by W. C. Taylor
and Lloyd Ross

ARISING from the failure of the political parties existing in the seventies and eighties of the last century to satisfy the needs and aspirations of the people, the Australian Labor Party aims to improve the economic and social conditions of the people, to widen their opportunities, to improve their status as individuals and as citizens of an Australian Commonwealth. The final step in forming a new political party, independent of the existing parties, was taken by the trade unions, thereby not merely giving a major bias to the policy and control of the Party, but providing a backlog of strength, loyalty, and power.

Whatever may be the later developments of social and economic policies in Australia, there can be little criticism of the view that Labor obtained its chance to express the unsatisfied views of the people because non-Labor had for the time come to the end of its capacity to produce ideas and leaders that a democracy of the free equalitarian Australian type constantly demanded.   As significant as the widespread circulation of Edward Bellamy's *Looking Backward,* Henry George's *Progress and Poverty,* and Laurence Gronlund's *Co-operative Commonwealth* was the development in the nineties of an Australian literature and political writings based on nationalism, land reform, republicanism, trade unionism, and socialism.   The Labor Party gathered together a movement which included dissentients of many origins and idealists of many dreams.

The Labor Party was socialistic from the beginning in the vague sense that its members demanded state assistance whenever they were in difficulties, either because their unions were unable to raise standards quickly enough or because the geography and economics of the Australian continent assisted the development of industrial monopolies and large landed estates.   There were active Socialists in the Party from the beginning—generally the most active men and women have been professed socialists—but the Party has been more concerned with solving immediate problems in a pragmatic way than in guiding its legislation according to socialist theory.   Yet the objective, frankly stated at the head of the Party's platform, is socialization of the means of producing and distributing wealth.   This is both an indication of the strength of Socialists in the Party and an example of the way in which social development in Australia is controlled by geographical and economic needs.   No political party in Australia has been able to avoid state interference and state control when faced with the job of settling particular problems.   No political party in the Australian democracy can hope for success in normal times without increasing social services.   But if it be argued that Australian socialism is only a rounding-off, a logical development from the demands of Australian geography and democracy, there has always been in the Labor Party, or on its borders, in the unions or encircling them with influences, a collection of Socialists, reinterpreting Marx and Lenin, publishing pamphlets and establishing ephemeral parties, running candidates against Labor and seeing the futility of such ways, pushing the politician further to the left, watching for the slightest sign that Labor governments are failing the people. The story of the Labor Party cannot be understood apart from the socialist influence both within and without, but also the significance of the role played by Australian Labor can be judged only if set against the complete failure of socialist groups to gain electoral support or to exercise a major influence except through the Labor Party itself.

Labor is socialistic, it is democratic, it is Australian. Even though members of the Communist Party have captured important positions in trade unions, which are affiliated with the Labor Party and have exercised an influence on trade-union behavior, the Labor Party has successfully resisted all their attempts to infiltrate and undermine its organization, to compel affiliation with the Communist Party, or to accept the communist view on political issues.

The two guides selected by the Labor Party as tests by the electorate and by its own members are the winning of full employment and social security. In a white paper issued by the Commonwealth government in 1945, this aim was stated in Keynesian rather than socialistic terms. Abroad at the Bretton Woods, San Francisco, and Philadelphia International Labour Organization (I.L.O.) conferences the Australian representatives emphasized their view that all countries should take full employment as the test of domestic policy. If the problem of unemployment were solved, then the national income of every country would increase, standards of living would be improved, purchasing power would be increased and hindrances to the development of world trade would fall into their proper place as minor causes of depressions.

State Labor governments had introduced schemes of unemployment insurance and had improved social services from time to time, but not until the coming of the Curtin and Chifley Commonwealth Governments had there been a comprehensive attempt to secure social security by state action. Taxation is the main method of providing the necessary funds for these benefits. Although as a result of the war taxation has extended down the scale into the low income groups, Labor believes that taxation should be placed on those best fitted to pay.

Every government must have a plan for the rehabilitation and re-establishment of its service men and women. Comparisons with other countries are unnecessary, but the plan of the Labor government has two outstanding features —its background policy of full employment and its comprehensive nature. We may leave to the political philosopher a discussion of the theoretical aspects of such policies; what is important to note is that they are consistent with democratic socialism, while the determination of the government to achieve full employment offers a better guide to policy than the earlier method of state interference.

State Labor governments have at various times established state concerns such as brickworks and cattle stations. The Queensland Labor government summarized its policy on this point in the slogan "Socialism in Our Time." Though this slogan has not been generally accepted as yet, Labor continues to adopt such methods. Recent advances in government enterprise are to be seen in the National Air Lines Commission, established by the Commonwealth, in the measure for nationalization of banking, and in recent proposals to re-establish the Commonwealth Shipping Line.

Labor believes that the increasing demands of the modern world for security lead inevitably to increasing state interference both in private industry and in economic development. For this reason Labor welcomes state interference and state control, although it does not always socialize an industry when a problem arises. Problems of the Australian constitution, which limit the power of the central government, have created major difficulties, but the Labor Party believes that there are more ways of increasing the power of the state than confiscation and that its variety of methods and approaches is in accordance with the desire of the Australian people and in harmony with Australian democratic development. In this connection the recent legislation regarding coal production may be cited both as an example of Labor tactics and as an important policy on a basic national issue.

Labor is the party of the working masses. With rare exceptions the worker has always voted Labor; generally in the states the small farmer supports Labor. The upper income groups vote anti-Labor—but there is a large swinging group composed of a few unionists, a few more wives, still more farmers and still more middle-class white collar workers. As the voter rises in the income scale the swinging group leans away from Labor except in periods of crisis as in 1943. The unique greatness of Labor's wartime prime minister, John Curtin, in Australian political history was the national leadership that he provided when the leaders of both the other political parties failed.

The task was not easy, for not always is it possible to reconcile the conflicting demands of the trade unionist, the small farmer, and the petty bourgeois. The recognition of this problem has produced a series of cynical comments from commentators both anti-Labor and pro-Communist. The academic theorist often argues that trade-union influence leads to a dull, unimaginative, illiterate policy that is certain to fail; the Communist or pure Socialist argues that the conflict of ingredients makes a socialist advance impossible. The answer to the first is that Labor more often than any other party has succeeded in holding together the diverse elements that make up the Australian people, and in holding them together for policies that on the whole have met the major problems of Australian development. There are weaknesses, gaps, and failures—all known to Labor supporters and regularly the subject of a cleansing, free discussion at Labor Party conferences. But the final achievements of Labor remain: the ever widening educational opportunities extended to the people; the planned improvement of social security so that more and more gaps are filled; the extension of state powers in an attempt to control economic processes in the interests of the people; greater equality of incomes by legislation and administration; the appreciation of the importance of education and culture. All these may be found paralleled in the actions of anti-Labor governments; the external critic who followed through the story of childhood endowment or old-age pensions with the piecemeal party additions to the amount and the regular pushing out of the circle of recipients by different governments will find difficulty in separating Party responsibility. But the major drive for social services has come from Labor just as the positive policy of state control has been limited to the Labor Party.

Yet while the answer to non-Labor will be based on an emphasis on drive, freedom from antistate inhibitions, and mass influence, the answer to the anti-Labor Communist or non-Labor Party Socialist is based on the inescapable necessity for any Australian political party to hold the support of nonsocialist elements.

The Labor Party was founded by the trade unions. It expresses the political needs of trade unions and they look to the Labor Party for assistance in winning their demands.

BIBLIOGRAPHY

AND INDEX

Bibliography

ALEXANDER, F. *Australia and the United States*. World Peace Foundation, Boston, 1941.

AMOS, D. J. *The Story of the Commonwealth Fleet of Steamers*. E. J. McAlister and Company, Adelaide, 1945.
———— *The Story of the Commonwealth Woollen Mills*. E. J. McAlister and Company, Adelaide, 1934.

ANDERSON, G. *Fixation of Wages in Australia*. Melbourne University Press, 1929.

ATKINSON, M., ed. *Trade Unionism in Australia: Report of a Conference Held in June, 1915*. Workers Educational Association, Sydney, 1915.

AUSTRALIA:
  Commonwealth Immigration Advisory Committee. Report. Canberra, 1946.
  Conference of Youth-Adult Employment, Canberra, 4–6 December, 1939. Short Summary of the Proceedings. Government Printer, Canberra, 1940.
  Convention of Representatives of the Commonwealth on Proposed Alteration of the Commonwealth Constitution . . . Canberra, 24th November to 2nd December, 1942. Record of Proceedings. Canberra, 1942.
  Full Employment in Australia. Canberra, 1945.
  Official Year Book of the Commonwealth of Australia, Nos. 1 to date. Canberra, 1908 to date.
  Royal Commission on the Constitution of the Commonwealth. Report. Canberra, 1929.
  Royal Commission on the Wheat, Flour and Bread Industries. First to fourth reports. Canberra, 1935–36.
  ———— Attorney General's Department. *Post-War Reconstruction: A case for Greater Commonwealth Powers:*

Prepared for the Constitutional Convention at Canberra, November, 1942. Canberra, 1942.

———— Army Education Service. *Australian Resources and Prospects.* 4 parts. Melbourne, 1945.

———— Commonwealth Bureau of Census and Statistics. *Census of the Commonwealth of Australia: 30 June, 1933.* Detailed tables. 2 vols. Canberra, 1939.

———— Commonwealth Electoral Office. *Statistical Returns in Relation to the Submission to the Electors of a Proposed Law for the Alteration of the Constitution ... Together with Summaries of Referendums, 1906–1944.* Canberra, 1945.

———— Department of External Affairs. *Current Notes on International Affairs.* Fortnightly. Canberra, 1936 to date.

———— National Insurance Commission. *National Insurance: A Summary of the Principles of the Australian National Health and Pension Insurance Act, 1938.* Canberra, 1938.

———— Parliament. *Joint Committee on Rural Industries. First to Fifth Progress Reports.* Canberra, 1941–42.

———— Parliament. *Joint Committee on Social Security. First to Eighth Interim Reports.* Canberra, 1941–45.

———— Parliament. *Joint Committee on Wireless Broadcasting. Report.* Canberra, 1942.

———— Post-War Reconstruction Ministry. *Commonwealth Housing Commission. Final Report, 25 August, 1944.* Canberra, 1945.

———— Post-War Reconstruction Ministry. *Re-establishing Pamphlets.* Canberra, 1945.

———— Post-War Reconstruction Ministry. *Rural Reconstruction Commission. First to Fourth Reports.* Canberra, 1944.

———— Prime Minister's Department. *Commonwealth Board of Inquiry into the Coal Mining Industry, 1945–1946. Extracts from the Report.* Canberra, 1946.

———— Prime Minister's Department. *The Federal Guide: A Handbook of the Organization and Functions of Commonwealth Government Departments and Special War-time Authorities, January, 1944.* Canberra, 1944.

———— Social Services Department. *Social Services, Embracing Invalid and Old Age Pensions, Widows' Pensions,*

Child Endowment, Maternity Allowances, and Unemployment and Sickness Benefits. Melbourne, 1946.

AUSTRALIAN INSTITUTE OF INTERNATIONAL AFFAIRS. *Australia in a New World.* Pamphlet series. The Institute, Sydney, 1943.

————— *The Austral-Asiatic Bulletin.* Bimonthly. The Institute, Victorian division, Melbourne, 1937 to date.

————— *Australian Supplementary Papers: British Commonwealth Relations Conference, Lapstone, 1938. Series A: Australian Population. Series B: Australian economic policies. Series C: Australia in the British Commonwealth. Series D: Australian policies, political and strategic. Series E: Australia and the Pacific.* The Institute, Sydney, 1938.

The Australian Quarterly: A Quarterly Review of Australian Affairs. Sydney, 1929 to date.

BAILEY, K. H., and others. *Problems of War and Peace in the Pacific: data presented at the Institute of Pacific Relations Conference, Quebec . . . December 4th–14th, 1942.* Australian Institute of International Affairs (Victorian Division, Austral-Asiatic section), Melbourne, 1943.

BARNETT, F. O. *The Unsuspected Slums.* The Herald Press, Melbourne, 1933.

BARNETT, F. O., and A. G. PEARSON. *The Poverty of the People in Australia.* Christian Social Order Group, Melbourne, 1944.

BEAN, C. E. W. *War Aims of a Plain Australian.* Angus and Robertson, Sydney, 1943.

BENHAM, F. C. *The Prosperity of Australia: An Economic Analysis.* King, London, 1928.

BLAND, F. A. "The Administration of Government Enterprises" in the *Economic Record,* Melbourne, May, 1929.

————— *Government in Australia: Selected Readings.* Government Printer, Sydney, 1944.

————— *Planning the Modern State: An Introduction to the Problem of Political and Administrative Reorganization.* Angus and Robertson, Sydney, 1934.

BRENNAN, T. C. *Interpreting the Constitution: A Politico-Legal Essay.* Melbourne University Press, 1935.

BRIGDEN, J. B. *Escape to Prosperity.* Macmillan, Melbourne, 1930.

BRIDGEN, J. B., and others. *The Australian Tariff: An Economic Enquiry.* Melbourne University Press, 1929.

BROWN, W. JETHRO. "The Judicial Regulation of Industrial Conditions" in *Australia: Economic and Political Studies,* edited by Meredith Atkinson. Macmillan, Melbourne, 1920.

——— *Prevention and Control of Monopolies.* John Murray, London, 1914.

BROWNE, G. S. *Education in Australia: A Comparative Study of the Educational Systems of the Six Australian States.* Macmillan, London, 1927.

CALWELL, A. A. *How Many Australians Tomorrow?* Reed and Harris, Melbourne, 1945.

Cambridge History of the British Empire, vol. 7, part 1, the article on Australia. Cambridge University Press, 1933.

CAMPBELL, D. A. S., ed. *Post-War Reconstruction in Australia,* by R. G. Menzies and others. Australasian Publishing Company in conjunction with the Australian Institute of Political Science, Sydney, 1944.

CAMPBELL, E. W. *History of the Australian Labour Movement: A Marxist Interpretation.* Current Book Distributors, Sydney, 1945.

CAMPBELL, P., and others, eds. *Studies in Australian Affairs.* Issued by the Institute of Pacific Relations, New South Wales Branch. Macmillan, Melbourne, 1928.

CANAWAY, A. P. *The Failure of Federalism in Australia.* Oxford University Press, London, 1930.

CHILDE, V. G. *How Labour Governs.* Labour Publishing Company, London, 1923.

CILENTO, R. W. *The White Man in the Tropics.* Government Printer, Melbourne, 1925.

CLARK, COLIN. *The Conditions of Economic Progress.* Macmillan, London, 1940.

CLARK, C. G., and J. G. CRAWFORD. *The National Income of Australia.* Angus and Robertson, Sydney, 1938.

CLARK, V. S. *The Labour Movement in Australasia: A Study in Social Democracy.* Constable, London, 1907.

CLEARY, P. J. "Industrial Relations After the War" in *Australia's Post-War Economy,* issued by the Australian Institute of Political Science. Australasian Publishing Company, Sydney, 1945.

CLEMENTS, F. W. *Australian Activities in the Field of Human Nutrition.* A supplement to the *Australian Journal of Science,* June 21, 1945.

COGHLAN, T. H. *Labour and Industry in Australia: From the First Settlement in 1788 to the Establishment of the Commonwealth in 1901.* 4 vols. Oxford University Press, London, 1918.

COLE, P. R., ed. *The Education of the Adolescent in Australia.* Melbourne University Press, 1935.

———— *The Primary School Curriculum in Australia.* Melbourne University Press, 1932.

———— *The Rural School in Australia.* Melbourne University Press, 1937.

COOMBS, H. C. *Industry and Post-War Reconstruction.* An address delivered at a meeting of the Institute of Industrial Management in June, 1944. The Institute, Melbourne, 1944.

———— *Problems of a High Employment Economy.* The Hassell Press, Adelaide, 1944.

COPLAND, D. B. *Australia and the World Crisis, 1929–1933.* Cambridge University Press, 1934.

———— *The Australian Economy: Simple Economic Studies.* 4th ed. Angus and Robertson, Sydney, 1941.

———— *Credit and Currency Control with Special Reference to Australia.* Macmillan, Melbourne, 1932.

———— *The Road to High Employment.* Harvard University Press, Cambridge, Mass., 1945.

———— *Towards Total War.* Angus and Robertson, Sydney, 1942.

COPLAND, D. B., and R. M. CLARK. *Profits and Price Control.* Angus and Robertson, Sydney, 1941.

COPLAND, D. B., and C. V. JANES, eds. *Australian Marketing Problems: A Book of Documents, 1932–1937.* Angus and Robertson, Sydney, 1938.

———— *Australian Trade Policy: A Book of Documents, 1932–1937.* Angus and Robertson, Sydney, 1937.

———— *Cross Currents of Australian Finance: A Book of Documents.* Angus and Robertson, Sydney, 1936.

COWPER, NORMAN, and others. *What the Census Reveals,* edited by G. V. Portus. F. W. Preece and Sons, Adelaide, 1936.

CRAMER, J. F. *Australian Schools Through American Eyes.* Melbourne University Press, 1936.

CRAMP, K. R. *State and Federal Constitutions of Australia.* 2d ed. Angus and Robertson, Sydney, 1914.

CUMPSTON, J. H. L., and C. M. HEINIG. *Pre-School Centres in Australia: Building Equipment and Programme.* Health Department, Canberra, 1945.

CUNNINGHAM, K. S., ed. *Review of Education in Australia.* Annually. Melbourne University Press, 1938 to date.

DEAKIN, A. *The Federal Story: The Inner History of the Federal Cause,* edited by Herbert Brookes. Robertson and Mullens, Melbourne, 1944.

DE BRUNE, A. *Fifty Years of Progress in Australia: 1878–1928.* Halstead Press, Sydney, 1929.

DENNING, W. E. *Caucus Crisis: the Rise and Fall of the Scullin Government.* Verity Hewitt, Canberra, 1937.

DRUMMOND, D. H. `*Australia's Changing Constitution: No States or New States.* Angus and Robertson, Sydney, 1943.

DUNCAN, W. G. K., ed. *Australia's Foreign Policy.* Angus and Robertson, Sydney, 1938.

———— *Educating a Democracy.* Angus and Robertson, Sydney, 1936.

———— *Marketing Australia's Primary Products.* Angus and Robertson, Sydney, 1937.

———— *National Economic Planning.* Angus and Robertson, Sydney, 1934.

———— *Social Services in Australia.* Angus and Robertson, Sydney, 1939.

———— *Trends in Australian Politics.* Angus and Robertson, Sydney, 1935. Seven papers read at the Third Summer School of the Australian Institute of Political Science.

DUNCAN, W. G. K. and C. V. JANES, eds. *The Future of Immigration Into Australia and New Zealand.* Angus and Robertson, Sydney, 1937.

The Economic Record: Journal of the Economic Society of Australia and New Zealand. Melbourne University Press, 1925 to date.

EGGLESTON, F. W., ed. *The Australian Mandate for New Guinea.* Melbourne University Press, 1928.

———— *State Socialism in Victoria.* King, London, 1932.

EGGLESTON, WALKER, ANDERSON, and NIMMO. *Australian Standards of Living.* Melbourne University Press, 1939.

ELKIN, A. B. *The Australian Aborigines: How to Understand Them.* Angus and Robertson, Sydney, 1938.

ELLIS, U. R. *New Australian States.* Endeavour Press, Sydney, 1934.

EVATT, H. V. *Australian Labour Leader: The Story of W. A. Holman and the Labour Movement,* 2d ed. Angus and Robertson, Sydney, 1942.

———— "Control of Labor Relations in the Commonwealth of Australia," in the *University of Chicago Law Review,* June, 1939.

———— *Foreign Policy of Australia: Speeches.* Angus and Robertson, Sydney, 1945.

———— *Post-War Reconstruction. Temporary Alterations of the Constitution. Notes on the Fourteen Powers and the Three Safeguards.* Government Printer, Canberra, 1944.

FITZHARDING, L. G., and others. *Nation Building in Australia: The Life and Work of Sir Littleton Ernest Groom.* Angus and Robertson, Sydney, 1941.

FITZPATRICK, B. C. *The Australian People.* Melbourne University Press, 1947.

———— *The British Empire in Australia: An Economic History, 1834–1939.* Melbourne University Press, 1941.

———— *British Imperialism and Australia, 1783–1833: An Economic History of Australasia.* Melbourne University Press, 1939.

———— *Public Enterprise Does Pay: A Story of Successful Government, Industrial, and Financial Enterprise in Australia, 1911–1944.* Rawson's Book Shop, Melbourne, 1945.

———— *The Rich Get Richer.* Rawson's Book Shop, Melbourne, 1944.

———— *A Short History of the Australian Labor Movement.* Rawson's Book Shop, Melbourne, 1940.

FOENANDER, O. DE R. *Solving Labour Problems in Australia.* Melbourne University Press, 1941.

————— *Towards Industrial Peace in Australia: A Series of Essays in the History of the Commonwealth Court of Conciliation and Arbitration.* Melbourne University Press, 1937.

————— *War-Time Labour Developments in Australia.* Melbourne University Press, 1943.

FORSYTH, W. D. *The Myth of Open Spaces: Australian, British and World Trends of Population and Migration.* Melbourne University Press, 1942.

GEPP, HERBERT. *When Peace Comes.* Robertson and Mullens, Melbourne, 1943.

GIBLIN, L. F. "Financing Full Employment" in *Economic Papers, No. 5.* Economic Society of Australia and New Zealand, Sydney, 1945.

GRATTAN, C. H. *Introducing Australia.* John Day, New York, 1942.

HANCOCK, W. K. *Australia.* Benn, London, 1930. Reissued in the Australian Pocket Library, 1945.

HARRIS, H. L. *Australia in the Making.* Angus and Robertson, Sydney, 1936.

————— *Australia's National Interests and National Policy.* Melbourne University Press, 1938.

HEATON, H. *Modern Economic History with Special Reference to Australia.* 3d ed. Workers Educational Association, Adelaide, 1925.

HENDERSON, N. K. *Christian Tradition and Australian Outlook.* Australian Student Christian Movement, Melbourne, 1923.

HIGGINS, H. B. *A New Province for Law and Order: Being a Review by Its Late President for Fourteen Years of the Australian Court of Conciliation and Arbitration.* Workers Educational Association, Sydney, 1922.

HUGHES, W. M. *The Case for Labour.* Worker Trustees, Sydney, 1910.

————— *The Splendid Adventure: A Review of Empire Relations Within and Without the Commonwealth of Britannic Nations.* Benn, London, 1929.

INCE, G. H. *Report on Unemployment Insurance in Australia.* Government Printer, Canberra, 1937.

Isles, K. S., and B. R. Williams. *The Truth About Compulsory Savings.* Robertson and Mullens, Melbourne, 1941.

Jauncey, L. C. *Australia's Government Bank.* Cranley and Day, London, 1933.

Jose, A. W. *Australia: Human and Economic.* Harrap, London, 1932.

Jose, A. W., H. J. Carter, and T. G. Tucker, eds. *The Australian Encyclopaedia.* 3d ed., 2 vols. Angus and Robertson, Sydney, 1926–27.

Kandel, I. L. *Impressions of Australian Education.* The Australian Council for Educational Research, Melbourne, 1938.

Keith, A. B. *Responsible Government in the Dominions.* 2 vols. Oxford University Press, 1928.

Kerr, D. *The Law of the Australian Constitution.* Law Book Company, Sydney, 1925.

Kinnear, W. S. *Report on Health and Pensions Insurance.* Government Printer, Canberra, 1937.

Knowles, G. S. *The Commonwealth of Australia Constitution Act.* As amended to July, 1936, with all the amendments, notes, tables, indexes, and appendices. Government Printer, Canberra, 1937.

Latham, J. G. *Australia and the British Commonwealth.* Macmillan, London, 1929.

Lyng, J. *Non-Britishers in Australia.* Melbourne University Press, 1935.

McGuire, Paul. *Australian Journey.* Heinemann, London, 1940.

MacLaurin, W. R. *Economic Planning in Australia, 1929–1936.* King, London, 1937.

Madgwick, R. B. *Immigration into Eastern Australia, 1788–1851.* Longmans, Green, London, 1937.

Madigan, C. T. *Central Australia.* 2d ed. Oxford University Press, Melbourne, 1944.

Maughan, David, and others. *Constitutional Revision in Australia.* Australasian Publishing Company, Sydney, 1944.

Mauldon, F. R. E. *The Economics of Australian Coal.* Melbourne University Press, 1929.

MILLS, R. C. *Colonization of Australia (1829–1842)*. Sidgwick and Jackson, London, 1915.

MOORE, W. H. *Constitution of the Commonwealth of Australia.* 2d ed. Maxwell, Melbourne, 1910.

MUNN, R., and E. R. PITT. *Australian Libraries: A Survey of Their Conditions and Suggestions for Their Improvement.* Australian Council for Educational Research, Melbourne, 1935.

NORTHCOTT, C. H. *Australian Social Development.* Columbia University Press, New York, 1918.

O'BRIEN, E. M. *The Foundation of Australia (1786–1800): A Study in English Criminal Practice and Penal Colonization in the Eighteenth Century.* The Remainder Centre, London, 1937.

PENTON, BRIAN *Think or Be Damned.* Halstead Press, Sydney, 1945.

PHILLIPS, P. D., and G. L. WOOD, eds. *The Peopling of Australia.* 2 vols. First Series, 1930; Second Series, 1933. Melbourne University Press, 1933.

PICK, J. H., and V. R. ALLDIS. *Australia's Dying Heart: Soil Erosion and Station Management in the Inland.* 2d ed. Melbourne University Press, 1944.

PORTUS, G. V. *Australia Since 1606.* 6th ed. Oxford University Press, Melbourne, 1937.

———— *Free, Compulsory and Secular, A Critical Estimate of Australian Education: Being Three Joseph Payne Lectures for 1936–37.* Oxford University Press, London, 1937.

———— *Studies in the Australian Constitution.* Angus and Robertson, Sydney, 1933.

PRICE, A. GRENFELL. *Australia Comes of Age: A Study of Growth to Nationhood and of External Relations.* Georgian House, Melbourne, 1945.

QUICK, J., and R. R. GARRAN. *The Annotated Constitution of the Australian Commonwealth.* Angus and Robertson, Sydney, 1901.

RAWLINGS, J. N. *Who Owns Australia?* Modern Publishers, Sydney, 1939.

REEVES, W. P. *State Experiments in Australia and New Zealand*. Grant Richards, London, 1902.

ROBERTS, S. H. *History of Australian Land Settlement, 1788–1920*. Macmillan, London, 1924.

———— *The Squatting Age in Australia*. Melbourne University Press, 1935.

ROSS, I. CLUNIES, ed. *Australia and the Far East: Diplomatic and Trade Relations*. Angus and Robertson, Sydney, 1935.

ROSS, L. R. M. *William Lane and the Australian Labor Movement*. Published by the author, Sydney, 1937.

SCOTT, E. *A Short History of Australia*. Oxford University Press, 1929.

SHANN, E. O. G. *An Economic History of Australia*. Cambridge University Press, 1930. 2d impression, 1938.

SHANN, E. O. G., and D. B. COPLAND, eds. *The Australian Price Structure, 1932: Documents Illustrating the Phase of Financial Reconstruction, November, 1931 to November, 1932*. Angus and Robertson, Sydney, 1933.

———— *The Battle of the Plans: Documents Relating to the Premiers' Conference, 1931*. Angus and Robertson, Sydney, 1931.

———— *The Crisis in Australian Finance, 1929–1931*. Angus and Robertson, Sydney, 1936.

SHARKEY, L. L. *Communist Theory and Practice of Trade Unionism*. Published by the Communist Party of Australia, 1942.

SHARKEY, L. L., and E. W. CAMPBELL. *The Story of Government Enterprise in Australia*. Published by the Communist Party of Australia, Sydney, 1945.

SHAW, A. G. L. *The Economic Development of Australia*. Longmans, Green, London and New York, 1944.

SHEPHERD, J. *Australia's Interests and Policies in the Far East*. Institute of Pacific Relations, New York, 1940.

SMITH, A. N. *Thirty Years: The Commonwealth of Australia, 1901–1931*. Brown, Prior, Melbourne, 1933.

SMITH, N. S. *Economic Control: Australian Experiments in Nationalisation and Safeguarding*. King, London, 1929.

SPENCE, W. G. *Australia's Awakening: Thirty Years in the Life of an Australian Agitator.* Worker Trustees, Sydney, 1911.

———— *History of the A. W. U.* Worker Trustees, Sydney, 1911.

SPENCER, F. H. *A Report on Technical Education in Australia and New Zealand.* Carnegie Corporation, New York, 1939.

Stability and Progress. Institute of Public Affairs, Sydney, 1945.

SUTCLIFFE, J. T. *History of Trade Unionism in Australia.* Macmillan, Melbourne, 1921.

SWEETMAN, E. *Australian Constitutional Development.* Macmillan, Melbourne, 1925.

TAYLOR, T. GRIFFITH. *Australia: A Study of Warm Environments and Their Effects on British Settlement.* Methuen, London, 1940.

———— *Australia in its Physiographic and Economic Aspects.* 5th ed. Clarendon Press, Oxford, 1928.

———— *Environment and Race.* Oxford University Press, London, 1927.

THORNTON, E. E. *Trade Unions and the War.* Current Book Distributors, Sydney, 1942.

TURNER, I. S. *The Training of Teachers in Australia.* Melbourne University Press, 1943.

WADHAM, S. M., and G. L. WOOD. *Land Utilization in Australia.* Melbourne University Press, 1939.

WALKER, ALAN. *Coaltown.* Melbourne University Press, 1945.

WALKER, E. R. *Australia in the World Depression.* King, London, 1933.

———— *Unemployment Policy.* Angus and Robertson, Sydney, 1936.

———— *War-Time Economics.* Melbourne University Press, 1939.

WARNER, K. O. *Introduction to Some Problems of Australian Federalism: A Study of the Relations between the Australian States and the Commonwealth with Special Refer-*

ence to Finance. University of Washington Press, Seattle, 1933.

WATSON, J. F., ed. *Historical Records of Australia.* Issued by the Commonwealth Parliamentary Library Committee, Canberra. 1914 to date, Sydney.

WILKINSON, H. L. *The Trust Movement in Australia.* Critcheley Parker, Melbourne, 1914.

———— *The World's Population Problems and a White Australia.* King, London, 1930.

WILLARD, M. *History of the White Australia Policy.* Melbourne University Press, 1923.

WILSON, R. *Capital Imports and Terms of Trade Examined in the Light of Sixty Years of Australian Borrowing.* Melbourne University Press, 1931.

WINDETT, N. *Australia as Producer and Trader, 1920–1932.* Oxford University Press, London, 1933.

WISE, B. R. *The Making of the Australian Commonwealth, 1889–1900: A Stage in the Growth of the Empire.* Longmans, Green, London, 1913.

WOOD, F. L. *The Constitutional Development of Australia.* Harrap, Sydney, 1933.

WOOD, G. L. *Borrowing and Business in Australia: A Study of the Correlation between Imports and Changes in National Prosperity.* Oxford University Press, London, 1930.

WYNES, W. A. *Legislative and Executive Powers in Australia: Being a Treatise on the Legislative and Executive Powers of the Commonwealth and States of Australia under the Commonwealth of Australia Constitution Act.* Law Book Company, Sydney, 1936.

Index